Frances Northam
-1936-

WHAT I LEFT UNSAID

BOOKS BY
MAJOR CHAPMAN-HUSTON

A CREEL OF PEAT: Essays and Appreciations.

THE MELODY OF GOD: Essays and Biographical Studies.

SIR JAMES RECKITT: A Memoir.

LIFE OF GENERAL SIR JOHN COWANS, G.C.B., the Quartermaster General of the Great War. (In collaboration with MAJOR OWEN RUTTER.)

EDITOR OF

DAISY, PRINCESS OF PLESS: by HERSELF.

BETTER LEFT UNSAID: by DAISY, PRINCESS OF PLESS.

SUBJECTS OF THE DAY: by the MARQUESS CURZON OF KEDLESTON, K.G.

BY THE CLOCK OF ST. JAMES: by PERCY ARMYTAGE, C.V.O.

FROM MY PRIVATE DIARY: by DAISY PRINCESS OF PLESS.

IN COLLABORATION WITH H.R.H. PRINCESS PILAR OF BAVARIA

ALPHONSO XIII. A Study in Monarchy.

BAVARIA THE INCOMPARABLE.

The Authoress

From a Portrait by Szankowiski

WHAT I LEFT UNSAID

By

DAISY PRINCESS OF PLESS

Edited with an Introduction and Notes by

MAJOR DESMOND CHAPMAN-HUSTON

With Four Plates

NEW YORK

E. P. DUTTON CO., INC.

Publishers

FIRST EDITION

To

The Memory

of

My Father and Mother

CONTENTS

LIST OF PLATES

EDITOR'S INTRODUCTION

I

AS the Princess of Pless becomes increasingly confidential with her readers her editor's task becomes increasingly difficult. It is true that the seven years that have elapsed since she published *Daisy Princess of Pless*, and the four that have gone by since *From My Private Diary* appeared, have, to some extent, enlarged her freedom as a writer, while at the same time curtailing it by the inevitable fact that what she has so far left unsaid is more personal and private than anything that has gone before. Even in these outspoken days there remain certain feelings and prejudices which should receive due consideration but never, in my view, an exaggerated deference.

Frank, fearless and impulsive by nature, the Princess, as is now well known, has no desire to conceal anything personal. Is it possible for the writer of a volume of reminiscences to be absolutely unreserved about herself and the events of her life and, at the same time, be cautious and reserved about everyone and everything else? Clearly, it is not. There are, however, two ways of being outspoken: One is in a subtly malicious and scandalous sense; the other in an honest spirit of objective realism.

I knew the delightful grandmother and mother whom the Princess so markedly resembles, and while both were amazingly frank, witty, personal and subjective, neither was ever in any circumstances malicious or merely scandalous; those who have read Princess Daisy's two previous volumes know well her warm, sympathetic and chivalrous heart, and will agree that in these respects she is very like Lady Olivia FitzPatrick and Mrs. Cornwallis West.

This volume seems to me to reveal even more fully than did its two predecessors the mind and heart of the writer, and, like them, it gives us a generous measure of her penetrating, shrewd observations on people and events. While it reflects faithfully her varying moods, the sympathetic reader will not fail to note that her views have ripened, her judgment matured, her conclusions acquired weight. She has had leisure—unfortunately too ample—to ponder on all that she has seen, heard and learned of the great world of the Europe of her day and generation.

In an earlier volume the Princess confessed the chagrin and alarm that almost overwhelmed her when she first realized during the South African War how little the statesmen, politicians and people of Germany and England understood one another.

Is this understanding any more complete to-day?

The events of the past few years hardly suggest that it is.

Now, as always, the Princess does her utmost to help Germany and England to face realities; she has some unpalatable things to say to Germany, Austria, France and England, but they are said as from friend to friend.

2

It is conceivable that narrow-hearted people might charge the Princess with indiscretion in making such generous use of private letters, but it is not a charge that could legitimately be sustained. When letters are good they are the richest and most rewarding form of literature, and it is noteworthy that during the Great War, people who ordinarily could not write a line, often became eloquent; furthermore, owing to the tragic circumstances in which they were written, such letters cease to be merely personal and become, in their degree, contributions to history.

The Princess could, of course, have paraphrased in her own words most of the actual facts contained in these letters; she could never have succeeded in giving their content. I therefore strongly advised her not to make the attempt but, wherever at all possible, to let the writers speak for themselves. If that was a mistake the fault is entirely mine.

Throughout the war Princess Daisy, like thousands of other women, charged herself with the onerous task of regularly exchanging letters with hundreds of soldiers. A proportion of her correspondents, such as those represented in this volume, were either relatives or intimate friends; the majority, however, were unknown to her except for a casual meeting, or by reason of their having passed through one of her hospitals or hospital trains. Herself an exile, the Princess realized how apart and cut off from all familiar intercourse a man felt once he was at the front, and how what she calls the "fathomless nostalgia" of the soldier was assuaged by letters of any kind; her feminine intuition told her that this intolerable loneliness was definitely relieved by regular correspondence with a sympathetic and charming woman. It is not without significance that while the young soldier on leave liked to amuse himself light-heartedly with girls who were more than a little free and easy, once he got back to the fighting line he speedily forgot all about them, and kept everything that was finest and best in him for women of quite another type and class. Again and again the letters of Prince Clary and Prince Eitel Friedrich of Prussia remind us that to go into the trenches without some secret source of sweetness and light within the heart was to go into them naked and alone. Another notable thing is that, although written during war, these letters are, in essentials, not about war at all. If it was mentioned it was as a rule only for the purpose of wishing it over. The writers preferred to look before and after—ignoring, so far as they could, the horrible present; in a passage memorable for its simple humanity Prince Eitel Friedrich begged the Princess never to mention the subject. And both the Austrian and Prussian soldier were more chivalrously concerned that the Princess should pass on her troubles to them rather than that they should pass on theirs to her. We have had in English some noble letters written by our own soldiers. Here then are examples, intimate and authentic, of how finely our enemies felt and thought and acted behind their own lines.

It should also be noted that all these letters are markedly sane and healthy. England, France and, more particularly, Germany, have had a surfeit of neurotic, even beastly, records of war experiences. As a rule their authors made the war responsible for the fact that they were writing filth. In all probability the truth is that, in war or in peace, writing filth of one sort or another would have been their inevitable occupation.

Consider, for one moment, the subjects instinctively and frequently chosen by Prince Eitel Friedrich: Birds, flowers, gardens, courage, "my beautiful soldiers!" Joyously he listens to—of all things—Handel's *Largo* almost on the battlefield, and to Schumann. His experience bids us hope that, while the melodies of Handel and Schumann are immortal, the hideous noises made by the huge death-dealing machines of modern warfare will soon, by common consent, be outlawed by our collective civilization. Then, on Christmas Eve, this man whom many would dismiss as a Hohenzollern and a "typical Prussian soldier" had to "bite the teeth rather hard" while he sings German hymns in a French church. His frequent references to the German *Muschkote* or simple private soldier gives the lie direct to the belief that the relations between German officers and men were less fine, close and human than they were in our own armies. To the Prince, officers, generals, army commanders, are fine leaders or good men, but the men themselves are always both brave and beautiful. And so they were: in all nations. On Christmas night the Prince goes out and watches "the nice English boys with their little Christmas trees" only seventy or eighty yards away! His deep love of his own Fatherland was unsullied by any hatred for lands that were alien. Side by side with the Prince's chivalrous regard for his enemies and his sense of oneness and equality with his own men should be placed his simple, humble gratitude to God that he was spared when comrades standing by were taken.

In the past we have heard far too much about hymns of hate; let us now hear through Princess Daisy something about hymns of love.

Prince Clary's love for the England where his sister found a sanctuary throughout the war was little less than his love for his Austrian homeland; while on a visit to Ostend the Grand Duke of Mecklenburg-Strelitz flings his love across the narrow channel to England, and wishes he could follow it; Count Fritz Hochberg, brother-in-law of the authoress, clings tenaciously to his almost worn-out clothes because they were made in England and smell of the New Forest, and declares that he is "stupidly homesick for that beloved little island."

As between the writer and the receiver the letters quoted in this book were healing; they eased their hearts and hers. Because they were written during the war by Germans to an Englishwoman they have a part to play in the healing of the nations, and, therefore, cannot be allowed to perish. They are first-hand, authentic, indelible little war etchings; above all they paint matchless portraits of the writers and the recipient. Amongst the many letters quoted there is not one that does not help to justify our belief in the essential beauty and fineness of our poor humanity. They reflect credit on Germany, on Austria, on England. And surely there ought to be something of deep humility in our English pride as, when reading them, we realize afresh the existence of that inexplicable, uncommunicable national English characteristic that somehow impels even her enemies in arms to love her.

Other friends of the authoress, who had not such close ties with England, were equally magnanimous. The Emperor and Empress, the Crown Princess Cecile, the two sisters of the Emperor, Princess Adolf of Schaumburg-Lippe and Princess Friedrich Karl of Hesse, Prince Joachim Albrecht of Prussia, Duke Ernst Günther of Schleswig-Holstein, only brother of the Empress; King Ludwig the Third of Bavaria, Prince and Princess Ludwig Ferdinand, Princess Pilar, Duke Wilhelm and Duke Luitpold, and indeed all the members of the Bavarian Royal House: General von Plessen, Aide-de-Camp General to the Emperor; Countess Brockdorff, Mistress of the Robes to the Empress; practically every member of her German family—all these, and many more, gave Princess Daisy throughout the whole war love, sympathy, understanding and courage. To these illustrious personages could be added the names of hundreds, nay thousands, of simple German soldiers, doctors, nurses, humble friends, miners, woodmen, foresters, gamekeepers, servants and dependants at Fürstenstein and Pless.

The Princess knows it well and would here acknowledge her great debt.

As was perhaps inevitable, her first book dwelt at some length on all she suffered during the war: this, her third and perhaps her last, is deliberately a work of love and reconciliation.

The chapters entitled *A Perfect Friendship* and *Der Rosenkavalier* are worthy of their titles. They are included by the Princess in the deliberate belief that they supplement those entitled *A Gallant Austrian Soldier* and *A Prussian Soldier Prince* by showing beyond all question how perfect and satisfying a thing real friendship between a man and a woman can be.

All her life the Princess of Pless has occupied a position of quite unusual prominence in Germany. It was therefore inevitable during the war that she should become the target of all that was low and vile in the beastly organs of war propaganda. She was *die Engländerin* and anything said against her was a direct blow at England. The most shattering thing about anti-enemy propaganda is that it can, and does, debase the highest and best, prostituting virtues into infamy. A vast system of internal espionage and censorship existed in Germany. Letters to and from the Princess were opened; garbled versions of their contents passed from mouth to mouth; sentences, often deliberately distorted, appeared in the Press. In any country echoes from evil take long to perish.

By giving here fully and accurately her complete correspondence with such men as the late Grand Duke of Mecklenburg-Strelitz, with Prince Eitel Friedrich of Prussia, and with Prince Clary, the Authoress advisedly removes them for ever from the shadows of conjecture and gossip and places them in the white light of historic reality and truth.

The Princess speaks of her more serious passages as footnotes to history, and that is exactly what they are; as footnotes they have a definite value inasmuch as they are made by a broad-minded, shrewd, intelligent, courageous, independent woman of the world, whose personal knowledge of the Europe of the past thirty-five years, and of those who played a prominent part in contemporary history, can have been equalled by few memoir writers of our times.

People who do not like reality will not like her book because it has the acrid smell, the salt taste of life itself.

D. C.-H.

Söcking uber Starnberg, Bavaria.

WHAT I LEFT UNSAID

CHAPTER I

SITTING BY THE FIRE

We sit beneath the dark old balk
When the heart of the peat is red,
My crony and I, we sit and we talk
Of the days that are long since dead:
We gossip together, I and he,
And he knows what I know and he sees what I see.

When days are dressed in gold and green,
And the birds are all gone asleep,
The shadows lie in the long boreen,
In the boreen lone and deep:
But other shades move to and fro,
And they see what I see and they know what I know.

THOMAS EKENHEAD MAYNE.

I

I SIT by the fire. One of the oldest of human pastimes, it is not half so dull an occupation as either the young or the incurably restless might think. The Irish sit by a peat fire; the English by a coal one. That is the unbridgable difference between the two peoples: We prefer the glamorous, the quick, the pungent; they the lasting and substantial. I think it was the late Lord Durham, a great coal magnate, who used to declare that the principal advantage of owning coal mines was that he could afford to burn wood; but then, being married to an Irishwoman, he may almost be said to have had Irish blood in his veins! Of course, I am only half Irish, and half and half Welsh; but, like all half-castes, I like both in Ireland and Wales, to pretend that I am one hundred per cent pure!

I see that like a true woman I am contradictory at the very beginning in describing sitting by the fire as both an occupation and a pastime. But, even so, I am neither as wrong nor as illogical as a mere man might think. A woman can always see both sides of a question; a man seldom. Therefore I will not rewrite my first sentence. Sitting by the fire can be not only one of the most serene and satisfying of human pastimes; it can be the most rewarding of occupations. Had Watt sat a little longer watching the kettle boil, who knows but that as a result one would be able to buy a teapot that would pour out without dribbling.

Nowadays everybody rushes around everywhere and I, God knows, have done more than my share of gadding about the world; yet I doubt if we were, or are, really any the happier for all this movement. Some of the richest and most contented lives I have known have been those of people who have spent all their days more or less in one spot. Be that as it may, travelling in any extended degree is over for me. My adventures henceforward must be interior—of the mind and the spirit; not exterior or of the body.

My fireside occupation just now is the writing of another book. Of course I am flattered, and I venture to think rightly so, that there should be a demand for a third volume of reminiscences from my pen. Those who have read my two previous volumes know that since I was a child I have always desired to write. Probably I came to it too late to do anything significant and lasting but, as the Germans beautifully say, I have done it all with love and that I feel sure is why my pen has won for me hundreds of welcome correspondents, and many thousands of readers in all parts of the world.

Long ago a dull old Israelite said disparagingly that of the making of books there was no end whilst, at that very moment, manlike, the wretched creature was himself adding to the number. Why should there be an end? There may be too many books in the world; there certainly are far too many firesides still without books. The other day I visited the house of a very great lady, who is also a very great personage. The daughter, literally, of a hundred kings, and the mother of a king, herself embodied history, and surrounded by historic souvenirs of the Europe of the past fifty years, she had not a single book in her house! That, indeed, is to exist in a tomb, because things, possessions, are dead, whereas a book—that is of course a real book—is alive. One of my girlhood's friends, Frederick, the great Lord Dufferin, said that a book, once printed, had put on a measure of immortality—by which, happily, he did not mean that all printed books are immortal.

Even after contemporary systems of education have succeeded in making the bulk of the population chronically illiterate, the writing of books will continue, because garrulousness helps to mitigate the most terrible element in human life—our eternal loneliness—and to satisfy our most human need, the cureless ache to communicate.

Thank God that for my own happiness and that of those about me I was never really one of those intense brooding women who leave things unsaid, harbour unquiet thoughts, dwell on fancied slights, nurse imaginary grievances and plot melodramatic revenges. Of course, I have had my phases of silent fretting. What woman has not? They were most frequent during the first ten years of my married life, before Hansel, my eldest son, was born. But I was never in any real sense a Hedda Gabler or a Paula Tanqueray. Give me a good old explosion and have done with it, and let sunshine quickly stream out of the midst of the storm. In other words, I am a woman who takes naturally to digression, so if you don't like that sort of woman better put this book down. Not for you the truth that amongst the best things in life are its asides—verbal or otherwise.

I am sure that the adage, silence is golden, was written by a man, because (as every woman knows) no man is capable of looking unaided into the heart of a matter, and every real man who succeeds in doing so is—fortunately for himself—

unwittingly led by the nose by some woman. How can one ever come to see both sides of a question except by talking it over? My experience is that men adore talking things over with a sensible woman, and the moment they seriously start doing so the woman has won.

You have only to glance at history to see how all men, even the very greatest, secretly like being ruled by a petticoat. From Adam onward they are all the same. Take, for example, Napoleon. I can understand the raw Italian soldier of genius succumbing to Josephine who, after all, was a woman of the world endowed with exhaustless charm and tact, and with a generous—perhaps too generous—experience of managing awkward men. The fire in her Creole blood called to the Tuscan fire in his. But why Marie Louise who, had she not been born an Archduchess, would have been only a dull little German strumpet, ready to fall into the arms of any man put in her way, and who didn't even care whether he had one eye or two! To fly from the tottering aerie of the golden eagle only to end in the nest of a cuckoo would be a sorry fate for any woman, much less for a great princess. To have the supreme good fortune to become the mother of the Eaglet and to mistake him for a croaking sparrow was surely the abyss of stupidity and ignominy.

Then look at the silly Antony, and the even sillier Cæsar, dancing to the tunes devised by the little Egyptian minx. What about the married Dante, father of several hefty children, mooning around Florence looking for a young female who probably never really existed; or the Duke of Wellington writing in his old age fatuous letters to a sex-starved school-marm. To come nearer to our own times, what about Parnell, a great man if there ever was one, throwing Ireland away because of his infatuation for a middle-aged married woman?

Since Hawarden Castle and Ruthin Castle, my birthplace, are quite near each other in Wales I, as girl, frequently saw Mr. and Mrs. Gladstone and, while Gladstone may have led the Liberal Party, Mrs. Gladstone certainly led him. Cleverer still; she did it with a silken thread so soft and fine that, for all his vision and foresight, Mr. Gladstone never once caught a glimpse of it.

Everyone knows that Gladstone's great political opponent, Lord Salisbury, was as putty in the gentle, tactful hands of his sweet and selfless wife. Disraeli was always dancing round some woman or another; if it was not a stately court minuet in the august presence of Queen Victoria, it was a homely polka with his elderly wife, or a mannered saraband with Lady Bradford or Lady Chesterfield. Wagner was hag-ridden, and quite miserable without a woman to bespatter him with praise and sympathy. Of course, the truth is that men are peacocks and must always spread their tails, and they prefer to do so before an audience of one—because they can hear the flattery better.

Then, think of my friend the Emperor Wilhelm the Second of Germany. He just had to have females everlastingly swinging incense in front of him. His first Consort, the dear charming Empress Auguste Victoria, might have been thought unambitious and unassuming, but, all her life, she successfully managed her volatile, clever, changeable, vain and unreliable husband. Better still, in spite of his innumerable mild flirtations (of which gossip had it I was one) she kept him, and that not one woman in ten million could have done. And when she died, within a year or so, he had ignobly treated Frau von Rochow who sacrificed so much for him; besought in marriage his own niece, getting badly snubbed for doing so, and espoused the pleasant, buxom Hermine of Reuss, widow of the Prince of Schönaich-Carolath.

Yes; history amply proves that any moon-faced girl with big eyes can catch a man—look, for example, at the ease with which the rather stupid Anne Boleyn netted the wily, ultra-experienced Henry the Eighth—but, as history also proves, it takes more than good looks to keep one. Nor, to take a man who was the antithesis of the sex-besotted Henry, must we forget Dr. Johnson, the most realistic mind of his period, the clearest-eyed of thinkers, who always firmly believed that his wife Tetty, twice his age and hideous, was a beauty. And after her death would he not on the slightest provocation, neglect Mrs. Williams or Mrs. Desmoulins at home, and go gadding off to the house of this woman or that—to Bloomsbury to call on Lady Diana Beauclerk, or to Streatham or Brighton or wherever it was to preen his wings in the presence of Mrs. Thrale? Perhaps it is not without some significance that Mrs. Johnson (how odd that sounds) was, as the widow of a Mr. Porter, possessed of eight hundred pounds in her own right, and that Mrs. Thrale was a rich woman.

Going back into the dim past, do we not all know how Adam's wife made immortal history with such scant materials as an eel and an apple, even though the Almighty himself was unable to make *her* without filching one of Adam's ribs. Although not mentioned in the chronicle (written by a male), we may be quite sure that it was Mrs. Noah who fed the chickens, managed her husband, put the children to bed, and kept everything going in the first house-boat in history until it safely reached Mount Ararat.

But what has all this to do with Daisy?

Well, only a woman who has had a great deal of admiration from men is in a position to know exactly what the creatures are like, and I have had my full share. Oh no; in spite of my title, I am not—not now at any rate—really giving any man away. A certain number of men whom I knew can rest quietly in their graves and their relicts—delicious Victorian word—to whom they hardly ever spoke in life, and the thresholds of whose bedrooms they had not crossed for years, can continue to go about with their noses in the air pretending that they were the heroines of a great married passion, the sole occupants of a fiery yet faithful heart.

Perhaps this paragraph may even *not* have a reassuring effect on some manly hearts still very much alive.

A few of the men who loved me were fine, honourable, reticent; many were egotistical, vain and boastful. Looking back I can see now that of the scores of men who, to use an odious expression, "made love" to me, hardly one was worth a serious thought, much less a tear: the sort of men who go in for "making love" are not. Emperors and Kings, Royal Princes and generals, famous politicians, great financiers, writers and artists, great sportsmen, simple soldiers in the war, and simple men in ordinary life, when they are "in love" are all equally stupid, tiresome and foolish. Poets one does not mention because as a matter of business the poor creatures are obliged to be chronically "in love."

For the purpose of this book I have again been poring over my old diaries and letters and recalling one by one the men who were, or professed to be, in love with me. The inexplicable thing is that, in retrospect, I am rather pleased and flattered by it all. Why? What is there for vanity to feed upon in the mere biological fact that, for her own unfathomable purposes, Nature has made the sexes attractive to each other? But we are so constituted that we do plume ourselves on this matter and, or so I think, always will. Read any book of reminiscences by a woman and you cannot fail to notice how, one way or another, she skilfully manages to dangle her scalps. Personally, I prefer to dangle them without pretence. Why not? Anyhow that is my nature. And I have good precedent. Did not Margot Oxford and Asquith, gifted with one of the quickest and acutest brains I know, boast in her incomparable autobiography of all the men, distinguished and undistinguished, who were in love with her? And, again, why not? An admiring glance, if only from the butcher's boy as he goes whistling past, can cause even a sophisticated woman to tilt her head heavenwards and battle more successfully with the trivialities of her lot. Each of us has an ideal picture of ourselves tucked secretly away in the heart and we all like to think that—because of its radiance and beauty—even a passing stranger can be so fortunate as to catch a glimpse of it at times.

But now I must stop meandering. I may return to this subject in a later chapter; but before doing so I must take thought. I know only too well that when a woman starts taking off her clothes she will take off far more than any man would dare to do. It is unwise (at any age) to be over-generous with one's charms. Some time after the war I remember the late Prince Napoleon going to see the wife of a distinguished English general who had injured her foot. She sat propped up in an over-gorgeous bed, feeling, no doubt, like La Pompadour receiving Louis the Fifteenth. The general's wife, as so often seems to happen to generals' and clergymen's wives, was skinny, very yellow beneath the artificially blooming face, and flat. Her exquisite lace nightie was open well below, shall we say, the etceteras. As the bewildered Prince—a true Bonaparte—said afterwards:

"But why? There was nothing to see."

2

And this business of communicating, trying thus to mitigate the doom of loneliness, pretending that by so doing we may even ensure to ourselves some remission of our sentence of oblivion—is it not indeed a curious and fascinating preoccupation. Closely linked to it is our innate worship of beauty. We cherish the strange belief that if we can unite these two we shall somehow defeat death. Not only to communicate, but to do so with at least a meed of honesty, sincerity, truth and beauty. That high longing is the source of all poetry, literature, art and adventure.

And always, or so it seems to me, the men who succeed in this strange traffic are more feminine than the ordinary man. The possession of feminine qualities does not, of course, make a man an artist; but no man can be an artist who has not a good slice of the woman in him. He must not be, like that monstrosity, the American film-fan's ideal, one hundred per cent. male. In fact, he must have had a father and a mother instead of two fathers. And this he can have without being in the least effeminate. A masculine woman may occasionally be attractive; an effeminate man is an abomination. However, the artist must, for example, possess a large measure of intuition because, otherwise, life is too short, and the way of art too long, for any significant accomplishment. To take a few names at random. Think for a moment of the feminine qualities in the man called Homer; he who understood Calypso as well as he did Penelope. Dante and Milton fall short of greatness in my eyes because neither of them seemed truly to understand women; and I doubt if Bunyan really knew or appreciated my sex.

In spite of all his adventures it seems to me that so far as true fellowship with women was concerned Balzac lived and died alone. Balzac was too masculine. He was one of those terrible men who early in life are so unfortunate as to conceive what used to be called an ideal woman whom they insist on continuing to cherish no matter how many disillusioning females may come into their lives. They never deign to look at the poor flesh-and-blood female trotting beside them, but keep their minds steadily fixed on "the ideal woman" firmly implanted in their boyish hearts by "their perfect mother," their first governess or some other ridiculously morbid creature. The mind of Balzac was, all his life, so befuddled by searching for romantic and impossible countesses and princesses, that he never saw in the exquisite friendship showered on him by Madame de Berny one of the loveliest and most perfect things in all literary history. But no; Madame de Berny was not an aristocrat; she was only the faithful wife of a *bourgeois* who selflessly bestowed a deathless friendship on an ungrateful man of genius.

In spite of Stella and Vanessa (or rather because of them), Swift, to my mind, knew and cared little or nothing about women; if he had done so he would not have transposed two real women like Hester Johnson and Esther Vanhomrigh into literary abstractions of such intolerable perfection. If you want inhumanly impossible women get a cynical man who has been a wayfarer to create them for you. Ultimately the cynic is always a sentimentalist. Spending his time in depriving other people of their illusions, he sticks like a bloated leech to his own.

Sheridan understood a certain rather artificial type of woman perfectly; Dickens seems only to have really known about charwomen and their better-off relatives; Thackeray comprehended perfectly what one may for convenience call a villainess; Becky Sharp is absolute; every mole and wrinkle, every mental kink is there; to me she is matchless. The only thing I could criticize is her family name. That family is of course enormous and we have its members with us in abundance in every generation, but Becky was so outstandingly unique that she should have been given at least a hyphen. The bald tribal name is too obvious, indeed a little cheap, too much in the facile manner of underlining words and phrases in letters, a fashion, one supposes, inherited in particular from the playwrights of the seventeenth and eighteenth centuries; I never could accept as valid such names as Mrs. Candour, Lady Sneerwell, Sir Benjamin Backbite and Charles Surface. I have often wondered why Becky and her type please and interest me so enormously. As I am a rather vague, rather haphazard sort of woman where practical affairs are concerned, I expect it is their efficiency and clear-headedness that astound me. I am fascinated by such unnatural decision of character as the rabbit is said to be fascinated by the snake. But Thackeray's good women are intolerable. Jane Austen, of course, understood women, especially those of the exquisite, if limited, world in which she chose to move; so did Charlotte Brontë—though her men are an unconvincing lot; mostly hopeless, self-deceiving prigs like Professor Héger or ponderous nincompoops like Rochester. But Jane Eyre and Shirley, and a score of lesser females created by Charlotte, are deathless. Charlotte's sister Emily, on the other hand, knew and portrayed men with uncanny skill. George Eliot understood both men and women and successfully created both, but, like her great contemporary, George Sand, she had a strong dash of the masculine in her intelligence. Had she lived to be old she would, like Rosa Bonheur, probably have had a moustache. George Sand in extreme old age would have had not only a moustache—but a beard.

Her best-known lover, Chopin, was more a woman than a man!

Of the novelists and creators of my own day it does not become me to speak. Hardy, by far the greatest of them all, knew women in and out; but his men are lumpy and unconvincing. Just imagine a real woman like Tess wasting five minutes of her thoughts over an Angel Clare; why his very name is enough to damn him. Conrad cared little or nothing about women. Mr. Bernard Shaw, for all his irritating complacency and self-satisfied smirking, doesn't know a woman from a feminist advertisement; because, whatever a woman may be, she is never merely an arid document or a piece of propaganda.

I find Galsworthy's women rather awful, though his men occasionally come to life. Where the chatterboxes in Mr. Noel Coward's plays come from I cannot imagine—not out of a normal female womb I vow. If one may use an expression from the racing stable, they seem to be by Jazz out of Hysteria, or by Disillusion out of *Hay Fever*. Like cocktails they are concocted rather than created. Alas! that they should so perfectly express the period in which they move with such delightfully unconvincing verve and life.

The one man who knew all about us from beginning to end was, without question, Shakespeare. French writers can dissect us into the most minute fragments; German writers pour forth endless incomprehensible tomes about our *Wesen;* Russians set us gyrating aggravatingly about our souls in cherry orchards and other unlikely and uncomfortable places; Scandinavians can portray us convincingly as heroic Amazons or bucolic drudges; English writers can describe and explain us; Shakespeare alone *understood* us.

But I must shut up, leave the podium and get back to my fireside; I have no title to write about such high matters.

3

A scientist friend tells me that it is because mankind has sat before fires for hundreds of millions of years that we all instinctively love doing so. A fire in the forest, it seems, was the first measure of protection devised by man against all his enemies, ghostly and animal. It shut out the great surrounding darkness with all its fearsome possibilities and kept the fierce wild beasts at bay. It was in truth man's first attempt at a home, if but a migratory one, and within its warm, protecting circle he not only enjoyed a measure of repose and safety, but it was in those comforting flames that he first began to envisage some dim sort of family and communal life. Looking intently for thousands of years into its quickening lights, or upon the shining faces of his fellow human beings around it, he somehow acquired his first far-off visions of an ordered society living in peace, safety and harmony.

All children everywhere go through a phase when they love lighting and sitting around camp-fires, and grown-ups who retain this longing always seem to have something simple and childlike in their hearts. To me a house without fires is dead, and the humblest abode, given a warm cheerful blaze, can become a real home. Wherever I have gone on the continent I have always had to make fireplaces and gardens, and it is these two fundamental urges that set the English people apart from all others.

And there are so many different sorts of fire to love.

The dining-room fire, its hospitable flames reflected in the crystal and the silver or, better still, in the rainbow colours of Waterford glass; the cheerful crackle of the wood a delightful obbligato to friendly chatter and laughter. How well in the old days did we know that moment when (everyone warmed and comforted by much good fare) our host or hostess turned to the butler and said: "Jenkinson, put the glass screen in front of the fire." The more serious part of the meal was over, but everyone felt an instinctive dislike to the ending of an hour or so of delightful and harmonious intercourse.

Such hours are amongst the best achievements of civilization; created only by exquisite skill, it almost seems like sacrilege to end them. In every age and clime, hospitality generously extended and generously received, has been prized as almost a fine art, as indeed it can be.

The glass screen in position, and tablecloth removed, fruit and flowers, silver and candles, wine red as rubies or golden as topaz make deep rich pools of light in the shining depths of the dark mahogany. The host (the right sort of host) surely said: "The ladies, I am sure, will not hurry away."

Nor did we.

In fact, we were as anxious to linger as the men were to have us do so. Now our best smiles came spontaneously, our wittiest remarks flashed forth, our tenderest glances were bestowed, our most understanding silences rewarded those who deeply attracted us.

The drawing-room fire to which in due course we moved in a rustling bevy was altogether a different matter.

As in grand houses the dining-room doors were thrown open for us by respectful footmen, or in simpler ones by the men guests in their becoming black and white evening uniform, did we sometimes between the firelight and the candlelight catch a masculine glance that seemed to say: Now that you go the room is empty. However that may have been, as soon as we reached the drawing-room many of us, manlike, found ourselves standing with our backs to the fire as Dr. Johnson loved to do. Whatever our personal relationships to some of the men left behind in the dining-room, however filled with love, or regret, or hope, for the next half-hour or so we were collectively their enemy. We immediately assumed the attitude of a phalanx of females, with man the eternal opponent. However much we might hate or despise each other individually we became—for the time being only—militant feminists. We announced in various ways our feminine independence. Proclaiming a superior allegiance which we kept discreetly vague, we let it be understood that we looked down on man and all his works, his futile ploys, his pipes, his guns, his golf-clubs, his primitive taboos and his silly ambitions and even sillier flirtations.

Then as the conquering males came drifting into the drawing-room, mentally and emotionally we women fell apart, the group disintegrated and, once more, for good or ill some man without any trouble whatsoever resumed his natural place as the orbit round which all our affairs were centred. Thus every evening after dinner was the eternal and unavoidable antagonisms between the sexes quickly aroused and just as quickly resolved.

Then think of the delights of the fireside in one's own private sitting-room, or, if we did not own one, in our bedroom. We would have no other light or, at most, but one soft and dim. There, before that quiet blaze, we become, as nearly as may be, ourselves. Jewels, smart clothes and tight shoes cast aside, and wearing only a loose wrapper, we nestle before the cosy warmth in a low comfy chair; we pile on with our own hands pieces of fragrant wood, not because of the cold, but to touch them, to see them blaze and hear them crack and cackle. How lovely and many-coloured are the flames; how pungently sweet and haunting the smoke. We are back ten million years in great, awesome primeval forests. We are alone. Here, and here only, do we summon forth visions of our best beloved ones, our dearest friends, our pet heroes and heroines, our secret ideals, our most precious hopes. How often in those flames did I see the eyes of my babies during those empty years before my babies came. In the dreams aroused, and to some extent satisfied by those flames, a woman often pictures the face of the ideal man, the perfect friend, the unfailing protector, the splendid guide . . . and it is not always the face of her husband. A bedroom fire is at once a luxury and a necessity: it can be a refuge and a sanctuary.

Another sort of fire I love is the welcoming fire in the entrance-hall. Outside Ireland one can hardly hope that it will be of peat. As a child I sometimes went to stay with Granny Olivia FitzPatrick and her husband at Cloone Grange in County Leitrim. They lived in a boggy, mountainous country with miles and miles of peat and many lakes full of brown peaty water, and their home had a great fireplace in the hall, as well as many other lovely "turf" fires distributed over the house. They burned blazingly and glowingly in a quick and vivacious way (as if they liked warming us) and gave out the most heavenly odour. They burned, as it were, with happiness, and ever since I have thought coal flames sulky by comparison. And if you watched from the outside of the house the peat smoke ascending it was never heavy, dark and depressing-looking like that of coal, but the tenderest, softest wisps of blue-grey-blue. There is only one thing more perfect, more aromatic, more delicious than a peat fire and that is a great, piled fire of fir cones on the edge of a forest in autumn.

When my husband bought and did up my Munich house for me after the war he made it comfortable in every way. The inner hall, while not spacious, is quite large enough to use as a sitting-room. The panelling and staircase are in a dark, rather heavy-looking German wood; but I lightened it up with gay brocades, warm wine-coloured velvets and cheerful lamp shades. Its worst feature was a great ugly green-tiled *Ofen* or stove, bang in the centre of the best wall. I hated it and, from the first, determined to get rid of it and substitute a large open fireplace. My sons, the architects, everyone—even little Dollie Crowther—assured me this would be quite impossible. I listened and said nothing. I waited.

Even now they don't really know Daisy.

After a time I quietly sent for experts and consulted them; they were unfavourable; I then sent for others, who proved to be equally unfavourable; I could never make an open fireplace and chimney there; it was structurally impossible; the whole house would fall down; and, even if I succeeded, the fire would not work; as English servants say "it would not draw." Now the only thing to do with experts is to go on searching until you find the ones who agree with you; then, armed with their backing, forge ahead. You need never despair, because there are always experts somewhere to suit everybody. The great thing about being an expert appears to be that it permits you the enormous satisfaction of disagreeing with all your colleagues and anyone else you come across whom you dislike, and agreeing with and supporting anyone of whom you are fond. I gave my third lot of German experts strong English tea followed by large quantities of German *Schnaps* (the combination is irresistible) and they were as wax in my hands: I was promised my open English fire.

The first thing to do was to get the dark green contraption hurriedly removed when no one was looking. I was quite Bolshie about it and watched the demolishing show with glee. There was a great hole right up to the roof, but both roof and walls stayed put. I had a charming fireplace of small hand-made bricks put in; the Germans are splendid craftsmen in wrought iron and I had a large simple fire-basket and a fender and fire-irons made. It burns beautifully and now, of course, everyone says it is the jolliest feature of the whole house, as of course it is.

I always thought that, as there is an outside wall, I could have an open fireplace made in the drawing-room in Munich and another, carried directly up from it, in the room above, which is my upstairs private sitting-room, And, if I make any money out of this book, I'm going to try it, whatever anyone may say. If the house falls down—well, let it.

Out of the profits of my second book I determined to turn an old walled kitchen garden belonging to the Munich house into an English flower garden with a pavilion and fountains—for I love the plash of a fountain as much as I do the music of a wood fire. The summer-house, of brick, is high and steep, the front almost entirely made up of folding glass doors with small square panes. It has a floor of slabs of soft-toned silver-grey russet Solnhofen stone, and I insisted on a fireplace. I got it, and it works, but the Germans are quite unused to building fireplaces and therefore the architect designed too large and massive a one; so that it is almost half as big as the whole little room itself. However, I pass many happy hours there watching the wood fire, listening to the fountains and the birds, cheered by the gay colours of the grass and flowers. For of course I have grass—as green and close as I can get it. But it has to be put down afresh every year because no lawn will stand the severity of the Bavarian winter. For seven months out of the twelve I have luncheon and tea regularly in the walled garden or in the little pavilion.

I quite forgot to say that, according to German law, I could not build a fireplace and chimney in my own summer-house in my own garden until I had got in writing a statement from all my neighbours saying that they had no objection! That, in my opinion, is typically German. They are unbelievably obstinate and conservative. The word *gemütlich*, meaning cosy or "homely," is never out of their mouths, but how on earth could anyone be expected to feel either cosy or "homely" sitting in front of that tiled or metal contraption known in Germany as an *Ofen* passes human comprehension. The only perfect thing about it is its name. That is exactly what it is—an *Ofen*—an ugly means of heating. Not even the most obstinate German alive could defend it as something *gemütlich*.

One of the nicest things about my unpretentious little villa near Cannes is that all the rooms have fireplaces, and I can have wood fires smouldering all the time whether they are necessary or not.

4

But truly, in my heart of hearts, I don't care for houses and have never been perfectly happy except in the open with Nature. For this reason picnic fires in the forest have always been my most intense delight.

A few years ago we had a bad outbreak of picnickitis and used frequently to visit the forest at Bad Kreuth on the property of the Duchess Karl Theodor in Bavaria, widow of the famous oculist, and almost at the very gates of the entrance to her summer home. We never went through the formality of asking for permission, but then in Bavaria trespassing does not seem to matter, and anyway I am quite sure the Duchess would not mind in the least. We would start off from Munich, was all that was necessary, and on our way through that my cook would not have time to prepare all the things we wanted for a party of six or seven persons. But a telephone message to Dalmayr, the Fortnum and Mason of Munich, was all that was necessary, and on our way through the city we would pick up a hamper and pack it on the back of the car with our own one from the house. A roast capon, cold ham, caviar, *foie gras*, to which Germans give the ugly name of *Gänseleberpastete* or goose liver, and so on. The house basket would contain all the essentials, including a Mosel or Rhine wine, liqueurs and, of course, Munich beer, hot coffee and, above all, potatoes for roasting in the red wood-ash. The sixty miles from Munich to Bad Kreuth would not take long, and there we would disembark ourselves and immediately start lighting a great camp-fire. Some of the men of the party would do this while Dollie, assisted by one of them, unpacked me and settled me in a camp-chair. Meanwhile, even more important, a footman and the chauffeur unpacked the luncheon and laid it out. And how the exquisite, crystal-like sheen of the frozen snowy ground made my beautiful table linen and napkins look tawdry and yellow! Presently the fire was roaring and the potatoes making a delicious smell as they baked. I ought not to touch them as they make me fat, but, except perhaps for a wing of the capon, I would make of them a large and greedy meal. I could never eat with real appetite and enjoyment except out of doors, nor could my mother Patsy who, to the end of her life, drove the servants crazy by partaking of half-cold meals in a chilly English "summer-house" on the banks of the lake at Newlands quite half a mile from the kitchens. How often at La Napoule have astonished visitors wandered in at lunch time, or even after dinner, found us sitting eating under dripping umbrellas on the damp terrace or lawn. Many of them, particularly if French or American, promptly fled at the ghastly sight lest they should be invited to sit beside us!

But to return to my baked potatoes. A friend (needless to say he is Irish) has a ravishing way of preparing these in the open. He does not cast them all into the fire at the same time, as most picnickers do, but religiously, one by one as he requires them. At the moment when it is a rich golden brown the first potato is snatched somehow out of the crimson embers, its top is cut off rather deeply like the top of an egg, and with a small spoon some of the flowery contents are scooped quickly out and cast to the birds, a little salt and pepper are drenched in, followed immediately by a large pat of slightly salted butter, the cap, which hangs by the toughened brown skin, is replaced, and in a few minutes one eats not a stodgy baked potato such as chefs prepare indoors in an oven, but manna, nectar, ambrosia and all the other things that come down direct from heaven without any intervention by man. I will never confess in public how many of these balls of perfection I can eat in such circumstances. Followed by a cup of really good coffee, the meal is a perfect one. It will thus be gathered that, in spite of my love of Nature, I am by no means one of those back-to-the-land sort of women. I like my comforts.

Now, everything being tidied up and the men-servants having discreetly—and gladly—disappeared to the nearest *Bierhalle*, some perfect hours are at hand. One or two of the more strenuous members of the party may seek to climb Hohlenstein, lying invitingly near on our left. But mostly we prefer to sit quietly and talk. As it is winter the afternoon is short. Soon the daylight begins to fade and a warm moon rises above Risserkogel; the waters of the Weissach almost at our feet reflect the waxing moonlight and sing the loveliest song I have ever heard a river sing. Just where we camp it is wide and winding, travelling over a stony valley and, for its size, making an extraordinary volume of sound, tumultuous, yet soothing. I always loved to arrive beside, and hated to leave, that magical orchestra. I cannot explain why this should be so, because I have seen and loved and fished many streams and rivers, but the little hurtling Weissach is dearest of them all.

On the fire fresh wood is piled; water is brought in our own kettle from the Weissach; tea is brewed. Ghost stories, fairy-tales, old, lovely, somewhat faded memories are recalled; the moon rises higher and higher; the great pine forest around us, every bough bearing a mantle of pure white snow, becomes dimmer, more shadowy, more mysterious; the fire flames shine brighter; the faces of those around it take on an odd, unearthly, fitful beauty; our voices are instinctively hushed. We fall silent.

Long-buried ancestral memories are now awake. Great beasts prowl in the forest and strange beasts make noises in the hills. Unseen presences creep up to the very edge of the little fire-lit clearing in which we sit. Eerie shivers run down our backs and we scarcely dare look around. How alone and apart from men we are at such moments and how close to Nature . . . perhaps, indeed, to Nature's creator and god. How mysterious, unknown and far away seem the souls of those beside us. Their faces look like the carved masks of strangers who have come unexpectedly amongst us from some unknown people.

Then, as the human ties between us loosen, all sorts of strange little birds and beasts and creeping things seem to steal out of the forest and, for that one hour, make us freedmen of their fairy kingdoms. The fir trees (the *Tannenbaum* worshipped for untold generations by our tree-loving Germanic ancestors) are awake—each one a separate entity and endowed with its own individual life. Moving softly they come forward one by one and commune with us, claiming kinship with that within us which is, it would seem, indeed their own.

In that moment we realize that life and death and Nature are truly one: The birds, the beasties, the flowers, the pine trees, we ourselves are all one. Abandoning personal identity we gain something more profound and significant . . . entity . . . reality . . . existence. For that hour we are; we do not merely seem. We are of the all; the all that comes out of the womb of Mother Earth, dwells for a brief time on her lovely bosom, and then too quickly returns.

Arising like an unknown river at some unknown source we travel inevitably to our home, the sea; the sea men call by the name of death. Whether we, like the Weissach, which between its rise in the Hochalpe a few miles west of Bad Kreuth and its fall in Tegernsee, only travels a few miles, or whether, like the mighty Danube, we journey magnificently half across a continent, matters in the end but little. The beginning of all and the end of all is the same. . . .

5

A motor-car travelling rapidly from Aachensee in Austria along the narrow valley road that follows the winding of the Weissach recalls us reluctantly to ordinary life. Through the pine trees we can see the distant lights of our own car on the highway half a mile or so away. The servants have lit them long ago, hoping thereby to awaken in us a little of what they consider common sense. Having reluctantly left their warm stuffy *Bierhalle* they are tramping up and down the white road telling each other that all *Herrschaften* or gentry are mad, and the English more so than any others.

Just as reluctantly as they left their fuggy *Bierhalle* do we leave our perfumed fire-lit clearing and, as we move, the pine trees over our head close out for a time ten million brilliant scintillating stars. Some men of the party stay behind to beat out the fire and as they do so the sparks spring heavenward like golden fountains: it is our customary farewell oblation to the high Gods who always gave us there such priceless, long-remembered hours.

Travelling rapidly along the valley we soon come within sight of Tegernsee, its chill waters burnished by the moon.

When directly under Ringberg we peer upwards to catch a glimpse of the Byzantine-looking castle of my old friend Duke Luitpold,[1] in Bavaria, perched dramatically on the very edge of a rocky plateau that overlooks the whole valley of the Tegernsee.

Now we are in the village of Tegernsee itself dominated by the enormous square castle, inhabited by another friend, the present head of the Bavarian Ducal House;[2] a monastery for over eleven hundred years, it looms on the very edge of the lake, seemingly large enough to house a whole town.

6

And so, like the little Bavarian river Weissach, I pass swiftly—all too swiftly—along the stony valley we call life. I know not whence I came, nor why, nor where I go. I only hope that, like the Weissach, I may on my journey bring to those who meet, or see, or hear of me, some refreshment, some flash of beauty, some echo of eternal music.

For the rest, the most that I can hope to do is to contribute a few footnotes to history (I am one of the few women who love such footnotes, often finding in them the very pith and marrow of the whole business). I gather here some old memories; disjointed ramblings, illogical, perhaps often contradictory. But, even so, does that greatly matter? Except for Chinese sages, Greek philosophers, nudists, faith-healers, higher-thought fanatics and vegetarians, life is rambling, contradictory and illogical.

One can hardly hope to catch the ear of the younger generations who, while denying that they have any roots anywhere, at the same time seem to count confidently on an enormously rich harvest. Nothing, so to speak, from

[1] b. 1890, s. of Duke Maximilian in Bavaria (1849–1893) and Princess Amalie of Saxe-Coburg-Gotha.

[2] Duke Ludwig Wilhelm in Bavaria, b. 1884, m. 1917 Princess Eleonore zu Sayn-Wittgenstein, widow of Prince Otto Viktor von Schönburg-Waldenburg K.I.A., Sep., 1914.

nothing. Surely a more fantastic creed than any of the old discarded ones.

I shall feel richly rewarded if my wandering thoughts and memories should serve to while away an idle or tedious hour for those of my contemporaries who, like myself, now sit quietly by the fire reliving with somewhat pensive pleasure bygone days.

CHAPTER II

WERE WE BEAUTIFUL?

I

I WANT to speak in this chapter of a little group of English women friends to each one of whom I was devoted, and of whom I, in one way or another, managed to see a good deal in spite of being married abroad. More or less the same age, interested in the same things, we all had a reputation for possessing more than ordinary good looks.

Were we beautiful? I don't quite know, but I hope so because, as Countess Olivia said to Viola, "It's a comfortable doctrine and much may be made of it."

A few years ago, when everyone had short hair and short frocks, I didn't think so; now that hair and frocks are again long, I think we were. You can be very, very pretty in a short frock and short hair; I defy you to be beautiful. A handsome friend of mine had her portrait done full length by a well-known and skilful artist when short skirts were the vogue, and the picture, with its two wooden-looking silk-stockinged protuberances, began to seem so absurd that she had to send for the artist and beg him to give her a long frock to match her train. This he did, and now all one can see of her legs are two tiny shoes peeping artfully out. And when you come to think of it, apart from nudes, there has never been a period in portraiture when the artist could successfully cope with female legs; which would seem to prove that one should be painted after the manner of Eve or of Georgiana, Duchess of Devonshire, who, to judge by her portrait, seems, like all Gainsborough women, to have had legs nine feet long. If the Duchess were suddenly to stand up, her head, like that of a Jack-in-the-box, would project miles above the picture frame.

When the artist attacks the difficult task of painting male legs he is, if anything, more ineffective. I once went to the National Portrait Gallery to look at Sargent's huge, rather dreary picture of the Generals of the Great War; all I could see was forests of vague-looking brown legs yet, in spite of this redundancy of understandings, poor Jack Cowans—who had a good pair of legs—didn't seem to have any at all! Our grandparents thought legs immoral; they are worse, they are mostly hideous. How many women does one know with really good legs—or men for that matter, though to either sex they are a great adornment. Judging from their portraits Victorian men had, as a rule, good legs, and Winterhalter and the others were not afraid to say so emphatically. But, apart from the rather tedious ultra-athletic type, most men seem to have not so much legs as things that they can just manage to get about on. And yet nearly all babies have lovely little legs.

But I must keep my wandering wits firmly fixed on my late Victorian and Edwardian beauties. Many of them, I swear, must have had good legs; they could walk, and no woman can do so unless she has. I remember Dame Ethel Smyth in her vivid reminiscences painting a fascinating picture of Queen Victoria and the Empress Eugénie at Balmoral bowing one another through a doorway, each, with exquisite courtesy, declining to take precedence of the other. To this I may be allowed to add a footnote. Dame Ethel describes the movements of the Empress as a poem, and goes on to assert that every bone, sinew and socket in her body must have been perfectly formed and perfectly proportioned and adjusted in order to achieve this enchantment of Andalusian grace. The Empress was an elderly woman when I met her for the first time at Cowes on a sunny afternoon in August, 1906, when she came to call on my hostess, Consuelo, Duchess of Manchester. After that I used to see her frequently at her lovely Villa Cyrnos at Cap Martin, or at Farnborough Hill in north Hampshire. When acquaintances came to tea it was not, of course, etiquette for anyone to leave the room before the Empress. She would solve this little problem in her own inimitable way, and at the same time afford us all an unforgettable treat by getting up, shaking hands with those nearest to her and then, going to the door, turn and sweep us all a curtsy which was the most graciously inclusive gesture that I have ever seen. This was the manner in which she always took leave of her guests and of her Household while still on the Throne of France. How marvellous must such moments have been in the billowing gowns of the period and with the salons and gardens of the Tuileries, Saint Cloud or Compiégne as the background.

Theresa, Lady Londonderry, mother of the present Marquess, was not tall but she had what used to be called a fine presence and she carried herself superbly. She once said to me: "My dear, always enter a room as if the whole place belonged to you." I have never forgotten this and, if there is any truth in a tribute paid to me in his *Memoirs* by von Bülow (he was much addicted to exaggeration) in which he says that I was "one of the prettiest women he had ever met, tall with a lovely figure, exquisite complexion, magnificent hair, splendid teeth, a typical English beauty," I perhaps owe its effectiveness to Lady Londonderry's wise advice. Because mere beauty is not enough; a woman must learn how to make the most of it, and can only do so by keeping strictly to her own type, whatever that may be. Nothing is more unconvincing than an imitation brunette, except, perhaps, an imitation blonde.

I often think that, as well as dancing, walking and riding are essential to a good carriage and graceful movements. The lovely Empress Elizabeth of Austria and her four almost equally lovely sisters were remarkably graceful, and they were all brought up on horseback, being trained by their father almost as strenuously as are circus riders.

I never saw Granny Olivia's legs [1] that I can remember, but they must have been excellent because she was active and graceful until her last day. Patsy [2] had lovely legs in a lovely body, and in all her movements had the grace, economy and ease of a bird. Both Shelagh [3] and I had excellent legs but, strictly speaking, hers were more beautiful than mine and she was, indeed is, a superb horsewoman and an unusually graceful skater and dancer. My poor legs, alas! prematurely deserted me—so we will say no more about them.

Such noted early Victorian beauties as Mrs. Wheeler and Mrs. Langtry were really before my time, although once when Lord Rosslyn was trying his fortunes on the stage I went with his sister, Milly Sutherland, to see him act with "The Jersey Lily" in a costume play. Her face was certainly beautiful in a rather heavy, statuesque way, but I found her figure clumsy and disappointing, and her movements were without grace. Of course, even then she was past her prime but, on the other hand, she had all the advantages of skilfully made clothes and a becoming background. As for Lord Rosslyn, he was just his usual hearty, handsome self—in fancy dress. His eldest sister Milly was one of the loveliest and most delightful personages in the Society of those days. Few women could preside over a great establishment with more ease or grace than she did in London, at Dunrobin, Trentham or Lilleshall. At the head of the famous staircase at Stafford House Milly would stand like an Empress receiving all that was best and most attractive in the social, intellectual and artistic London of the period. A woman of heart, wide

[1] Lady Olivia Taylour (1822–1917) d. of 2nd Marquess of Headford, m. 1853 the Reverend Frederick FitzPatrick (1815–1895) of Cloone Grange, Co. Leitrim, and Warren Hall, Cheshire.

[2] The Authoress's mother, Mary Adelaide Virginia Thomasina Eupatoria (1854–1920) d. of the above, m. 1871 Colonel William Cornwallis Cornwallis-West (1835–1917) of Ruthin Castle, North Wales, and Newlands Manor, Hampshire, g.s. of 2nd Earl de la Warre, Lord Lieutenant of Denbighshire 1872–1917. Throughout this volume the Authoress frequently refers to her parents as Patsy and Poppets.

[3] The Authoress's sister, Constance Edwina, G.B.E., m. 1901 Hugh, 2nd Duke of Westminster; secondly, in 1920 Captain James FitzPatrick Lewis, late R.A.F.

interests and keen intelligence, she attracted all types and may truly be said, in the real sense, to have had a *salon*.

The seven "handsome Hamiltons" were amongst the leading figures of my girlhood's days in London, and I, of course, knew them all although they were mostly too senior for me and I was therefore never quite in their set. The Duchess of Buccleuch, the eldest, gave magnificent if somewhat staid entertainments at Montagu House, a rather pompous but not undignified mansion in Whitehall; Lady Blandford was then in her prime and loved Society; Lady Mount-Edgcumbe preferred her country homes in Devon and Cornwall; Lady Winterton had, I always thought, an extraordinary charm, while Lady Lansdowne, the youngest—when not a Vicereine in Canada or India—lived of course in Lansdowne House—an unequalled background. As I love the Adam period, I liked it better than any house in London, and thought it far finer than the rather heavy style of Kent's Devonshire House next door, which was, of course, later on the London home of Lord and Lady Lansdowne's eldest daughter, the present Duchess of Devonshire. The Devonshire House rooms were too low, and although it was interesting in a way that Kent had not only done the decorations, but designed practically all the larger pieces of furniture, the result was ponderous and monotonous. The greatest exterior charms of Lansdowne House were its gardens at the front and back, and, in the interior, the fact that the hall, the staircase, picture-gallery and state-rooms were all designed as a background for the fine statuary and magnificent pictures it enshrined. It had that combination of dignity and lovableness only found, I think, in great houses in England. You can make a stately Georgian interior into a home if you will, but no one could succeed in doing that with either an Italian Renaissance or an Austrian baroque palace.

In Arlington Street dear Violet Rutland also surrounded herself with a unique and delightful circle, amongst whom artists and musicians were always to be found, as at Stafford House; Violet herself, as is well known, being an artist of grace and distinction. When she knew a sitter well, she could catch a likeness and reveal character with a skill that was sometimes uncanny. Poor darling, like all artists, she must have had to listen to a great deal of nonsense about her art. I have more than once at exhibitions and in private houses heard her work being praised for just those qualities which it does not possess.

No list of late Victorian and Edwardian Duchesses would be complete without the names of Winifred Portland and Consuelo Marlborough. The Portlands have always been my good and kind friends and Winnie was, and is, a woman of brains and quite unusual beauty and distinction. Perfectly as she looked the part of the great Society lady, I like best to think of her at stately Welbeck, the personality and the background matching to perfection.

I do not see much of Consuelo Marlborough nowadays because, somehow, although we both live a great deal on the Riviera, our lives seem to lie apart; but for years she was one of my dearest friends, and a sweeter, truer, finer woman does not walk this earth. Her great wealth was of course a help to Consuelo in a social sense, but her tall grace and stateliness, her charm and common sense would have enabled her to win her way anywhere. She was well fitted to be the wife of the owner of Blenheim, which is, in its pompous way, unique. Personally I never cared much for Sunderland House in Curzon Street, which was a wedding present from her father, Mr. W. K. Vanderbilt, nor, I imagine, did she. A new London house on the grand scale could perhaps hardly help being a little like an imitation of a French hotel. Artists have found it difficult to do Consuelo justice. It was the ensemble that was so attractive. The masses of soft dark hair—now a most becoming grey—the long slim neck, the sad-looking hazel eyes, above all the slender, willowy figure with its unusual height, had in their combined effect something so magnetic and distinctive that the artist seldom succeeded in capturing it. To my mind the only one who partially did so was the Frenchman Paul Helleu who, by the way, also did a charming portrait of Almina Carnarvon, and she is by no means an easy subject, her undoubted good looks being also of the sort described by lady novelists as elusive. Consuelo married as her second husband Colonel Jacques Balsan. Their large château at Eze, with its park and really magnificent gardens, is perhaps the greatest social centre on the Riviera, and there one meets English, Americans and French all mixed up in a delightful mélange.

Darling Rachel Dudley, whether at Carlton Gardens, Himley Hall, Witley Court, or at Viceregal Lodge, Dublin, was a perfect hostess. She too had grace, presence and charm. Perhaps owing to her Quaker blood there was about her something a little apart, some deep reserves, as if her tragic and untimely death stretched its long shadow over her whole path. All this, or so it seems to me, can be traced in Violet Rutland's delicate perceptive drawing made of Rachel many years ago. Another uniquely attractive woman was Gladys de Grey, whose husband, the best shot of his day in England, afterwards became Lord Ripon; Gladys's love of music was deep and sincere and her musical knowledge by no means negligible.

Frances Warwick, half-sister to Milly Sutherland and Lord Rosslyn, was not of a type of beauty that appealed particularly to me—being perhaps too much like my own. She had masses of blonde hair, perfect features and complexion, exquisite eyes, hands and feet and, as everyone knows, could have been Duchess of Albany and daughter-in-law to Queen Victoria had not Blanche, Lady Rosslyn, wisely declined the honour on her daughter's behalf. Her reign at magnificent Warwick Castle and at Warwick House, next door to Milly, was notably brilliant. Of late years she lives at Easton and devotes herself to literature, serious politics and her gardens.

No one who saw her in all her fresh young loveliness can ever forget Sybil Westmorland. Beautiful hair, complexion and figure and a pair of deep violet eyes were her chief charms. She alas! died too soon.

I don't know whether, according to the strict canons, Mrs. George Keppel would be considered beautiful, but she was and is one of the most brilliant and resilient creatures in London Society—or any other. She united wit and audacity to an unerring social tact to such a degree that she could keep a whole dinner party in roars of laughter yet never say an unkind or spiteful thing. Moreover, she charmed women as much as she did men. Nor were deeper gifts lacking. She was loyal and sincere, and her excellent brain made her advice always invaluable. I don't think she was in any way ambitious because, had she been, she could have accomplished simply anything. As it happens, she prefers the exquisite background of Florence (where my father was born) and the society of her chosen friends—chosen, be it said, with perfect discrimination—and her lovely garden.

The present Lady Londonderry I knew as Edie Castlereagh, and her father, dear old, unique Harry Chaplin, was a beloved friend of mine, and I have always admired immensely his daughter's brains, beauty and organizing ability. She, too, has in fullest measure that queer thing called distinction, without which mere beauty seems valueless. Her *Memoir* of her father is a fine piece of work and paints inimitably a spacious English life that has now passed away. Bee Pembroke and Juliet Duff always seemed to me two very lovely women. They are both tall, especially Juliet, and they also have their full share of impressiveness. Ava Ribblesdale, whom I first remember as Mrs. John Jacob Astor, was extraordinarily lovely and has brains and presence.

Aunt Min,[1] Patsy's younger sister, did a delightful thing for our family when she chose handsome Guy Wyndham as her second husband in May, 1892. She thus became the sister-in-law of George Wyndham and his wife, Sibell Grosvenor, Bend Or's mother; old Mrs. Percy Scawen Wyndham of Clouds became her mother-in-law and Madeline

[1] Edwina Virginia, widow of Captain John Monck Brooke of Summerton, Ireland, m. Colonel Guy Wyndham, C.B., late 16th Lancers, b. of the Rt. Hon. George Wyndham (1863–1913), of Clouds, Wiltshire.

Adeane, Pamela Glenconnor, and Mary Wemyss became her sisters-in-law. I doubt if a more handsome, more distinguished or more brilliant group of "in-laws" could have been found anywhere; better still, each one of them married charming and notable husbands. Lord Wemyss (long known as Lord Elcho), and Mr. Adeane have never sought the limelight but, had they cared to do so, would have gone far. Pamela's first husband, Lord Glenconnor, was a stalwart pillar of the Liberal party, her second, Lord Grey of Fallodon, arousing an intensity of admiration I never quite succeeded in sharing.

The Empress Eugénie, the darling Granny-Grand Duchess of Mecklenburg-Strelitz,[1] Mrs. Percy Wyndham and Granny Olivia were four of the handsomest and most distinguished old *grandes dames* I ever knew. Such graciousness, such charm, such a presence! Do people grow old like that now?

The story of how Madeline Wyndham came by her charm and beauty, although well known, will bear repeating. Anne Syms, known as Pamela, was said to have been the daughter of the noted Madame de Genlis by Philippe Egalité Duc d'Orleans. Sheridan, when a widower of forty, wished to marry Pamela, who was then only either fifteen or nineteen—her mother never seemed quite sure which! His first wife, the lovely Miss Linley—an ancestress of my old friend Frederick, Lord Dufferin—immortalized by Gainsborough—said to her husband during her last illness, "I should like you, when I am dead, to marry that girl." Pamela, however, preferred Lord Edward FitzGerald, the handsome second son of the first Duke of Leinster, the premier Duke of Ireland. Lord Edward joined the United Irishmen, became famous as the romantic and handsome Irish leader, and Pamela, because of her magical loveliness, her reputed Royal origin and her unconventionality, attained a legendary fame second only to that of her chivalrous and unpractical husband. She was

[1] Augusta Carolina (1822–1916), g.-d. of George III, elder sister of the Duchess of Teck, and aunt of Queen Mary; m. in 1843 Friedrich Wilhelm IV Grand Duke of Mecklenburg-Strelitz (1819–1904).

always scandalizing the Dublin ladies by very simple expedients, such as going to a ball dressed entirely in black, dancing, and speaking French, much too well, speaking English badly and thoroughly enjoying life. Lord Edward and Pamela had one daughter, also called Pamela, who married Sir Guy Campbell and became the mother of Madeline Wyndham. One of the first things I had to do when I reached England again in 1919 was to attend dear Aunt Min's funeral at Clouds in Wiltshire, where she died in October of that year. She and Guy had two children, Dicky and Olivia, both of whom inherited the good looks and talent of the family. After leaving the army Dick took up painting seriously and has already made a lasting reputation. Olivia can do well anything that she has a mind to.

A few years ago Guy married Violet Leverson; they are very happy, possess two good-looking children and have a nice little place tucked away on the Wiltshire Downs near Marlborough. Clouds, alas! had to be sold, as Dick could not afford to keep it up. The chief glory of the great hall was Sargent's remarkable picture known as the Wyndham group. I was so angry when it went to America a few years ago. No reproduction gives an adequate idea of its grace, at once alert and languid; its marvellous colouring was Sargent at his best, soft and persuasive, whereas his colours were too often loud and intimidating. Had I possessed the money I would have bought it for the National Gallery, where I think we really should have a few *Christian* Sargents. What a pity Sargent never painted George Wyndham, the eldest brother of the three sitters in the group. George was one of the most distinguished-looking and attractive men I ever saw; whenever I met him I envisaged Lord Edward and Pamela. George had much of Lord Edward's romantic flair for leadership, his personal fascination, his somewhat unrealistic idealism. The attempt to unite Irishmen under a single leadership broke George as it had broken his great-grandfather Lord Edward. The noble, and as yet unfulfilled, dream of a Settlement by Consent was indulged in before him by Gladstone and

Rosebery and, after him, by John Redmond and, most notably, by His Majesty King George the Fifth.

George had an Elizabethan sense of prose as those who know his essay on Francis Thompson will never forget. His last years were tragic; his end sudden. Very soon after his death his handsome only son, Percy Lyulph, who was in the Guards, was killed in action in September, 1914, a very short time after his marriage to a daughter of the fourth Lord Ribblesdale, "the Ancestor," whose marvellous portrait in the National Gallery is the finest thing of its kind that Sargent ever did.

2

Though I of course knew nearly all the ladies of the British Royal family, the only one whom I could, strictly speaking, claim as a friend was dear Queen Alexandra, and to her I have paid my devoted homage elsewhere.

I cannot honestly say that, apart from Queen Alexandra, many English Royalties could really be described as beautiful. Princess Louise was the prettiest of Queen Victoria's daughters, as the Empress Friedrich was the handsomest and cleverest. All the others, sons and daughters, were endowed with rich personality and a character such as prevented them sinking into the category of conventional Royalties—a fate that so easily overtakes those born to pomp and circumstance.

The first shall be last. I now come to Queen Mary. As a girl she was pretty; as a young married woman she was good-looking, always well, if somewhat severely, groomed, her lovely golden hair exquisitely *coiffeured*, her complexion perfect. For the past twenty-five years she has been one of the handsomest women in Europe. Her quarter of a century on the throne has given her whole personality poise and her manner assurance. To see the Queen on any state occasion is to carry away an unforgettable impression and, scores and scores of times, I have heard Americans and foreigners rave about the stately and imposing grace of Her Majesty's appearance and bearing at a Court, a Court Ball or other important function. I have never known any Empress or Queen who could wear a quantity of superb jewels with such ease and simplicity and without appearing in the least over-laden. Queen Alexandra could successively wear a great many jewels, but I have sometimes thought her slight figure a little overborne by them; it is never so with Queen Mary.

Queen Mary, quite rightly, has never gone in for extremes of fashion any more than Queen Alexandra, or any other member of the British Royal family, ever did. The Queen contents herself with the variety that is to be obtained by lovely tissues and materials, exquisite shades and half-shades, sumptuous embroideries and stitchings. Speaking generally, most of the Queen's public appearances are of a ceremonial nature and these call for a handsome, even imposing, style of dressing. Moreover, Her Majesty knows that jewellery suits her, likes to wear a certain amount, and this cannot successfully be done with either very simple clothes, or, as a rule, with clothes designed in the extreme fashion of the moment.

One and all, the ladies of the Royal House of Windsor have made it their practice to dress becomingly and suitably with the minimum of concession to extremes of fashion. After all, it is not fitting that they should act as amateur *mannequins*. The young members of course can, and do, allow themselves a little more freedom. Princess Patricia, being an artist, has always allowed herself a certain amount of variety in having her gowns designed to suit her tall, graceful figure and has a fondness for soft-textured materials and long, flowing lines. Princess Arthur of Connaught also adopts a style of her own, yet always contrives to look elegant and chic. As everyone knows, the Duchess of York has popularized her individual type of clothes, which indeed seems to be generally copied by all the young women of the day.

3

Were we beautiful? As I said at the beginning, I really don't quite know. The ascription of beauty is often a matter of fashion, and must always be a matter of personal taste. "If she be not fair to me what care I how fair she be," is as true as when Wither wrote it long ago. Each of the dear women friends, of whom I have tried to paint a simple pastel, possessed certain essentials without which mere beauty is too ephemeral to be taken seriously. As I have emphasized they had *esprit*, distinction, character, personality—and, above all, personality. As to externals, they not only knew how to buy clothes, they knew how to buy suitable clothes and how to wear them on all occasions—and wear them with a difference.

The Englishwoman who really knows how to dress realizes that a touch of apparent carelessness, a suggestion of unconcern that reveals personality, removes her from amongst those who never look anything but walking *mannequins*. Herrick enshrined this "sweet disorder" in English literature when he declared that such elegant trifles:

> Do more bewitch me, than when art
> Is too precise in every part.

Inheritors of a great and gracious English tradition, each of the women friends whom I have named adorned it, enhanced it, passed it on enriched and lustrous to the succeeding generations.

CHAPTER III

A PERFECT FRIENDSHIP

I

FEW things in life are to my mind more tragic than the way in which people waste their friendships. I have always tried to obey somebody's wise injunction to keep my friendships in repair. I take it that by that it is meant that not only should we be continually making new friends, but that we should not indulge in the foolish belief that because persons are your friends you can take them for granted, be rude to them, make use of them and . . . neglect them: and, all too often, neglect them for something and somebody relatively quite unimportant. For each of us, after middle age, the world is always emptying.

Thank God that, although by no means a wise woman, I was always able to recognize intuitively true friends from false. The consequence is that I can only clearly remember one false friend. A certain man, after professing friendship for me and mine over a long period of years, let me down when I badly needed help. An Englishman, I am sorry to say, was the exception that proves the rule. He is, or is supposed to be, very rich. During the German inflation I was at my villa near Cannes and, as my German income was practically worthless, I was in a very bad way indeed. The French who can be so charming when one has money to spend, can be quite the opposite when they discover that one has none. When I am obviously in funds they only see in me a delightful Englishwoman who can give them pieces of land for cemeteries, war memorials or other public purposes, subscribe to all their endless local charities, a comrade and

Ally of the French—many of whose relations and friends even enjoyed the privilege of laying down their lives for *La Patrie.* When I am hard up or have to postpone paying my bills—and more than a month's credit they will not give anyone—then I am only the wife of an infamous *boche!* This was how it was at that particular time. I saw in the Cannes paper that my old English friend was at the most luxurious hotel on the Riviera and, accustomed all my life to turn to the nearest men when I needed help, I sent him a note explaining the circumstances and asking him to cash for me a post-dated cheque. (It was Dollie who put this into my head.) He replied that, as owing to the war, etc., his resources were very much depleted, etc., and must regretfully decline, etc. etc. I have often wondered why it is that when people want to be untruthful or evasive they always wander off into foreign phrases. My countrymen, who don't know any foreign languages, are particularly apt to overwork that beastly little Latin contraction, "etc." I hope my English friend reads this and realizes that I only asked him because he happened to be on the spot. I never liked him—even if my husband did—and, although he often stayed with us in Germany and enjoyed marvellous sport, I never once put foot across the threshold of one of his many houses. Also, when some day he publishes those wonderful reminiscences of his, of which we have all heard so often during the past thirty years, I hope he will tell the *whole* story. Always very proud of his sportsmanship, he was, and is, in my opinion, a poor specimen of his sex and, as Beatrice says, "he that's less than a man is not for me."

Dollie and I were so vexed by all this that we decided we must make a desperate effort to cheer ourselves up. I had in those days a sort of "lady-in-waiting," or companion, a Baltic Baroness provided by Hans Heinrich who, even after our separation, still insisted on such encumbrances. She was called Olga Vladivostockuralovna, or some such name. Of course she was a refugee and, like many refugees, had quite a good business sense; indeed, she had elevated her rickety social and financial status almost to the dignity of a profession. Like all my other affairs, her salary was arranged and paid by the *Hausmarschallamt*[1] at Pless, and she, of course, had sufficient foresight to insist that she should always be paid in sterling. I, of course—I am always a fool about money—received my allowance in German currency. The consequence was that for the time being I was a pauper, while my Baltic Baroness was, comparatively speaking, a millionaire. Dollie went to her and tried to borrow twenty pounds. But she was adamant where money was concerned. Then, to annoy her and enjoy a sort of revenge, Dollie and I concocted a little plot. Pretending that it was their birthday, we sent her off to Cannes to buy a large box of chocolate for the little dogs—two lovely Pekinese, *Chang*, a dog, and his little friend, *Tusan*, who is of course a bitch, but who doesn't really in the least like males—unless they are St. Bernards! The car came round; Lindenau and the footman, between them, pushed in the Baroness who, for a refugee, was of a quite inappropriate rotundity. Then we all started giving her the money to pay for the chocolate. We piled it beside her, at her feet—everywhere—wads—wads and wads of German paper Marks. She protested, declaring that she would pay for the chocolate in English money, whereupon Dollie reminded her that she had just sworn she hadn't a penny of any sort of currency in her possession. At last she was driven off from the door and, as the car passed out by the little gate lodge, we all fell down with laughter, the servants—who did not like her—appreciating the joke quite as much as Dollie and I did.

But Providence never really lets Daisy down, or at any rate not for long. A day or two later Bend Or's[2] huge black and gold yacht, the *Cutty Sark*, dropped anchor in Cannes harbour. I sent a footman in with a note and—because he is an authentic and not a make-belief sportsman—my messenger was back with a nice fat packet containing, so far as I can remember, two to three hundred pounds in clean, crinkly

[1] Office of the House Marshal or Comptroller of the Household.

[2] The family little name of the Duke of Westminster. *See* p. 27 (footnote).

English bank-notes—and what an authentic and reassuring feeling they had after the German Marks made of infamously bad paper. Also, by order of Bend Or, the footman was given a whisky-and-soda, English tobacco and cigarettes and ten shillings.

I forgot to say that the Baroness returned from her shopping expedition with a dreadful headache, because the shops in Cannes were furious when she proposed their taking the motor-load of almost worthless German money. We never dared to ask for details, because Cannes was overrun with refugees and, as they were always begging, the shop people hated them: but she came back without the money and *with* the chocolate, and that evening both *Tusan* and *Chang* were quite besottedly seasick. . . .

This foolish little story again reminds me that, in spite of all I suffered there, I have, as I always had, the greatest respect and admiration for Germans and Germany. I am proud when I remember that the nation, which only twelve years ago was in such low state that a motor-car load of her currency would hardly buy a sweet or a flower, is now once more almost at the top of the tree.

So we dismiss my English friend and, with him, the memory of little personal resentments. Deliberately forgetting them, we are enabled to cherish with pride the nobility of purpose and the disinterestedness that animates mankind as a whole. Above all, it is wisest and best to cultivate personally the spirit of gaiety and courage because, so long as they endure, if we cannot be happy and victorious, we can at least elude unhappiness and defeat. And this brings me back to my favourite theme, real friends and real friendship.

2

All of that seems a very roundabout and frivolous prelude to the story of one of the great friendships of my life. I will call its hero, for no less a word will do, simply Prince Maxl. He belonged to the Austro-Hungarian branch of an illustrious

Bavarian family which had spread into Württemberg and Prussia. Down the centuries its members occupied some of the greatest places in the Holy Roman Empire, and had frequently married into Imperial and Royal Houses.

I first met Maxl in 1896 at Castolowitz, in Bohemia, at the home of my dear friends the Sternbergs.[1] At first we were not much interested in each other. Maxl was shy and reserved and (in spite of all my boasted powers of intuition) it was five years before I got to value him at something like his true worth. As a matter of fact, in those days I was far too busy with social trivialities to have time for intuitions, or indeed anything else that really mattered. Then we became friends. Maxl fell in love with me. Really in love. Now that can be either the ending or the beginning of friendship. With Maxl it was the beginning of a friendship, fine and beautiful, that lasted as long as his life. I feel that to give a frank account of it here is to make for him an honourable memorial and, at the same time, remove for ever all occasion for stupid and malicious gossip.

Writing in my Diary in July, 1906 (that is five years after I *really!* got to know Maxl), I said:

"Our relationship is indeed a perfect example of what I have always said is possible. In spite of the man, for instance, feeling passion and wishing for more than a platonic relationship, a real, fine, close friendship is *quite* possible between two people who, even when perhaps experiencing a bodily sympathy or attraction, can transmute and exalt this feeling with their thoughts, ideas, intellect and common interest in everything around them, such as politics, art, religion, literature and sport. Thus they sustain and inspire one another and hold together throughout the sundering years. I only pray he may come to no harm now that he goes far away."

On re-reading Maxl's letters I find that they tell the story so honestly and completely, with such manly frankness and

[1] Leopold 6th Count von Sternberg, b. 1865; m. 1895 Countess Franzisak (Fanny) Larisch von Moennich (1870–1935).

simplicity that I will just give them as they come—only writing something in between when I cannot avoid doing so:

"*Schloss S. . . . Bohemia, Dec.* 8*th,* '01.

". . . To leave you for months—without saying nicely God bless you and good-bye; for *months*—and heaven knows *whether*, *where* and *when* we shall meet again—that is *more* than even *I* can bear. And that I can bear pretty much even you must admit—for you told me enough these last days! Adding up all that I seem to you, I come to the following charming picture of myself: 'A small effeminate black mole, badly dressed, sometimes a dreadful bore, with hair only growing where it shouldn't (!), wasting his time in thinking about things he shouldn't even dream of, bad tempered and too weak to carry you in his arms, etc., etc.' A nice picture, isn't it?

"Nevertheless I am the fool who, after all that, tells you again and again: I cannot live without you; and though I am such a monster 'on whose shoulder you wouldn't even for a single moment lay your head' and 'for whom you *never* felt anything'—*though* I know all that, and heaven knows how often you have told me—I want to be and will be, your friend. And, believe me, you never had such a true and good one! You are perhaps right when you say that I am 'not enough of a man'—not because I cannot carry you about the rooms—but because another man 'wouldn't waste his time,' as *you* call it, and would try to comfort himself in one way or another—even if he were a monster like me.

"But this monster is *so full* of you, so awfully, madly fond of *you*—of all of you, not only your face, your eyes, your dear, dear hair—but also of your soul, of your thoughts, of all that is in you and comes from you—that the monster cannot go to someone else and succeed in perhaps 'not wasting his time.' It is a nasty, cruel phrase: 'wasting your time.' Think about it and you will admit that it is rather bad of you.

"Now look here, angel, only to-day I got a letter from somebody very nice, telling me to come to Vienna this week—a nice letter from a nice person whom you know, I think, and where perhaps I wouldn't waste my time. But stupid or foolish or what else you will think, I am too *full* of you to forget you. For isn't it 'forgetfulness' if one begins something serious elsewhere? I don't think I *could* do it; all would be a lie, a lie, and a lie, and I am not *false;* even in your nice repertoire of all my splendid qualities you don't say that!

"Dear, dear *Rattie*, if I wasn't sure that I am going to see you on the 18th, I wouldn't know what to do. I look forward so tremendously to seeing you again, even if it is only to say good-bye! And now good-night my dear, sweet friend, my only interest in all this stupid life. Write me a line, please *do,* to say what has happened in Pless. . . .

"I am here till Thursday, then in Vienna at the Jockey Club. . . . And on the 18th I come for one day—the last one—to my sweet angel. . . .

"God bless you.

"Yrs. MAXL."

"*Vienna, November 29th*, 1902.

"I got your dear letter to-day and I thank you so much for it, my dear, dear *Rattie*. I can only tell you what I often and often have told you, that I love you, not only as somebody 'in love' does it, but also as a true good friend—a friendship that ever grows stronger. You are such a nice, fair, and gentle little woman that one must be fond of you; to think of you—and heaven knows that it happens often—makes me always feel as if one were thinking of somebody or something above all human troubles and dirty things. All the good that is perhaps in me is developed by the love I have for you. Forgive me, angel, but I cannot but love you. I will and shall not trouble you with it for I know love cannot be enforced, but in my heart the first place will *always* be for you, and even if 'the storm passes' it will be so for ever and always. Don't think that I will bore you with my love, I will only show you friendship, because you will it so, but believe me, dearest, the time when *only* 'friendship will shine as a bright star and the storm of passion has passed away' is still very, very far off. But you know I am your 'thing' and I can only do what you want me to do. I *like* not to be proud with *you*, I want to be, and will be, in your hands; do with me what you like. Tell me to do this or that, whatever you want, and be sure that the only wish of my life is to please you. And though already years ago you told me that *you* never felt anything like wanting to rest with your head on my shoulder, please allow me to do it sometimes—only sometimes when I am tired and weary of all that one has to stand in this stupid beastly world—which reminds me of a lunatic asylum. Dear *Rattie*, you are so much to me, what would become of me without you! Forgive the stupid letter I wrote to you the other day from the mountains; it *was* stupid I am sure, but it is certainly a comfort to me to write to you, my dear, dear angel. . . .

"Good-night, dearest angel, I am awfully tired, for I had the whole day to work and to talk to Generals and to G.; they all want to say something very important about affairs and know less than I do—and that means *nothing*. But one has to listen and to do so as if one were awfully interested! My thoughts were always and everywhere with you and so they will be always.

"Dear angel, I send you my best love (pardon—'friendship') and one friendly kiss on the dear hair.

"Yrs.

"MAXL."

"*Dec. 2nd*, 1905.

"Many, many thanks for your dear and nice letter. At last it was a long one; but even short ones I haven't got from you for a very, very long time—white devil. And strange—as often as I am in Fürstenstein I never can have you (I mean for a private talk, of course), because it is always: 'Maxl, I must write letters; oh, you have no idea *how many* letters!' I wonder if all the other 'victims' go through the same experience! . . .

"I had to go to Vienna to pass an examination for the General Staff to become a Major. This examination is considered very important; it is therefore funny that they write me now that—by order of the Emperor—I need *not* to make it, and am to become a Major without it! I think such an exception was never made before, and I am rather pleased about it.

"It is really extraordinary what a chatterbox R. is! How

did she know about 'my new love!' 'New love'—good gracious, how exciting that sounds! At any rate, I must say that the person in question is awfully nice and that I was very sorry when she left—that is true. . . .

"What are *you* doing, old *Rattie?* I feel, I don't know why, that you are making many 'victims,' but, whatever their number, I hope you have not quite forgotten *this* one.

"Now good-bye my dear old white *Rattie.* It is funny, but the longer I cannot see you the fonder I become of my old golden-haired Angel, and I hope you too will forget your black—I just wanted to write sheep, but I mean—victim!

"Please write me soon—it will mean a good mark in heaven for you—as I hear so little from you and it always makes me feel better when I get news from the white *Rattie.*

"A lot of nice, really nice, thoughts of every kind,

"Yrs. always, MAXL."

Vienna, July 19th, 1906.

". . . You look so well in Fürstenstein that I can hardly imagine that you do not feel well now. But with me it is just the same; I never felt quite well since I was ill and now I often get so tired and at the same time so depressed that I hardly know what to do. Does it mean anything, or will it go by? I don't know. I only know that I long for you more than ever. We always will be great friends, and I will never do anything to spoil our friendship, as you fear; but still I think things are not exactly as you describe them. If two people are really and truly fond of each other for a long, long time, nothing that could happen really matters. . . .

". . . I was foolish enough to think when we were together the last time in Fürstenstein, that you had begun to care a little for me, and it made me awfully happy, gay and full of joy. For you see I felt less shy and not so frightened as I am sometimes when with you. I thought: Coming back in Spring we shall really be awfully happy together, quite, quite natural, knowing that each cared for the other.

"'Now I will write more often,' so you said, and I *nearly* believed it. But I have been here about a week and still no word from you, and yet the day is so long and it takes so little time to write a few nice lines. And I keep on all the time thinking of you and writing to you, while I can so easily imagine how my letters are received. I *see* it all in my mind:

"You come back from skating or sleighing at five o'clock. Letters are scattered about the table in the hall, and you look quickly at them: some bills, one or two letters from 'victims,' one from home, and of course a letter from me. You sit down and read first the letter from England (either about the acting in Lymington, or from your mother or something like that), then you say 'damn' or 'excellent,' gather up all the letters, bills, etc., and go slowly upstairs. 'Again a letter from Maxl. It is so dangerous and he always keeps on writing in the same way; the poor fellow really loves me, I believe.' So you reach the door of your dressing-room, you enter and ring for Mariechen. Meanwhile, you open my letter and begin to read it. 'Oh, he has sent me the pelt of the white fox he shot, that *is* nice of him, I must write him one of these days,' but more you cannot read as just then the little Prince comes in and you begin to play with him. Then Mariechen arrives, you change your dress and go into your boudoir, where you have tea and keep on playing with the baby. Then Missy, Freytag, perhaps a few guests, or a just-for-a-few-days-asked victim make, one by one, their appearance, till about half-past seven. Hans Heinrich the Seventeenth—or is he the one-hundredth-and-seventeenth—has to be put to bed and then you have hardly time to dress for dinner. As Mariechen arranges your hair (*my* dear golden hair) my letter comes again into your mind: 'I quite forgot that letter' and you continue to read it. But Mariechen has finished to curl and to arrange the whole hair, before you have read very much. You are already a quarter of an hour late and so you must hasten downstairs. 'I cannot leave this letter lying about,' you think almost angrily, so you hurry into the boudoir to lock it up in your writing-table, and then go downstairs. Late—after eleven o'clock—you come back upstairs and *if* you think at all of the letter, you take it out of your writing-table and just glance over it. Then you give a long, long yawn, smile rather wearily and throw my poor letter almost unread into the fire: 'I will answer him—but—Lord—I have *so many* letters to write—all about that Chatsworth acting business' and you go on meditating about—who will act and who not—and go slowly out of the room to undress for the night. And my poor letter shares the fate of so many of its predecessors: it is not answered to-morrow, nor in some days—nor—at all! Honestly—hands up—isn't it so—angel?

"I *know* it *is* so—for I know how such things happen. I too get sometimes such letters; therefore I realize how little I am to you, and still I keep on writing—loving—*adoring* you! It *is* a little sad, but, dearest, you are so much to me.

"Here it is not over exciting. I arrange my apartment —which will be quite nice. Will you ever see it I wonder? The town is quite deserted, everybody is away; people don't come back before January. I have just returned from the Club where I met only two or three stupid people, so I came straight home and—looked at your new photograph for a long, long time; then I kissed it, with the hands on my back, quite from very far: 'It is dangerous, Maxl, somebody might come in. Oh, my neck! you hurt me so dreadfully! Maxl!'

"Good-night, my precious angel—I *love* you.

"M."

How wrong dear Maxl's assumptions were! I treasured and carefully preserved every single one of his letters—else I could not be writing this chapter now. And I always felt bound to discourage him and, for his own sake, give him the impression that, although I of course valued his friendship, it was by no means of vital importance in my life. Thus did convention and worldly prudence introduce an element of deception into a friendship that should have been "artless as the air and candid as the sky." Maxl's nature was such that it craved for a home and love and married friendship; I could give him none of these things and I always tried, as it were, to force him to seek for them where they might be found. I have always thought that a married woman who keeps an unmarried man tied to her is a despicable creature.

"*Berlin, January 7th,* 1908.

"I have just got your letter and really didn't know for a moment whether to be angry or not; then I laughed, because you really are too funny! I wrote you a long letter from Vienna wishing you a happy Christmas and New Year, and telling you how I hope that 1908 wouldn't change our old friendship which began with the first snow, and which will, I hope, only end when one or the other has to face the last snow! Then you sent me your photograph in the snow, which I thought was your answer to my letter. When I arrived here I found the pencil and your telegram, and wired to you at once. So you see you have no earthly reason to be 'awfully hurt' as you say! And then, dear old thing, even if I hadn't wished you a happy New Year, I don't think it would have mattered so much! You know that my feelings for you will *always* be the same; and whether we write 1907—1908—or 1960 has really nothing to do with all that I feel, and shall always feel for you. I am not only very fond of you, as you know very well, but I have the greatest confidence in you, and that gives me a true feeling of lasting security.

"How I should like to come with you to the Riviera now, but I cannot even think of asking for leave to go so far, as I would never get it. At any rate I shall be here and receive you with open arms on the 28th when you come to that lovely place called Berlin.

"The little Rosalie is still quite delighted with your *séjour* in Potsdam; she simply adores you, which gives me pleasure, as I like it when people know how to appreciate you.

"Good-bye, dear old angel—stupid old thing. I send you all the best love I can dispose of, and am always

"Yrs.,

"MAXL."

4

"*Berlin, January 23rd,* 1908. *Thursday.*

"MY DEAR OLD ANGEL,

"You must be the first person to whom I say this—and now don't be too much surprised—that I am nearly engaged to a sister of the little Rosalie! What do you say to that? It is not yet official, so please keep it as a secret till I send you a telegram about it. I go on Sunday to their place in the Hungarian mountains, where I was with the family all last week, and there I think it will be *déclaré*. But I wanted you to know it beforehand, my dear old angel, as I am sure you will be pleased to hear it. It is Gabrielle, the third daughter. I don't think you know her, but I am sure you will like her as she is such a nice kind-hearted and really charming girl.

"Please, my dear old angel, do be nice to her, first on account of our old friendship and then later you will do so for her own sake, as you will see very soon that she is much, much nicer than I deserve.

"We, my dear old angel, shall always, I hope, be the same good, true and sincere friends we have always been, and if I thank you to-day for all kindnesses and everything you did for me in the course of the last ten years—that is not a phrase but a gratefulness which comes from the depths of my heart. I never shall forget all those nice times in Fürstenstein I had with you, and I am sure—as I know you, dear angel—that all that won't change, and that you really will be kind and good to Gabrielle. She will be a charming little wife, of that I am sure, and I am awfully fond of her. I don't doubt for a single moment but that you will appreciate her and I assure you that this certainly adds to my happiness. Please write me a line soon and tell me that you will be the same good, dear friend to *both of us* that you have always been to me.

"I don't know your address, so have to send this letter to Fürstenstein, whence I hope you will get it as quickly as possible. As soon as the thing is *déclaré* I will send you a telegram to Fürstenstein.

"Good-bye, dear old angel, I know you will think of me with all possible kind and affectionate thoughts, and I feel glad for that.

"Always yrs., and always the same true friend,

"MAXL."

"*Schloss T. . . . Hungary, February 2nd*, 1908.

"MY DEAR OLD THING,

"I must write you a few lines to thank you for your kind letter by which I was really very, very much touched. Please don't think that we shall be less friends than we have been for so many, many years. I wrote you that already in my first letter, which unluckily you must have got *after* my telegram. You will see what a charming and extraordinarily nice creature Gabrielle is, and I am sure you will like her very much. She is such a kind-hearted clever little girl, understands everything so well, that I am perfectly sure that all my friends will in the shortest time also be hers. As you are one of my best friends I am sure that she will like you from the beginning. So don't be sad and say that all is changed now; it makes me sad to think that you could imagine I could ever forget you.

"You understand, I am sure, how happy I am that, after so many years of a life, largely passive, I am at last to have my own home and the right to care and work for somebody. That the person who will be my companion for life is such an extraordinarily nice woman, is something which I really believe I have not deserved.

"I leave for Vienna to-morrow and there I shall see what the Emperor has decided, whether I can stay on in the Army or not. So far as one can know the marriage will be in May; at any rate I shall be in Berlin at the end of February for some time.

"And now good-bye, dear old friend, and be sure that I shall always be your greatest and truest friend, and always interested in everything that concerns you.

"Always yrs.,

"MAXL."

Vienna, May 15th, 1908.

"MY DEAREST PRINCESS DAISY,

"I thank you so much for your kind and nice letter which really gave me great, great pleasure; I am sure we shall always remain the same true friends that we have been for years, and the only thing by which you can make me angry is to say that 'you have lost a friend.' You mustn't say that, because it is not true.

"My wedding is fixed for the 3rd of June, and I shall be more than glad when all the fuss is over. What a bore all those preparations for marriage are: it really seems as if people tried to make it as difficult as they could. God knows what papers one has to have, and this and that; I will tell you all about my amusing adventures, and of how I believed for a time that I had never been christened—and wasn't at all sure that I had even been born—because I couldn't find the baptismal certificate! You will laugh. Now, thank the Lord, everything is there and all the bores who every day wanted something fresh are satisfied.

"In the famous Ödenburg, where my Regiment is, I couldn't find a single house for us to live in, so I don't know at all where we shall go in the autumn. Till then we shall stay in the country, perhaps travel a little, and I hope—we shall meet somewhere. Perhaps if it suits you, we could come in summer or later; at any rate I hope we shall meet as soon as possible.

"It is awfully nice of you to give me a wedding present, and I shall, of course, like anything you give us; what I value and always shall value most, is your friendship, my dear old angel, and I am sure you will always have the same nice and kind feelings for me.

"I must say I am rather glad that the engagement festivities are over, for I am always on edge here in Vienna, living only out of my trunks for months, and without anything to do; one gets lazy and doesn't care for anything, and certainly indolence and laziness are the greatest enemies to happiness.

"So I look forward very much to being at last alone with my future wife, who is really awfully nice and very gay and amusing. I hope and believe that you will like her.

"And now good-bye, dear old friend. I too think very often of you, and am always your old 'victim' and now old friend."

Mähren, June 24th, 1908.

"My Dear Princess Daisy,

". . . Thank you very much for asking us to Fürstenstein now, but I am awfully sorry that we can't come; we must leave here to look for a house where we can live in the autumn and near the Regiment to which I am posted. Either Ödenburg where I was for some years—you surely remember—or Steinamanger, the place where we caught the train coming from Keszthely with Erni Hoyos.[1]

[1] Count Ernst Karl Hoyos, of the Catholic line, b. 1856; m. 1883 Countess Marie Larisch von Moennich (1862–1886).

"Then we come back here in the middle of July and are going to Styria later, and shall then have lots to do in arranging our home. But I am sure we could manage to come to you at Promnitz in the second half of September, and I must say I should like awfully to come there and am sure it would be very amusing. Have you also had such great heat? I am sure it was always fresh and cool in dear old Fürstenstein. . . .

"I really hope you are quite well again—you know how much I like to know you well and happy.

"Always yours, my dear Princess, with my very best love,

"MAXL."

September 13th, 1908.

"DEAR PRINCESS DAISY,

"Last week I was in Pardubitz, where I had to look after different things in my old apartment, and then I was at Castolowitz with the Sternbergs. We had a duck shoot which was quite nice, but the people there were awfully dull. . . . Then other people, such as a fat old H. (eldest son of the late C. . . .), his dreadful wife, and so on; you know the hostess well, but I didn't know her as a Bridge player. Quite a horrid performance as she hardly knows the difference between hearts and spades. I had to play with her and two other people in the same *genre* for two hours and a half—not for money, only *so!* It was quite awful! I left with Tonio H. (you know him) in a motor-car for Chotzen; the tyre burst and we had to finish our journey in a wagon in which the farmer was carrying manure to Chotzen. I thought I would have had time to change my smelly clothes at the station, but only managed to undress before the train arrived. I hurriedly put on my overcoat and was fortunately able to jump into an empty carriage—like *Monna Vanna*—while my faithful servants ran after me with all the bits and scraps that mercifully hide one's nakedness!

"Good-bye, dearest Princess Daisy. My wife really thanks you very, very much for thinking so kindly of her and is tremendously looking forward to seeing you as soon as she is again all right. Then you must ask us to Fürstenstein.

"Many nice thoughts and best love,

"Always yours,
"PRINCE MAXL."

"*September 30th,* 1908.

"DEAR PRINCESS DAISY,

"Many thanks for your kind letter which I have just got. I was awfully sorry that I couldn't come to Promnitz, but it was impossible. We had really bad luck; in coming here the main roads were closed for military purposes and we had to go by awfully bad side roads, so that we were shaken about in the auto in a frightful way. I was very much afraid as I was sure it would be bad for Gabrielle: but at first it seemed that there were no consequences. But finally —she made a *fausse couche!* Of course she was quite in despair, and so was I—for all that is not very pleasant, as you can imagine. But, thank God, she recovered very quickly and to-day, after the *faux évacuement* she is almost quite well again, and the whole thing did her no harm; so I hope she will soon be as usual *et l'affaire,* I hope this time a real one, *sera à recommencer.* We leave here in two days for Baden, where we shall stay a fortnight, and then I shall take her somewhere where the air is good in the mountains, or to the sea, before I again assume the warrior pose at Ödenburg! So please excuse my not coming to Pless just now. I really wonder when I shall see you again *at last*—as I must tell you—I am longing to do. . . .

"Rosalie was here for a week; I was out shooting with her the other day and got two stags; she is in Vienna now with the old Queen of Spain who is a relative; the young couple[1] are in Pest and get to Vienna on the 3rd, where I must go on the 4th to meet them—which bores me immensely. Then they come here, but we shall leave before their arrival as there will be *un énorme trouble, chasses, dîners, bals,* and so on; and I really think it is better for Gabrielle to live quietly for the next two or three weeks.

[1] King Alfonso XIII and Queen Victoria Eugenia, married in Madrid, May, 1906.

"Please write me if you have a minute to spare: you know how glad I am to hear from you. I always hope the year will not end without our seeing each other.

"Gabrielle (without knowing you yet) sends you her best love and so do I, dearest Princess Daisy, as I always do when I think of you.

"Yrs. *very* sincerely,
"PRINCE MAXL."

"*Ödenburg, March 20th,* 1909.

"DEAR PRINCESS DAISY,

"I thank you very much for your nice and kind letter from Cannes and send you at last the coat-of-arms for the watch.

"How are you and how do you feel? I hope very well and no longer like a 'stumbling horse,' as you wrote you do feel sometimes! It must be lovely now on the Riviera; even here spring is beginning and I take all the nice rides in the woods which I used to have so many years ago.

"I wonder if we shall have war or not; it becomes a bore at last that one cannot make out if yes or no; every day we have contradictory news. If there is war I should be only too glad to have my part in administering to the Serbs the licking which they so much deserve.

"We live very quietly; sometimes there are people coming from Vienna, which is so near. The Tecks[1] were here before they left Vienna—awfully sad! I must say I understand it because they will never enjoy life anywhere more than they did in Austria-Hungary. I told the Duchess last year that if I ever have a son for whom I have to choose a career, he will become 'an English Duke in Austria-Hungary,' where he will have the nicest shootings, the best horses to hunt, the nicest places in town and in the country to live in.

"And now good-bye, dearest Princess Daisy, Gabrielle

[1] Adolphus, Duke of Teck (1868–1927), afterwards 1st Marquess of Cambridge, eldest brother of Queen Mary; m. 1894 Lady Margaret Evelyn Grosvenor, 3rd d. of 1st Duke of Westminster. The Prince was British Military Attaché in Vienna, 1904–1909.

sends you lots of messages; she greatly hopes to see very much of you in all the years to come.

"From me all the same nicest thoughts as in all the many years since I began writing to you.

"Always yrs.,
"MAXL."

Ödenburg, December 24th, 1909.

"DEAREST PRINCESS DAISY,

"I was just about to write you when I got your telegram. I just wanted to send you our very, very best wishes for a merry Xmas and happy New Year. You know that my wishes for you are always the very best, but still I want to tell you so on great occasions.

"I hope you are well and happy. I often think of you and it makes me always feel pleased and content when my thoughts go back to the old times, when we were at Dresden or at Pardubitz—or Fürstenstein for the first shootings when the whole bag amounted to two pheasants, one hare and three squirrels! Once I shot two foxes! Now the shooting has become splendid, but surely it was just as much fun in the old days when the head-huntsman blew with a flourish of trumpets all the customary calls if only we bagged a weasel!

"To-night we have our own Xmas tree! First the servants get their presents, then the tree arranged by Gabrielle is lit up and the 'Crown Princess' will be brought in and get presents from us, the grandparents, and so on; but I don't believe she will appreciate them very much. Then Gabrielle and I give each other our precious personal gifts; and at last come the dogs. . . ."

"*Ödenburg, February 11th,* 1910.

"DEAR PRINCESS DAISY,

"Many thanks for your telegram which Rosalie has sent me in a letter. It is *such* a pity that we cannot come to Berlin while you are there, but it is really impossible. . . .

"We have been in Vienna several times, to balls, dinners, and so on; nothing wildly amusing, but still it was quite interesting to see lots of people—most of them running after something—'the only thing' they want for the peace of their life—and as soon as they have got it, there is already another thing to run after! It always makes me laugh, and the older I get the more I feel that contentment comes rather from within than from outer circumstances. Forgive these philosophical reflections, but as we have always shared our thoughts, why not now?

"I heard from different people that you are very well and *très en beauté*. How did you find Rosalie? Is she already very fat and heavy? Do write me once—if you sit down to answer 6,000 letters as you always used to do when I was in Fürstenstein for one poor single day! 'Maxl, won't you play the piano for me, I have lots and lots of letters to write,' and you went upstairs, *perhaps* opened the window into the hall, and I had to play till you had written to two or three hundred 'victims,' and then we went out to put order into the demesne and the garden! However—good-bye, dearest Princess Daisy and many nice thoughts from:

"Yrs. always,

"MAXL."

3

After many postponements and disappointments, Maxl was able to bring Gabrielle to Fürstenstein in July, 1910. Both for Maxl's sake, and the sake of her sister Rosalie, whom I loved, I was prepared to love Gabrielle. There was no need to make any allowances; she was all, or more, than Maxl had painted. She was devoted to shooting and, I think, liked Fürstenstein.

My youngest son Bolko[1] was born in the autumn of 1910. I was most dreadfully ill with blood-poisoning and all sorts of complications, some of the after-effects of which remain to this day. I really thought for a time that Daisy was going to be asked to give up the ghost—but Providence thought better of it, which seems to prove that even the most exalted can sometimes change their minds with advantage. This explains Maxl's next two letters:

[1] Count (*Reichsgraf*) Cecil Bolko Conrad Friedrich von Hochberg, b. Berlin-Lichterfelde, Sept. 23, 1910.

"*Wien, Palais Archduke Salvator.*
"*December 25th,* 1910.

"My Dear Princess Daisy,

"I was so glad to hear that you are better at last and have left for Cannes, so I hear, or somewhere in the South. These lines not only bring you my very best wishes for Christmas and New Year, but tell you at the same time how much I thought of you all these weeks when you were so ill, and how glad and happy I am that you have got over all that now. I am sure you will be all right very soon and when we meet again I suppose you will already have forgotten all about it. . . . I couldn't think it possible that anything *could* happen to you, as I am sure you will live for many, many years.

"We are going back to Ödenburg for the winter until May; then I leave the Regiment altogether and we go to Baden, near Vienna, where Gabrielle will wait for the arrival of No. 2. No. 1. is already quite a grown-up person and very much admired by everybody!

"I hope that by autumn we shall have found somewhere to settle down, for it is tiresome not to be really at home anywhere. On the other hand, it is so difficult to find just the thing you are looking for. Twice we thought we had found it, but either it was not for sale after all, or something else happened, and it was nothing again.

"Please do write me a word or a line, *where* you are, and *how* you are, as I don't like not to know. Gabrielle sends you her best love and all the nicest thoughts and wishes.

"Good-bye, dear Princess Daisy; I hope you *feel,* even if I cannot express it, as well as I wish to do, how much I thought of you all that time, and how sincere and from my very heart all my wishes are—which I form for your recovery. Always yours, since many years,

"Maxl.

"Best wishes to Hans Heinrich. I write to Fürstenstein not knowing your address."

After receiving one of my pessimistic effusions, Maxl replied as follows. I put his letter in because the advice proved effective and I therefore commend it to any of my readers who may have to face similar experiences:

"Many thanks for your nice letter and the beautiful sketch of the white angel and the *schwarzes Kind.*

"If you feel depressed I advise you to do this: Take a bit of paper and write down all your sorrows on one side, and all you can do to cure them on the other side. You will see that most of them vanish as soon as you give them an objective reality; whimsies produced by nerves (as well as genuine sorrows) will grow less when one endeavours to find means to banish them.

"Do try to follow my advice, even if you think it stupid at first. At any rate, you will see by it that I think very much of you and that all my feelings for you are, and always will be, the *same*—and that is the *best* ones.

"All my heartiest wishes for Christmas, dear old girl, and I hope to hear very soon from you that you are well and try to be happy.

"Yours as always,

"MAXL."

"*Vienna, January 5th,* 1911.

"MY DEAR PRINCESS DAISY,

"I cannot tell you how much pleasure your letter gave me; first of all because I saw by it that you are so much better and will be quite well again—of that I am sure. Then because all you say is so nice and kind, and it is just the way I always feel about you—dear old thing.

"I understand so well all that you felt when you were ill and low, how little you cared whether you were to die or not. Even if one is in good health one often gets so tired of everything, that one simply longs to have done with all the nonsense of this world. Now it is different with me, as I know that Gabrielle wants me and the child —and later the children—so one doesn't think of the 'how it would be—if all were over'; but in former days I wanted so often—not to die (because one has to go through such a lot of unpleasant performances till it is done)—but to *be* dead. *If,* and *how*, life will be after death, I cannot envisage, but I always think that the greatest blessing will consist in the realization of eternal peace. This I think will happen to all good people, whereas the few bad people (for there are not so many really bad people in the world) simply won't feel anything at all. Perhaps it is wrong not to believe in hell and all the eternal punishments, but I really do not think that one could do anything so bad during those miserable few years we spend here, that would deserve *eternal* punishment.

"You are quite right when you say that one has chosen the best part by living only for one's family. Of course I was at first a little sad at having to give up my soldiering because, after so many years, one takes an interest in working and feels pleased—or not—at having done this or that and watching the outcome. But after all, in any profession one has to depend too much on other persons and still more on luck, and I find that all who have taken any part in public life over a long period and can retire without having suffered a painful check—have had rare good fortune. And then independence is so agreeable; therefore, after all, as soon as we have got our house, I wouldn't go back into *any service*. But there is no danger that I shall ever be asked to do so, as it has been decided that on account of Gabrielle's health it would be impossible.

"I was in Hungary the day before yesterday for the funeral of poor Friedrich Carl Hohenlohe, Baby's husband. The Prussians are all so ridiculous; poor Friedrich Carl was simply a private person—indeed, anything but an official personage. The funeral was in the country, yet all those fools were dressed up as if they were at a Court Ball. Plumes, decorations, swords, spurs, top-boots and God knows what; just the thing for people like Max Fürstenberg and Hugo Reischach.[1] Perhaps it has to be so, but I cannot help finding this rage for dressing-up simply ridiculous.

"The Emperor Wilhelm, of course, adores it. I saw him this year in the autumn when he was shooting at my father-in-law's, with golden spurs, yellow boots, and whole birds on his hat; in short, all the paraphernalia which you know so well and which always makes me think of a circus-master!

[1] Hugo Baron von Reischach (1854–1933), for many years Master of the Horse to the Emperor Wilhelm II; author of *Under Three Emperors*. London, 1927, Constable.

Poor man, he means so awfully well; everything he does is intended for the best, and still he is so completely destitute of tact that everything turns out exactly opposite to what he intends; so that I have come to the conclusion that the most indispensable quality for a Sovereign is tact. The merest animal, if he has tact, will thrive better than the most intelligent man, if he has none.

"I wonder how things will go in Germany after the new elections; very badly I think, thanks to the blunders of the conservatives who either can't or won't understand that they must make concessions in order to safeguard the position. Everywhere things are drifting towards an internal crisis—in England, Germany, Russia, in our own country, everywhere. I don't think there is any fear of the slightest international complications, because they are too much afraid of each other. I am quite sure that *that* man will be the saviour of the world who finds something to put in the place of all the different parliaments. As it is to-day it is a completely unsound institution and will end as every institution has ended—by the errors of its representatives. Kings have been beheaded, monarchies abolished, all because the representatives of the régime—the sovereigns, their mistresses, their ministers, and so on—abused their power; and to-day, in the same way, deputies and representatives of the people abuse their position, and will therefore end by undermining the parliamentary system.

"But enough now, dearest Princess Daisy; I hope you won't mind all this nonsense; but I love to talk to you and to tell you what I think, as I know you will keep it all to yourself.

"Gabrielle sends you very best love and the photo of herself with our 'Crown Princess!' She was not so ill as she was the first time, thank God.

"Many, many nice thoughts from your *great* and *true* friend, who likes you very, very much.

"MAXL."

"*Ödenburg, May 10th*, 1911.

"DEAR PRINCESS DAISY,

"Many thanks for your letter; it was such a long time since I had news from you! I am sorry that you are still far from well; it does last a long time and you must have quite forgotten how one feels if one is well and *not* expecting a baby! But I am sure that now in summer, when you are as much as possible in the open air surrounded by flowers, all will be right very soon. At any rate, I wish it for you with all my heart, and so I hope that you may still be very far from becoming a real angel!

"I am awfully sorry that we cannot come to Pless now. Gabrielle doesn't want to travel and I myself have promised the Festetics to go to Pest for a few days. The last days in May we go to Baden, near Vienna, where the new baby is expected in July; why Princess Metternich thought Gabrielle had already got it, I don't know! At any rate, I *shall* be glad when everything is over, and look forward to the time when Gabrielle will be able to enjoy life again. Life is not so long after all, and altogether the baby-getting performance takes more or less a whole year—which really is rather much!

"Now I must tell you something that will make you laugh. A fortnight ago I was shooting capercailzie with Charles Kinsky at his place in Bohemia. There was a Belgian lady there, a Vicomtesse S., whom you have surely met somewhere, and to whom Feri Metternich is devoted, I think. Well, this lady pestered me all day long to write something in her album, where masses of people had already written very high-flown sentiments—Paul Bourget, and other people of that sort; and then lots of people who sweat blood and water to prove their *esprit*, which is conspicuous by its absence. I hate to make a fool of myself by writing something affected at which everybody laughs behind your back. So I said I would put only my name, but as she insisted I should write some 'exquisite sentiment,' just before I left I scribbled in her dam'd book:

> 'Past errors of duty towards others always bring us back to the moment foreseen in advance.'—*Mullincourt*.

"Needless to say I invented everything, including the name of the *soi-disant* author. At first everyone tried to explain the meaning of this profound sentence, then, grasping that I was pulling their legs, they all laughed heartily, as I hope you will.

"And now good-bye, dear Princess Daisy. I should like very much to see you after all that long time! Do write me about your plans and don't forget that I very often think of you and all the fun we have had together!

"With best love from Gabrielle and myself.

"Yrs. MAXL."

Maxl, accompanied by Gabrielle, who had a cold, joined us again for Christmas, 1913, at Pless—the last before the war. The party included Christa and Emmanuel Salm-Salm, Gottfried and Henriette Hohenlohe, Hansi and Olivia Larisch,[1] and some others whom I have forgotten. I am happy to remember that I then gave Maxl the greatest proof of friendship that a woman can give . . . her trust. According to my Diary this is how it happened:

"They all seemed happy here, and last night, just as in the old days, little Maxl came into my upstairs sitting-room and played the piano while I dressed for dinner, and we talked through the open door. As he had been playing Bridge he could not come up earlier, and so in order to join him I dressed hurriedly in thirty minutes.

"He played all the dear, favourite tunes and songs of mine which we have known for years and as I left the room to go and dress, I leant down and kissed the top of his bald head as he played an old song called 'How can you expect me to forget you,' and, my dear Diary, this was the first kiss I have ever given him—and he in all the years has only once or twice just touched my hair or forehead.

"My eyes were full of tears—and he saw them—and tears came to *his* eyes also, remembering Fürstenstein as it used to be, the blue sofa I used to rest upon while he played to me in the evenings before dinner, while Hans was enjoying Bridge or Patience downstairs.

[1] Emmanuel, e.s. of 7th Prince Salm-Salm, b. 1871, K.I.A. at the battle of Pinsk (near Brest-Litovsk), Aug. 19, 1916; m. 1902 the Archduchess Christina, e.d. of the Archduke Friedrich and aunt of King Alfonso XIII; Prince Gottfried of Hohenlohe-Schillingsfurst (1867–1932), Austrian Military Attaché, St. Petersburg, 1903–1907, m. 1908 the Archduchess Marie Henriette, sister of the Archduchess Christina; Johann (Hansi) Count Larisch von Moennich, b. 1872, m. 1912 Miss Olivia FitzPatrick, first cousin of the Authoress.

"He took my hands and held them, and said he had no friend like me, and he was ever and always would be the same true comrade.

"I had him on my left-hand side at dinner and we talked—of all things in the world—politics! And then I turned often to the right and spoke with the Crown Prince Wilhelm of old times."

When Maxl got home he wrote me as follows. The last letter of his that I shall quote, it makes a fair end to a beautiful story:

"If you had only one ace in your hand the struggle would, of course, be unequal and I could well understand your discouragement; but as it is, you hold not *one,* but many, trump cards, so don't get nervous and play them all. Be a good diplomat and you will still do with people whatever you like. Everybody is fond of you, you know how to take people, how to talk to them, and so forth. Last, but not least, you are in a position where you can do lots of good. You hate snobbism and 'pretending' as you call it; and so do I, but one has always to play one's little part in one way or another. So play your part now as the gracious Princess; you will remain yourself—my dear old white angel—all the same! Take it as a new page in your life-book—one has to turn its pages sometimes. The first part of this book was 'Princess Daisy'; the new one will be 'the reigning Princess,' and I know it will be just as attractive as the first one; you can not only *do* what you like, but you will do it *well.* So let it appear as the new book for Christmas, 1913; *you and* the whole world will enjoy it!"

§

If it be correct to describe as home the place from which we come, then Maxl has gone home. While here, he did much that was good and beautiful, and he created one very rare and utterly lovely thing . . . a perfect friendship—of which this chapter is a very inadequate, but most sincere and grateful, record.

Maxl, prince amongst men and man amongst princes, I salute you here by a name that is not yours, but which you will recognize. I selected it with deliberate care because it is a common *Kosename* in your beloved Austria and, therefore, typifies you as in every way a humanly representative figure in such fashion as your native modesty and inimitable loyalty would approve.

How often did we laughingly wonder together as to what would happen "after the last snow" had fallen for us. On a November day a few years ago "the last snow" fell for you, and there is no telling when my "last snow" may fall. . . . Let all the snows of all the future be in their pure and radiant beauty a heavenly memorial to a friendship pure and beautiful as they were . . . but, unlike them, imperishable.

CHAPTER IV

POLITICIANS I HAVE KNOWN

I

THE title of a chapter in a book seems to me to be like a new hat—seldom, if ever, entirely suitable. Almost as I write the words at the head of this one I begin asking myself, does one ever know a politician? A more cynical person than myself might follow that up with what parliamentarians call a supplementary question: In the ordinary politician is there ever anything very much to know?

Gazing back into the mists of a childhood which now almost begins to assume for me the dignity of the prehistoric, I see the greatest of them all, Mr. Gladstone, as merely a venerable old country gentleman, kindly and gracious to children, enshrined in my recollection largely because of a deep and musical voice.

Mr. Gladstone was a huge success because he was to perfection the product and mirror of his age. Rhetorical, romantic, fanatically Puritan, self-appointed Christian arbiter of the morals of Turks, Moslems and Jews, a man of first-class intellect who could with the greatest ease delude himself—and often others—into believing almost anything! Why, he even believed—to give one or two examples from memory—that one had only to be born an Armenian and to be persecuted, to become perfect; that if you directed verbal thunder loud and long at any evil it would crumble like the walls of Jericho; that rhetoric moves mountains, whereas it only moves mutton-heads; that Queen Victoria could, with impunity, be treated as if she were a public meeting; that Disraeli had horns and hoofs; that Marie Corelli and Mrs.

Humphry Ward had made permanent contributions to English literature; that Liberalism, both political and religious, really lived up to that great name; and that you could convert gay and erring females, induce them to leave the London streets and to adopt the career of ill-paid domestic drudges in horrid institutions, by meeting them in Jermyn Street after midnight on the sly and giving them modest half-crowns and a generous measure of good advice. And, in spite of these, and many similar absurdities and contradictions, Mr. Gladstone was a great man—and a great Christian in the sense that he was quite prepared to disestablish and disendow anything or anybody (even erring females) for the good of their souls.

Of Lord Salisbury I can only give one clear personal recollection. It happened some time between 1895 and 1902, during his last Premiership. For some reason or other which I have now forgotten I stood beside him at the head of the staircase of his house in Arlington Street on the occasion of a great political reception. By way of conversation (he was not an easy person to talk to nor are such occasions propitious) I remarked what a lovely sight it was to see the beautifully dressed ladies, nearly all wearing tiaras and fine jewels, slowly climb the imposing staircase as in a great canvas by Paolo Veronese. "If you had lived forty or fifty years ago you would have found the sight far finer—all the long necks and bare shoulders." His unexpected reply immediately evoked for me a Court at Buckingham Palace or a great party at Windsor when Queen Victoria was in her hey-day, the Prince Consort stalwart and watchful beside her, and the women graceful as swans on water—a mass of flowing, billowing lines. I have since often wondered if this incident could be adduced in support of the popular belief that all politicians, however austere, are susceptible to feminine influence!

Sir Henry Campbell-Bannerman I knew but slightly, having only met him once or twice at dinner parties and on one occasion heard him make a speech at Chester. He struck me as an agreeable nonentity, an amiable stop-gap, who would be quite in place as Chairman of a Missionary or Philanthropic Society, but no fit head for what was then still the British Empire. I have heard it argued that in England a nonentity always makes the best Prime Minister. If that be so, then Sir Henry is high up on the list, indeed could hardly be beaten by some of the members of the present English Cabinet.

When Lord Salisbury left office in 1902 he was succeeded as Prime Minister by his nephew Mr. Balfour.

I have in mind an unforgettable picture of him a year or so earlier at Shelagh's wedding to Bend Or at St. Paul's, Knightsbridge, at which he looked like a mislaid and slightly bedraggled archangel. Of course the Conservative party pretended that he was both a great leader and a great politician, but that was nonsense, and they conspired to do so only because they had no one else convenient. His political career was aptly epitomized by the criticism made in the House of Commons by an opponent after Mr. Balfour had delivered himself of one of his long and halting orations: "The speech of the Right Honourable gentleman," said his opponent, "has illuminated every single aspect of the subject under discussion—except how he means to vote." Naturally no one could ever know how Mr. Balfour meant to vote, for the simple reason that he seldom quite knew himself. His aloof and critical intelligence never succeeded in grasping that great, British, fundamentally democratic dogma that if only you could endow cabbages with votes and induce them to exercise the vote when they had got it, then they would all somehow turn into intellectual and moral supermen. Mr. Balfour, with all his mental dexterity, could never quite bring himself to believe that. As a matter of fact, he entirely lacked Mr. Gladstone's unassailable capacity for belief, and it is very interesting that two men so directly opposite in every way should successively become venerated elder statesmen of the British people. Mr. Balfour was quite impossible at the head of a political party because he would neither make decisions nor lead in any definite direction.

Nevertheless, there he was, and we had to deal with him. During illness one's mind can be both agitated and, in a way, abnormally clear. After Bolko's birth I lay week after week worrying as one does at such times about my two chronic preoccupations—England and Germany—during December I wrote Mr. Balfour the following somewhat feverish letter:

"*Gross-Lichterfelde-Ost, Jungfernstieg,* 11.

"Dear Mr. Balfour:

"I have been very ill and even now am not really allowed to write letters or see a soul. Thank God I am allowed to read my books and the papers; but the latter I generally end by throwing to the foot of my bed in disgust when I read what L.G. and Winston say. Now Blatchford begins to mordle again on a subject which, although very important, is at the present moment not of immediate urgency—that is, to make men realize the necessity of electing a Government that will provide an efficient Army and Navy.[1]

"What England must now trouble about, and fight for, is the very existence of England. Dear Mr. Balfour, do not think my illness has made me mad, as I can assure you that both nurse and doctor would tell you that at the present moment my temperature is normal!

"Living in Germany as I have done for so many years, and realizing the power and steady purpose of this great government machine, I am made miserable when I compare it with the present degradation of England where my heart will always be. That England, proud mother-country of many Empires, should now be ruled by *Ireland* and a few Labour members and Socialists *is* a degradation.

"Do the people realize that the first thing the present Ministry did was to raise their own salaries; that . . . .'s present income is, for him, like the finding of a gold mine; and that without his ministerial salary . . . would be living on £1,500 a year.

"But now, Mr. Balfour, to my real point. As, anyway,

[1] Robert Blatchford, b. 1852, the well-known Socialist, was then writing on these subjects in the *Daily Mail.*

you probably think me insane, I may as well go ahead and say what I want.

"Well, what are old traditions? Let them go like the poor hansom cabs. What are the Liberals now but Socialists? That being so, let there be no more Unionists in England, but Conservatives, prepared, because it is unavoidable, to give *Home Rule to Ireland.* That cry of Home Rule I have heard since I was a child—it is *bound to come.* And for God's sake don't let the present Government give it, for, if they do, later on it will mean Home Rule for Wales and Scotland, and Great Britain will cease to exist.

"Give Ireland Home Rule; it would *not* be treachery on the part of the Unionists, because it would be the saving of England, and if England is lost Ireland is surely lost. Join hands even with Redmond. I believe he does not trust the Asquithians and, as he is a gentleman, would be glad to join with gentlemen.

"And then, when that poor little Ireland (I must own years and years ago ruined by England through the difference in religion) gets Home Rule, she won't know what to do with it without the advice and co-operation of England. She is a country absolutely full of uneducated people (both high and low), and down trodden by ignorant, suspicious priests. It is not speeches from platforms that will turn the Irish people into loyal friends of England, but common tasks carried out shoulder to shoulder and man to man.

"Forgive me—but I must intervene. *Call, call* together all the Conservatives and Unionists and make them, yes, make them face realities. Could there not be a *private* meeting (no newspaper reporters), and let your battle cry now be, Home Rule *for Ireland?* It might well be the saving of England for all the years to come. Anyhow, one dare not go on like this.

"What does it matter if you *do* feel it to be a lie; then *lie* to save a friend, and that friend Great Britain.

"America will not continue to send money to Ireland.

"Please forgive this letter and laugh as much as you like, but I feel frantic here, lying uselessly in bed and reading Lloyd George's speeches . . . miserable, with no one to speak to. You must be very tired and very bored. I hope you are feeling very well.

"With best remembrances, dear Mr. Balfour,

"Yours,

"DAISY OF PLESS."

Mr. Balfour was the soul of courtesy and to this screed he promptly replied as follows:

"*Whittinghame, Prestonkirk, N.B.*

"*3rd, January,* 1911.

"DEAR PRINCESS PLESS:

"Your kind letter reached me in the hurly-burly of the election and gave me much pleasure. I am glad that you still take so keen an interest in our domestic politics, and follow our fortunes with so keen and sympathetic an eye. The present position is curious and critical: no man can, I think, say with confidence what the ultimate issue is going to be; though he must be of a very sanguine and confident temper who is capable of looking forward into the future without feelings of grave anxiety.

"I was so grieved to hear of your serious illness: but your letter, and some talk I had with the Duchess of Westminster, give me every hope that things are going well with you.

"Pray believe me,

"Yrs sincerely,

"ARTHUR JAMES BALFOUR.

"Every good wish for the New Year."

The vapourings of an emotional woman suffering from the abnormal mental excitement inevitable after an illness that brought her almost within touch of the grim outstretched arms of death? Perhaps. But what would have been the result if the Conservative and Unionist Party *had* voluntarily, freely and magnanimously given Ireland the fullest measure of Home Rule in 1910 or 1911? Would Ireland not now be a contented and prosperous Dominion within the Commonwealth—the Irish emerald the loveliest jewel in the Imperial crown? Would a United Kingdom, truly *united* in heart and purpose and ideals, have prevented Germany declaring war in 1914? And, had the war unluckily come, would it not have meant a whole Irish Army serving spontaneously and wholeheartedly and heroically in France? Would not the tragic farce of Irish conscription, and all its terrible aftermath, have been avoided? It is hard to say—but it would, at the worst, have been a great, a gallant, a noble adventure in the old spacious English tradition of courage, magnanimity, brotherhood and hope.

The niggling way, from beginning to end, in which the Conservative Party handled the whole Irish question dealt a blow to the Empire from which it will not soon recover, that is, if it ever does. I am a convinced and life-long Conservative, but in all Conservative parties in every country there is a substrata of crusted, narrow, unprogressive non-entities who still think that the world is flat. At this moment they are very vociferous over the Indian question and, if they have their way, we shall lose India as we lost the American Colonies—with which the names of West and de la Warr are so proudly associated.

George Wyndham could, and would, have solved the Irish question. With the blood of Pamela FitzGerald in his veins, he was Elizabethan in his vision, his courage, his charm, intuition, his fine presence, his gift of oratory, all combined to make him sympathetic and attractive to the Irish people. He was on the very edge of success. The little politicians, yapping at his heels, demanded blood. Mr. Balfour, his friend and chief, flung him to the yappers.

A truly great statesman would not have done that.

As Chief Secretary, Mr. Balfour had been himself the ruler of Ireland during a most difficult, and therefore most enlightening, period. He had vision and understanding. He neither saved the Irish situation himself, nor allowed his successor, George Wyndham, to do so. I therefore maintain against all comers that, however unquestioned his eminence in other respects, Mr. Balfour was not a great statesman. A child can see the outcome of his policy now; a statesman should have seen it then. He lacked neither imagination, courage, knowledge, disinterestedness nor opportunity. What, then, did he lack?

In my opinion what he lacked was faith—the faith that can remove mountains. Believing in nothing he accomplished nothing. That, in spite of all its brilliance, is the real reason why his political career was constructively sterile.

2

Lord Curzon was an entrancing eighteenth century figure and, like German baroque architecture, was perhaps most admirable when viewed from a distance. Close examination of all the manifold details that went to the making of a complex and contradictory personality was, somehow, displeasing. But, to stick to the simile, Lord Curzon was certainly an arresting figure. Almost startling. Like many pompous people he was in certain ways both shy and childlike, and his vanity was too naïve to be really annoying. I am quite sure that he never said he had twice married beneath him with complete success, or sent out dinner invitation cards with gilt edges and surmounted by a gilt coat-of-arms. But I am equally sure that he would have done either had he wanted to. He was a true aristocrat after the ancient French pattern in that he considered nearly everyone beneath him, and he despised the mob. The awful thing is that he was quite right; nearly everybody *was* beneath him and the mob *is* despicable. In conversation, presumably to flatter his listeners, or to put them at their ease, he would sometimes graciously refer to "people like ourselves," but I doubt if in his heart of hearts he really believed that there was anyone quite like himself. And again he was right. There wasn't. Cheap people thought themselves witty when they declared that he looked like a butler. If he did (and I deny it) princes can afford to look like butlers—if they want to—and no butler ever looked like Lord Curzon. In the intimacy and privacy of affection and friendship George Curzon looked like a mischievous, delightful child: the Marquess Curzon of Kedleston like a graven image. He certainly, when he wanted to, could make people tremble like the junior houseboy when summoned to the butler's private sanctum for a good wigging; the uncomfortable and dangerous gift of being able to make anyone feel in the wrong was fatally his. I never saw him preside in state at a Durbar, but I am told that when he did so he outshone in presence and dignity the most illustrious of the Indian Princes. That is the sort of thing even the best butlers cannot do.

A man of the greatest intellectual brilliance, with the clearest of brains, Lord Curzon valued inordinately the trappings of eminence. Entitled by birth to wear a name as good as any and far better than most, fortunately he disdained to hide it under a brand-new territorial designation; but he bedizened it a little ridiculously with the insignia of rank—stars and ribands and mantles, prefixes and affixes, and cluttered it up with what was in a personage of his eminence largely meaningless addenda. The splendid simplicity of the Garter or the austere simplicity of the Order of Merit perhaps—but nothing more—and certainly nothing less, because the V.C. was not within his reach; had he been a soldier he would certainly have won it. I particularly dislike quantities of minor orders and decorations because they are so characteristic of German *Bürgermeister*. Even so, it says much that he never quite succeeded in divesting himself of simply being "Curzon." That was his signature to the end although occasionally as a sort of afterthought he would add an "of K."

No one who once spoke to him for five minutes could ever again liken him to a butler. The wide intelligence, the piercing thrust of the brain, the love of culture, of poetry, of great prose, of fine architecture, the selfless fanatical devotion to high public service, all combined to make an unforgettable impression.

And women? What were his reactions to women? For by that must a man be ultimately judged. He was courteous, considerate, with, when he occasionally cared to exercise it, a resistless charm all his own. He flattered one by questions and, more subtly still, by silence and an appearance of the closest attention while we answered them. I do not think one could say that he was ever married; rather did he contract two alliances in the regal manner and, like many such arrangements, neither gave him the son he would have liked to carry on his name.

Modern democratic conditions do not favour the production of such men as George Nathaniel Curzon, and the loss to modern democracy is incontestable.

3

I fear that in Germany it will be many a long day before they outlive the delusion that King Edward the Seventh willed the Great War, that Lord Haldane secretly prepared the British Army to win it, that Lord Grey of Fallodon artfully chose the moment when it suited England to have it declared and, in order to screen those evil plotters, that Winston Churchill, Haldane, Lord Lonsdale and some others made by order loud and frequent protestations of Anglo-German friendship. The following note, made by a German friend of mine in 1917, shows how another legend, that of Lord Grey's infamy, has gripped quite intelligent German people. The letter from one of Grey's foreign colleagues which it quotes contains a quite unjust estimate of his character and limitations which is, I am sorry to say, still prevalent in Germany and on the continent. Lord Grey had many admirable qualities, including a not unusual fondness for birds and their ways, and the sentimental English thought that—joined to a sufficiently imposing façade—these made him into a great statesman: Well, they just didn't. Circumstances cruelly cast Sir Edward Grey for a rôle for which, in my humble opinion, he was quite unfitted, and for which he was in no sense equal. There is, therefore, a certain amount of justification for the following letter:

"A letter from a well-known foreign politician, written at the time of the Conference of Ambassadors in London,[1] is very remarkable as the analysis of the personality of that man who stands in the first row of those persons who bear the criminal responsibility for the provocation of the present war: 'For those who know Grey from the beginning of his career it is rather entertaining to watch how he is impressing his continental colleagues. They seem to suspect in him something that in reality does not exist at all. He is one of the best anglers in the United Kingdom and a very fair tennis player too, but he possesses neither political nor diplomatic talents, unless one would define his tiresome speech and his inflexibility as such. Rosebery once said that Grey makes such a concentrated impression because he has got no ideas of his own which could divert his mind from the brief that has been handed to him.

"A certain Secretary of Embassy, who is very fond of interfering, objected not long ago to a foreign diplomatist who spoke as follows about the manner of Grey's speeches: 'When a money-box is filled with gold it certainly does not clatter, but when there is not a penny in it, it does not clatter either. Some tricks of Winston Churchill make such a noise that they get on one's nerves; on the contrary those of Grey make none. Only he who takes the box in his hand would know whether it is full or empty.'

"It was rather cheeky, but well said.

"After my opinion Sir Grey has a very decent character, in spite of a certain stupid vanity which sometimes leads him to take part in affairs from which a person who is anxious to have his hands politically clean ought to stand aside."

"Be good, sweet maid, and let who will be clever" is not the most suitable of ideals for a British Foreign Minister, and however touching it was to see Sir Edward Grey and Mr. Roosevelt wandering in woods looking for birds, it can hardly be accepted as a satisfactory equivalent for political foresight and sagacity. To advance it as such is a typical example of English skill in evading the issue.

[1] i.e. in 1912 at St. James's Palace.

Whether the policy of any British Foreign Minister could, or could not, have postponed or prevented the outbreak of the Great War is not the point. The point is that Germany thought then, and thinks still, that Sir Edward Grey could certainly have postponed and, almost certainly, have prevented the outbreak of war, and in all international relationships it is not enough for statesmen to be guiltless; they must occupy unassailably the position of Cæsar's wife.

CHAPTER V

FRITZ THE MIRACLE MAN

I

FRITZ HOCHBERG was in many ways an extraordinary man endowed, or so I think, with a touch of genius, and with more than a touch of that eccentricity that seems so often to be its inevitable accompaniment. First of all, he felt that he and his family, his environment, and his country were in antagonism. Like most Germans of his rank he served for a time in the *Gardes du Corps,* but anyone more unlikely to fit comfortably into a Prussian cuirass never walked this earth. Moreover, like his elder brother Conny, he was imbued with a passionate love for England. He always had one or two houses in that country; he married Nancy Roche,[1] a charming Irishwoman; and, when the war broke out, he had already spent much time and wasted much money in having designed for him a large new English country house. For Halbau, his fine home in Silesia, which he at one time loved, he had developed a temporary dislike and, for long spells, never went there if he could help it—but then most of Fritz's likings and aversions were like the waves of the sea, beyond human control or reason.

I don't seem to have preserved any of Fritz's early letters, but an extract from my Diary dated 1904 will give a clear idea what I felt of my husband and brothers-in-law thirteen years after I was married. My dear father-in-law I always loved, but must in all fairness admit that he kept my husband too short of money; thus he never learned its true value

[1] Count (*Reichsgraf*) Friedrich (Fritz) von Hochberg (1868–1922) m. in 1905 the Hon. Nancy Burke-Roche, d. of the 2nd Baron Fermoy.

but, like a schoolboy, had to keep running to his father when he got into trouble. For instance, at the time of which I write Hans Heinrich wanted ten thousand pounds to put into some German business scheme in which Bend Or and the Duke of Sutherland[1] were interested. I wrote:

"Dear *Vater*: I do so hate him to be bothered. I would really much rather sell my jewellery and give the money to Hans. *Vater* was so well and good-tempered in Berlin and I am afraid this may upset him. And his sons are a funny trio —not a bit like him. Hans is the most so, only, of course, not quite the old-fashioned great gentleman that *Vater* is, nor has he such a powerful mind. Vater's first wife[2] may have been charming, as people say, but to my mind she did not bring up her three sons well; on the other hand, her only daughter Lulu[3] is enchantingly perfect. Fritz goes and builds a villa in Florence, which is now sold; is at present in Cairo, and talks of settling down in England. I don't wonder at this, but all the same it isn't natural. Conny is again in America; all the years I have known him he has never been to Court in Berlin or done a Berlin season, or tried to marry a German girl. Myself, being English, I understand this, but Conny is a German, so again this is not natural. Hans hates Berlin, talks of some day building a house and going in the winter to *Breslau:* he is *quite* serious about it, so much so that I really wonder sometimes if he is right in his head. Breslau! where there isn't a soul living, only Jew shopkeepers. All the Silesians who can afford it naturally go to Berlin where there are Court balls and functions, and a Society—of sorts."

When Fritz married Nancy, as neither were babies, we all hoped that both had found their true happiness. But it was not a success. In March, 1907, I put in my Diary:

[1] Cromartie Sutherland-Leveson-Gower, 4th Duke, Marquess of Stafford, etc. (1851–1913), m. in 1884 Lady Milicent St. Clair-Erskine, d. of 4th Earl of Rosslyn, now Lady Millicent Hawes.

[2] Countess Marie von Kleist (1828–1883), m. in 1857 Johann Heinrich XI (1833–1907), 2nd Prince and 1st Duke of Pless, Grand Master of the Order of the Black Eagle, etc. etc.

[3] Countess Ida Luise, b. 1863, d. of Hans Heinrich XI by his first wife, Countess Marie von Kleist, m. 1881 Friedrich, Prince of Solms-Baruth.

FÜRSTENSTEIN, SILESIA

From the Gardens and from the Air

". . . I wrote to a friend of Nancy's before the wedding and told her that Fritz could make a woman very happy or very miserable—he could be an angel or a devil. For he is a man with the most changeable feelings on many points; he is so full of the enjoyment and appreciation of everything in life: the flowers and mountains, the sea and sunsets; he worships the picturesque and the beauty in people and things. He fully believes in the religion of a future life, he loves animals and thinks they have souls, he lives a great deal *in* himself and his love of art, and he is so very pure and open-minded that the least little thing jars on him, particularly from someone whom he loves and admires. He is a man who wishes to paint his life as one paints a picture, and frame it in the gold companionship of a woman who would understand things as he does and feel things in his way."

Reading that over now I still think it was pretty accurate. But essentially it was a selfish ideal and not one on which a true marriage could be based. All the Hochbergs suffered from a sort of hallucination where women were concerned. To Hans Heinrich I was a lovely English picture and Fürstenstein and Pless my splendid gilt German frames. To poor old Fritz he was himself the centre of the picture, his wife merely part of the background!

During 1912 and 1913 my life was all upside down and then, as always, Fritz was splendid, striving to shepherd me into the paths of acceptance and contentment. Like many of us he could be very wise about the affairs of others and, at the same time, be very foolish about his own. This letter from Fritz was written from Halbau soon after my husband began the stupendous task of altering and rebuilding Fürstenstein:

April, 1912.

"My Darling Daisy,

"It is only here that I find a quiet moment to answer your dear pathetic letter. First of all I hope you are much better and able to enjoy life again, which is the principal thing. I went to Fürstenstein for Hans's birthday so that he shouldn't be quite alone and he seemed very pleased and was perfectly charming. What a queer fish he is. Having those two darling boys at Pless and not stopping with them for his birthday; and hating being alone for that day; and yet never dreaming of saying or asking somebody to come, yet being delighted if one comes.

"He belongs to that type of person who (like Hansel)[1] never really can show or demonstrate their feelings or emotions, and therefore are often misjudged. For instance, he positively longs, darling, for you to come back, and yet he's half afraid, half shy of asking you. He's an extraordinary creature, and the more I see of him, the older I get, the better I understand him, the more his nature amuses me. He's so totally undeveloped yet, his soul is still in its infancy; he's almost helpless in his childishness, as well as childish in his faults. And his queer bringing-up; the German, Prussian stiffness from which he can't emancipate himself. Poor boy, I can't help laughing at him.

"About this building (it's now too late to stop him), I must say that everything he is doing, he is doing well. That's one consolation. It is really going to be very beautiful, and very practical and fine, and, I'm now certain, even *gemütlich*. There's no doubt it will all be a vast improvement, and you will love the new place better than the old, in fact I'm positive of it. You won't be able to help it. Only in the state of health you're in at present don't go and live in that otherwise charming little apartment. We'll talk about that in Pless, as well as about lots of other things, you and I, because to please you and Hans, I'm coming there at once after Whitsuntide, or for it, with my saddle, for three or four weeks of peace and love and youth and happiness. As I have put off my return to England purposely for you, please do come to Pless as soon as you're well. We'll have such a time there with the boys. Only let's be alone. Don't ask anybody; anyway not at the beginning.

"About living six months here and six months in England,

[1] Prince Hans Heinrich (Hansel) of Pless, eldest son of the Authoress, b. Feb. 2, 1900; m. in Dec., 1924, Marie Katharina (Sissy), d. of Clement Count Schönborn-Wiesentheid.

darling, you talk about it like Shelagh. Please don't think of it a second time. Think (if not of yourself, who would be much more unsatisfied and unhappy, because aimless) think of those dear boys, darling Daisykins. You weren't forced to have them, yet you longed and prayed to have them. It is a privilege (mind I don't say a duty) to have them and to sacrifice even a lot for them. This six months here and six months there business is always injurious to children, and besides yours being boys—German boys—having forcibly to go through the schools, you couldn't get them away for six months; moreover, other influences would become the strongest, and you would lose them mentally entirely. And after all, darling, you used to be happy here, in a way. Don't you think you could be so again—for the sake of all of us who do really love you so much? And, everybody here does love you. Everybody's asked me about your health in real genuine compassion. All the people at Pless and Fürstenstein adore you. And your old silly 'Tommy'[1] loves you too, believe me, darling, though he doesn't show it. . . . At the bottom of his heart it's you, darling, he really loves. He's always talking about you, believe me.

"Anyhow, now do get well and come to Pless, and the sun will shine again as in olden times.

"Just fancy, when they dug out underneath Mother's old bedroom in Fürstenstein, they found a huge male skeleton, evidently having been murdered, as it was buried in bits, scattered about in various places. No wonder he came and haunted you when you used her rooms. Now Hans will have him buried properly by a priest in a Christian graveyard. He said himself he was certain it was this poor man's ghost that haunted you.

"Alas, my morning's peace is gone, as I am expected to be present at lunch. Lulu's youngest boy is here.

"Ta-ta, and best love to Shelagh, and God bless you, darling.

"A happy day,
"Your loving
"FRITZEKINS."

[1] The pet name of the Authoress for her husband.

The next two letters were written some six months later from Great Bowden, near Market Harborough, a place Fritz adored and where, surrounded by his lovely hunters and half a score of Irish wolfhounds, he was as near being perfectly happy as he could be anywhere. The uncanny insight shown in the first one regarding the dangers of the European situation is, even now, startling. Fritz had without doubt a strong mystical strain in his make-up. It was developed in a lop-sided way and without direction; nevertheless, he fore-felt much that was to happen, and this faculty made him, to many people, an uncomfortable person to know, and an impossible person with whom to live. One of the great bonds between us was that I not only understood and liked his psychic gifts, but that at times I derived distinct help and inspiration from their exercise.

Bowden, November 25th, 1913.

"My Darling Child,

"What can I say about your letter except that it made me so miserably sad? To think of you, beautiful creature, who used to be like embodied life and sunshine and happiness, a human sunbeam, a sun-ray incarnated, having to go through all this sadness and depression—and loneliness! If people like myself have to learn their bitter, cruel lessons it doesn't matter; that, I expect, is what we were meant for, what we came into this world for. But people such as you ought never to learn the bitterness of disappointment, the terrible depression of loneliness. And yet I expect, if God sends it it must, like everything in this world, have its good reasons, because, darling, everything has; and therefore is, finally, for our best. But at the moment it is always difficult, nay, sometimes even impossible, for our shortsighted human eyes, to see the good, because they are so blinded by human tears. But know and realize my poor darling child that God never puts more on our shoulders than we can bear and that we are really never tested beyond our strength. I do so wish I could help you, be something encouraging and sustaining to you—a difficult thing. Yet how I understand it all. . . .

"Thank goodness you've only got one more month of

that shooting business at Pless and then you'll fly off to your lovely place on the Riviera where, as I say, you can live your own life, see your own people, be with your own chosen friends. So cheer up. And then you've got the whole summer in front of you*, and great changes will take place next year everywhere*—Just have a little bit more patience, and keep well. . . . Don't lose your confidence, dear child, don't get rattled. It will come all right. Don't for God's sake do anything rash, for your own sake. Wait a little longer till I have a house of my own in England where you can come for a week, a month, or longer, just as you choose, and rest and sleep . . . and learn. I could teach you such a lot, do you such a lot of good. You would be surprised. Because, darling, I've gone through it all—I know. That's why I am so sorry for you, because I understand. They don't. Don't say, don't even allow yourself to think, that that awful weary illness might come back again. Because it won't. I banned it; and unless you open the door wilfully by your thoughts, it has no power to return. So keep that door well shut and leave only the door to sunshine and happy thoughts open, and don't bother about other people at present. Put your mental cloak around you, let your thoughts be like a huge bed of pansies, but only bright-coloured ones!

"A happy day,

"Your devoted,

"FRITZEKINS."

". . . Many thanks for your long and certainly not cheerful letter. So glad to learn from your wire that my last letter had a calming effect on you—and I expect the Emperor and the Empress having been nice to you has made you feel almost regal (I think one ought to write that with a capital R.; I apologize for my lack of etiquette) and your husband a little more kindly disposed towards 'his humble slave girl.' All this sounds most Oriental and thousand-and-one-nighty, and fits in badly with your having to cross a cold Silesian courtyard for each meal, live in a glorified stable,[1] and having—oh God, how I pity you—sixteen

[1] While the rebuilding operations were going on.

smoking Germans for dinner. Oh, the conversation—don't I know them? One hears them dimly from far off, like a fog horn; one's interests and ideas, one's life is leagues, not mere miles away from them and theirs. Worlds, fortunately, lie between them and us. Does not the talk—one cannot call it conversation—go like this: *ach wirklich: jawohl: wie interessant: es ist ja erstannlich: natürlich*[1] and all the cheap little words one can throw in politely without really owning mentally the gulf that separates—yes, isolates one. And because one feels isolated, one feels lonely, and perhaps gets sad—but don't. (Just look at them with the telescope because they are so far yonder.) Look at their little cabbage-state in spite of all their '*kolossal*' Orders and Decorations and Tummies! Would you exchange your living, loving, throbbing, *knowing* soul for their little cabbage-stalk? Go on! *Poverina!* And, you know darling, you'd find a good many cabbage-stalks over here, especially in the hunting set, although it's a smarter type of cabbage. But cabbage-state they are.

"Now don't give way to these depressions and morbid moods, beloved child, just cheer up. 'The other side of every cloud is bright and shiny. I therefore turn my clouds about and weave them with the inside out, to show the lining.' (But you see one has to turn them about *oneself!* Mind that!) And the sun is going to shine again. You must be a little more patient; it's all on the mend. And live your own inner life; it's entirely by that that one exists—and by prayer. We all, who have reached a certain mental development, must be lonely, darling; we can't develop in a crowd, nor get strong if we cultivate a permanent stoop. We have to stand upright and alone, look upward in order to grow and be blown about by the storms and winds and shaken and bent backward and forward to make us thrive spiritually and grow strong; to enable the invigorating life-sap circulate within. The old dead leaves must all be blown off before the new ones burst forth and the flowers come—and the fruit. So just have a little more patience. It's winter now. But spring will come, is coming. And with it all the glory, all the happiness and delight and all the

[1] Oh, really! Yes, indeed; how interesting; how surprising; of course.

peace. The thrush and the nightingale will sing again, child, in your new spring. And its song will be sweet to you because the fragrance of the cast-off old dead leaves in the ground will mingle with the sweetness of the violets. Don't despair. Trust. *Gott wird machen, dass die Sachen, gehen wie es heilsam ist.*[1]

"I'll smack you. Surely I never told you that it wasn't wrong to take one's life; somebody else must have told you that, and you have confused it. I might have said I don't condemn them. Ah! that's quite a different thing. I know, and I'm sorry for them, *tout comprendre, c'est tout pardonner.* But I know also that the poor things who commit suicide don't gain anything, because they have to go through their discipline just the same and are not freed over on the other side; they have to come back here and to learn the bitter lesson all over again.

"I had a bad spill last Thursday, over a big post and rails, and hurt my shoulder and ribs again. It wasn't the poor darling's fault, because the ground was so frightfully greasy; he slipped taking off and, as he is one of my best timber jumpers, I was happily sailing behind hounds, never minding how stiff the timber might be. So we came a regular somersault and on me he rolled. But that's only to tell you. . ."

2

The war had no effect whatever in damping Fritz's love for England, nor Conny's for that matter, although both had hurriedly to fly the country. Fritz was tenant of Minsted Manor in Hampshire at the time—which he had taken to be near Newlands—and Patsy whom he loved—had to leave all his beautiful horses, motor-cars and so on. His hunting-box at Great Bowden and all its contents were seized. He had the greatest difficulty in scraping together enough ready money to pay local bills and buy his ticket. He had to go to Mr. Edward Hutton and other personal friends because he found, just as I did when I asked the Ritz Hotel to cash a cheque for me, that most persons of the tradesmen class suddenly

[1] Which might be paraphrased as "God doeth all things well."

changed their natural subservience for insolence. In all countries your born tradesman is the quickest to change his flag or turn his coat.

Fritz's next letter I quote simply to show how straight and truthful he could be—even when he had something unpleasant to say. Probably I resented it a little at the time—I don't remember—but I am grateful for it now:

"*June,* 1914.

"Darling Daisy,

"Having received your second wire, sent on from Holzhausen where I'm going to-day, I have again changed all my plans *through you,* and have, to *please you,* arranged to be at Fürstenstein on June 16th. So I hope you'll be satisfied at last. What a much happier person you would be if all the men you have met in your life (except your husband) hadn't always, at your whim, changed their plans and thrown other people and other duties over. Then you might not have developed into what dear Dr. S . . . so rightly calls 'Princess Caprice,' and you certainly would have been ever so much happier. You really ought to have that nice little bottom of yours well smacked. Of course you'll be furious and indignant. . . . You are a pet and I love you and am awfully sorry for you, but as you wire please help me, I'll try to do so, and I will come. . . . If for God alone knows what reason you find you can't go to Fürstenstein for June 16th, then please let me know at once to Holzhausen. . . .

"I certainly am the last to take anyone's part against you; on the contrary; but when I come to Fürstenstein I flatly refuse to listen to all the old rigmarole . . . darling child, I know it all by heart and, as I tell you, it's no use raking up old unpleasant thoughts and memories. *It's unhealthy. . . . I'm living and alive* and I've seen too much of real suffering and unhappiness and misery, and still more of real pluck and courage and patience and endurance, to attach very much importance to the lighter things. . . ."

Fritz was quite unfitted for any sort of military service. An accident, while still a young man, had seriously disabled him, so much so that he could not ride astride. He therefore rode on a lady's saddle and in Leicestershire was known as "the side-saddle Count." All the same he could go, and was not afraid of anything.

Early in 1915 he started organizing a Field Hospital unit, largely at his own expense and, as was to be expected in "orderly" Germany, met with many difficulties. As I was at Pless he was at the same time trying, in Berlin, to help me to get the staff I wanted for the Red Cross Hospital train or *Lazarettzug* that I was then organizing. Fritz wrote:

"*April,* 1915.

"That old swine Perthes[1] refuses officially to give us Sisters Edith, Clara and the two others, saying that they are wanted here and that they were too young. Also, the one male nurse I wanted he won't give, nor the seven Franciscan monks. I went to see him yesterday and he told me most pointedly that 'after all I was *merely a private individual*' (these are literally his words) 'and *therefore* they had no reason to do anything for me.' I nearly laughed in his face. But I was very polite and amiable, told him I was sorry I had taken up his valuable time, and then left him.

"Afterwards I remembered that Perthesi is a bosom friend of Fritz Solms, and that he is the creature who, last autumn, made all that unpleasantness with Conny about not sending sisters, medicines and instruments out to St. Quentin, for which I had asked only because they were absolutely necessary. He looks like a red alligator. I must still laugh when I think of him and his impertinent questions. What amused me highly was his saying I was merely a private individual. Thank the Lord I am. But I think there'll be very few private individuals who have done, and are ready to do, for their country what I have done.

"This morning I got a charming letter from Baroness Wangenheim[2] from Therapia (the summer residence of our Embassy, near Constantinople), in which she advises me not

[1] Rudolph Eduard Von (1843–1918), Infantry General on Reserve, Military Inspector of Voluntary Nursing.

[2] d. of Baron Spitzenberg, wife of Baron won Wangenheim, German Ambassador in Constantinople.

to go to Djemal Pascha's Suez Canal Corps, as at present nothing was going to be undertaken there, but to come and nurse with her, where there would be work for us both. So there. Try and get these Franciscan monks from Falkenhayn[1] or the Emperor—or shall we give up the big hospital idea and just collect two or three ordinary nurses (such as Lexel's[2]) and go quietly down with them to Baroness von Wangenheim, and not ask any favours from anyone?

"Anyhow, I have counter-ordered the tents, as in Gallipoli or Constantinople we wouldn't want them, and it seems to be unnecessary expense. Oh! what a funny world it is. . . . I tell you, darling, '*Germany doesn't want me.*' I found that out long ago. You see it again in old Perthes' answer. I'm by no means *pikiert,* darling, or sorry. *I'm simply delighted,* and it only proves what I knew *since years. All the more have I now a good reason for living in another country.* My conscience is absolutely clear. I have done my duty towards this blessed country. This is the third rebuke, and I can greet it with a clear conscience. If they don't want my work, *malesh,* as the Arabs say."

A little later on I am going to speak about my friend the Grand Duke of Mecklenburg-Strelitz,[3] whom we all called the *Rosenkavalier*. As, in spite of the frankness with which I wrote about him in my former books, my friendship for him has again and again been misrepresented. I will here quote a letter from Fritz which proves quite clearly that a whole year or more before his tragic death I was honestly and disinterestedly trying to find him a suitable wife, and that Fritz knew of my plans and was backing them up all he could; moreover, woman-like, I had even had ideas about planning his matrimonial future as far back as 1902 or 1903, when he first visited England:

[1] General von Falkenhayn, Chief of Staff of the German Field Armies till Aug. 29, 1916, when he was superseded by Field-Marshal von Hindenburg.

[2] Count (*Reichsgraf*) Alexander von Hochberg, 2nd son of the Authoress, b. London, Feb. 1, 1905.

[3] Adolphus Friedrich VI (1882–1918), g.-s. of George Duke of Cambridge (1819–1904) and cousin of Her Majesty Queen Mary.

"*Berlin, 23rd Feb.,* 1917.

"Aunt M. has just sent me an express letter telling me that you and the Grand Duke want to lunch or dine or visit them on February 27th, and implores me to be there. I had just written the G.D. a few days ago asking him to lunch with me in Munich on February the 28th, when I am on my way to Switzerland to Conny, who, I'm sorry to say, is not well. I expect the G.D. didn't get the letter, as I wrote to Strelitz, not knowing he was already at Munich or at Berchtesgaden with you.

As I really know M. and her girl very well, I take the liberty of saying that a first meeting of the little Grand Duke and the girl would be better without you, unkind though it may sound. But as you are the Grand Duke's real true motherly friend and, I'm sure, desire only what is best for him, I expect you'll want him to get a nice wife, which this girl really is. So, knowing them both well, I therefore strongly advise you, keep *at present* out of the picture. M. has lived of late years as a sort of recluse, not mixing with the so-called world, so is full of prejudices. . . . A shy, retiring woman, M. has recently been a good deal with Aunt Zita, who hates you, and you know how silly and idiotic people are—there was a lot of gossip about the Grand Duke being in love with you. Of course it's not true, but I mean one must realize what people are and what one has to deal with. . . . The glory of the whole thing, if it comes off, *will always be yours*. So, if you want this girl to marry him, better not come to Munich now. The girl is exceedingly clever and knows exactly what she wants, so it is better to handle her carefully at present, not to rouse suspicions in her, nor in any way to seem to press her. . . .

"She has got £1,000 a year income of her own which she inherited (I mean the half-million Marks capital) last year from Aunt Anna.[1] . . . Besides, there are two young men, both Princes with very large estates . . . who are very keen to please the girl. So it isn't a case of a little penniless

[1] Countess Anna Hochberg (1839–1916), aunt of the Prince of Pless, m. first, 1858, Prince Heinrich XII of Reuss (1829–1866), second in 1869, his brother Heinrich XIII of Reuss.

princess only too pleased to be *honoured* by this glorious marriage. . . .

"M. and the girl are lunching with me on February the 25th at one o'clock in Munich, so please ask the Grand Duke as, according to M.'s letter, he is staying with you at Berchtesgaden, if he will do me the honour of joining us at luncheon at the Hotel Continental on that date. And, please, don't come yourself.

"I'm off to Switzerland the next day. . . . So nobody need fear that I will interfere with their interests. I proposed two other girls to the Grand Duke, both of whom I'm positive would simply jump at the offer. The youngest H. girl, sister of Princess A.W., who hasn't even got enough to pay for her own stockings, and the W. girl, aged eighteen. I'm certain that either of them would even be sent on approval!

"Am hearing the most interesting lectures by Dr. X., I think quite the most developed mystic it ever was my chance to meet. . . . I'm sorry to give up his lectures here, but poor Conny is apparently quite ill, so I'm going to him. Hans was operated on the day before yesterday by Potter at the *Hedwigskrankenhaus*. Went to see him yesterday and again to-day. He's quite well, has no temperature, no pain, is in good spirits and hopes to leave for Fürstenstein on February 25. . . .

"Didn't you know Benckendorff[1] was shot? How strange! No! it wasn't in the German papers. I'm sure Princess Natalie[2] knows it. . . .

"The Grand Duke's sister[3] is, it appears, a fountain of babies."

Fritz's next letter gives a vivid picture of Hans Heinrich at Fürstenstein during the middle of the war (May, 1917):

[1] Alexander Count von Benckendorff (1849–1917), m. 1879 Countess Sophie Schouvaloff. He died in London and his body was deposited in the crypt of Westminster Cathedral, where it remains unburied to this day. He was Russian Ambassador to the Court of St. James's, 1903–1917.

[2] The Count's sister, Natalie, m. in 1872 Hermann 3rd Prince Hatzfeld and 1st Duke of Trachenberg, sometime Viceroy of Silesia.

[3] Princess Marie, b. 1878, m. first, in 1899, Count Georg Jametil, whom she divorced in 1908; second, in 1914, Prince Julius Ernst of Lippe.

"My letter to you had barely gone when a wire came from Hans asking me to come to Fürstenstein for two days. I had already begun a letter to him declining, when I was impelled to tear it up and write a wire saying I would come—and I went. I spent two glorious days in the beloved old place which, in the full beauty of lovely spring, enwrapped me with all its incomparable charm. What a heavenly, dear place and how I love it more than any spot on earth.

"Your Lord and Master was most charming and in excellent spirits, met me half-way up the drive, and was cheerfulness and amiability personified. Of course building, building, building the whole day long which I admit, interests me too, and especially at this place, where one knows and loves every angle. I must again say that what Walcher, the architect, and Hans are doing is splendid, bar the back part, which is, and always will be, too heavy, too high, too out of place. But the rest is magnificent indeed, and the interior very fine. Walcher is a genius.

"Lexel, looking very well and happy, and such a handsome boy, was very nice and seems to get on well with his new tutor. Bolko had just arrived as I left, as I had to be back here to receive Geheimrat Siler, the famous oculist, and a stiff Medical Inspector from the Ministry of War, who inspected everything; both were delighted with the work I have organized here for the poor blinded soldiers. It really proves a great success.

"A happy day,
"Yours,
"FRITZ."

As his next letter shows, Fritz never very much modified his opinion regarding certain stupidities practised by Germany during the war:

"*Halbau, Silesia, May* 29, 1917.

"MY DEAR OLD GIRL,

"I fully agree with you about what you say and think regarding this blessed country, and the idiocy of their policy and their vulgarity and all the rest. Dear girl, who feels and resents it more than I, whose whole heart and soul and spirit, whose whole ego is English—although as a strange freak I was this time reincarnated in this blessed country, with which I've got nothing in common!

"Yet, for the present, being incaged here, I have realized the necessity of keeping locked within myself what I feel and think and suffer . . . as I can't help those over there on our beloved little island, nor *bring about an understanding of them here,* I keep to myself and absolutely quiet, and do some work which benefits humanity. I, who am so stupidly homesick for that one place, that to-day when on account of the heat I had to put on an old country coat I hadn't worn since I left my beloved New Forest and its peace and harmony, tears came to my eyes and such a rage to my throat I could have knocked people down for the mere reason that they were Germans. . . .

"We must realize, and there's no getting away from it, that the whole world is in a delirium of madness. No nation seems to be in their present state of mind in their sane senses. Even beloved England. If a man like Lord Robert Cecil can allow such things as the propagating of those vile stories about Germans using corpses for munitions and so on . . . but never mind that. . . . Isn't it the only sensible thing to do for self-preservation and peace of mind and soul, to go on helping in a quiet corner, and out of the contact of these lunatics? Unfortunately, your temperament doesn't allow you to do this. Princess Caprice you always were; you flew from one thing to the other, hoping, poor dear, to quiet or soothe or banish the emptiness in your heart, the loneliness of your love. . . .

"How on earth the idea entered your head to go to Uncle Bolko[1] for help, darling, simply makes me laugh. Twenty-five years have you lived in this family, in this country, and never apparently realized its worth nor their feelings and sentiments. To that old fool of Uncle Bolko! Good God alive! Honestly, darling, I thought

[1] Count (*Reichsgraf*) Bolko von Hochberg (1843–1926), uncle of the Prince of Pless, m. 1869 Princess Eleonore von Schönaich-Carolath.

I could have credited you with more knowledge of the world and of people. Upon my word! His letter is typical!

"The other day I went for a day to Berlin because Alfred Salm[1] wants to send his second boy to Dr. Kisch's tubercular sanatorium and I took him there. My clothes are old and mended and shabby (I've been wearing them now for three years continuously; in fact, ever since I left my happiness). My boots are badly polished, because I have to do with an untrained Hungarian as valet, yet, old as they are, my clothes have an un-German cut, and I noticed the startled state of everybody in the streets and stations, defiant, hateful, ironical, contemptuous, insolent, furious, depreciating, as they looked at me. Well, my dear girl, that's the feeling that exists, and is a concrete fact in this country nowadays; first of all, against everything foreign, especially English; secondly, against the upper classes, against aristocracy. All these hungry, nervously overstrung, patriotically madly excited people would only be too pleased to spit at us, to throw stones at us. They are as a nation not right in their heads. They're all dancing on a volcano. Don't let's be the stone that starts the eruption by falling out of its proper place. . . . But keep quiet. These times require it. It's the only thing we can do."

3

That, certainly, was good war-time advice. But Fritz never failed to help me in every way both before, during, and after the war. And what way better than giving honest advice? Often enough I did not like it; rebelled, got angry, even sulked. But Fritz did not mind. He could be brutal in a kind and friendly way, and that attitude from a man to a woman is often a tonic, a necessary one. The following letters from Halbau dated June, 1917, reached me when I was in a very disgruntled state, and explain some things in my life better than I could:

[1] 1863–1924. 5th Prince Salm-Reifferscheidt-Krautheim.

"*Halbau, June 17th,* 1917.

"MY DARLING GIRL,

"Once a friend—always a friend? It's not I who changes. . . .

"I don't agree with what you say about L. For one thing he is a gentleman (so far as that thing exists in the mentality of this country) and that he is also a snob is only natural for one of his class, but that, my darling, you'll find in all nations. . . . If I could only convince you, my own pet, of the fact that *now* is really not the moment to undertake anything. . . . You are English, and in Prussian public opinion England is worse than all the devils in Hell combined. So, whatever you say, Prussia would always sanction anything done against *die Engländerin.* Keep as quiet as possible, not out of fright—you've got nothing to be afraid of—but, darling, out of cleverness. Wait your turn, as long as this war lasts it won't come, so patience. . .

"Look forward; don't turn round; don't rake up continually the old dead leaf-mould. . . . Haven't you got the faculty of remembering only the nice things in life? Damn your old Hans—he has never been, will never be, the centre of your life. If it pleases him to see you with less curls, well, have a good Viennese hairdresser, do your hair in the smooth 'Franz Hals' way all women wear it these days. . . .

"Now who told you since years you wore too many curls? Old Fritzekins! Who several times when your maids did your hair begged you to leave it un-toupéd and without curls? Fritzekins! Who always fluffed it up and pulled out curls in spite of him? Daisykins! Oh, you silly dear old noodle! You will never learn.

"Very sensible of you to go to Pless with the children. It's so nice there in summer. I know Prinz, the artist, who painted you; I went to his studio with Princess Vicky[1] for the last sittings of her marvellous portrait. He is a wonderful artist. So glad you have been painted by him. How much does he charge? Saw some lovely photos he

[1] Princess Victoria of Prussia (1866–1929), 2nd d. of the Emperor Friedrich III, m. 1890 Prince Adolf of Schaumburg-Lippe (1859–1916).

had done from his portrait of the Queen of Rumania, and those Prussian daughters and daughters-in-law. Please tell him to send me a photo of your portrait. I should love to see it.

"When the war is over . . . we'll have a real grave dug, we'll put all your dead remembrances and griefs and sorrows and disappointments into it. . . . We'll take the next boat and sail for our beloved little island . . . you'll make your main home at Arnewood[1] and come to your German hill house for a yearly trip. Now, why, for instance, didn't you go straight to Pless to meet the children, instead of going to Fürstenstein to meet Hans? You'll only quarrel. . . . Do leave him alone.

"What about the little Grand Duke whose birthday, by the way, is to-day? Is he ever going to make up his mind about the girl? It is a pity he is so shy and unpractical. They have left Munich now, where everything could have been managed so much more easily. Do you think he still thinks seriously about it? Because, as you know, darling, there are two other very good matches she could make . . . but it seems a shame to let the girl and him lose their great opportunity.

"So glad my blind people's work is going on so well, and proves such a success.

"A happy day,
"Yours,
"FRITZ."

"*P.S.*—So glad you had such a success at Salzbrunn. Of course they all love you. Now don't overdo it . . . don't make yourself too cheap. Play your cards well. . . .

"Mrs. Weisman sends me word, via Holland, that Patsy was very worried about you as she hadn't heard from you since Christmas. . . . Heard to-day the sad news that my nice English valet, who was with me for eight years, has been killed in action. Oh! this awful war.

"S. has a fortnight's leave and is coming here, I'm glad to say, next Wednesday. It will be nice having the dear boy

[1] A place in the New Forest, at that time owned by the Authoress.

again. . . . I thought it was settled that you were going to Pless, and found it very sensible. It's so nice there in the summer, real country, because, fine as old Fürstenstein is, somehow it isn't what I call country. We had such a glorious thunderstorm last night, and everything is refreshed, and the air, deliciously moist this morning, smelled and felt like England. Oh, that precious beloved country! The only country in the world! 'England, England, *über alles!*'

"Yours,
"FRITZ."

4

Fritz was one of those unlucky (or perhaps lucky) persons born out of due season. As I have said, neither his family, his environment, nor his country suited him. He was the queerest mixture of artist, democrat, aristocrat, sinner and saint that I ever came across. He had both heavenly and earthly wisdom and yet could do the most foolish things. All this would have been explicable enough had he been really a genius, but he was nothing of the sort; his mind was in many ways quite commonplace; it was his spirit that was in patches fine and beautiful. Then he understood women in an uncanny way; understood us perhaps far too well ever to want to be married to one of us. It is the kindly, honourable, evenly-sexed man, mentally a little below par, to whom woman is always somewhat of a mystery, who makes the most devoted and satisfactory husband.

Fritz should have been a Catholic priest during the late Renaissance—it would have to have been a Jesuit, because only they have freedom of thought—and, by means of his rank and wealth he would have been able to climb high while quite young and become a Cardinal with some ceremonial office at the Court of the Vatican, the duties of which he would have carried out quite charmingly, provided he was not asked to do so too often. He would have received all sorts and conditions of men and women and known only those, whatever their rank, whom he really cared for. He would have collected precious things, made lovely gardens, built houses here and there. He would have paid great public deference to the Pope, while secretly abjuring all the Sovereign Pontiff's pretentions to infallibility and so on. Above all, he would have been enchanted that although the White Pope was nominally his master, his real master, to whom he was bound body and soul, was the Black Pope, the General of the Jesuits, whom he would never want to see in the flesh and whose name even he would prefer not to know. Fritz was a German *John Inglesant.*

Having been born three hundred years too late, and a Protestant, it was perhaps inevitable that he should turn, first to mysticism, and in the end to spiritism. For a time, like myself, he was enormously attracted by the mystery of Egypt and the East—or what seemed its mystery. Bitten with the idea of reincarnation he went through a phase when he imagined himself an Egyptian priest, of course, with royal blood in his veins, because, in his own way, Fritz possessed quite a streak of the Hochberg dower of snobbery. It was more subtle, more childlike and less childish, than that of some of his relations, but it was just as real.

It will be remembered that in the spring of 1916 he was with his brother Conny in Switzerland, and from there he wrote me as follows—he often called himself "the Miracle Man":

". . . So your Miracle Man is not going to do anything of the sort, darling Princess Caprice, especially as he has serious work to do here; that is why he was sent here by his spirits. It's too long to explain, but I'm glad to say it's very successful and helpful, where it was to help. Thank God. Because darling, I neither came for my own pleasure, nor do I like the place, nor the people. But I was sent here for a certain purpose, and before this task is accomplished I can't leave: So there. So you see what a silly (pardon) ass you've been again to imagine I didn't come because I didn't care for you any more or didn't want to hear your griefs. Rest assured. I do. But I'm not so free as you imagine—although I haven't got a husband. . . .

"I look facts straight in the face. It does hurt sometimes, terribly. But it's a cruel strong pain, and it's over then. It doesn't drag on. It's like having a tooth out. It hurts terribly for the moment, but it's done for. And it's better than having sleepless nights from the tooth and having to go for days to the dentist to have that tooth drilled and scratched and poked about with painful instruments, then, patched up temporarily, and, after years, pulled out just the same.

"I'm awfully touched, darling, about your having written all those kind letters to English people I know. . . . That, perhaps, is the reason why poor King Edward has attached himself to me, and comes to me at each séance, in the most insistent way, imploring me to do something for his poor people. Me! As if I could do anything but pray. . . . I hope your Hospital Train will be a huge success, and wish you every possible luck. . . .

"You say, 'I expect you have made many friends.' I hardly make friends. I'm not a friendly person. I may have to make acquaintances, but I very rarely make friends. I've got mine—what the war has left me. That suffices. And my beloved spirit friends."

Now I am not one of those who laugh at spiritism or consider it all moonshine. After all, isn't even moonshine real? I can only say that, although I personally never got much out of it, I am quite prepared to believe that many people do. Thought is the only reality. All else is illusion. Because during the war many disheartened people went too far we must not blame the Spiritists. During those wretched, endless, morbid years, everyone, everywhere, went too far about everything. How could it be otherwise when the whole world was insane. But Fritz, in my view, went much too far. An old friend, the late Lord Knutsford, who was such a splendid champion of the London Hospital, told me that some of the people, mediums and others, who got hold of Fritz during and after the war, were charlatans or worse.

His guides, Fritz wrote, knew exactly what was best for him and others and, as he was directed, he acted—and one of his directions was to the effect that King Edward was sent to him to beseech him to help England during the war. One just couldn't believe it even if one wanted to! Poor Fritz. I will leave all that rather sad side of him alone. There was, however, no doubting his burning desire to help everyone, and me, let me repeat it, he helped more than I can ever say. He was loyal; affectionate; responsive. The frustrated artist in him gave him no repose, but it made him sympathetic and understanding beyond the ordinary. He travelled quite a lot in India, Australia and Japan, and, as his very entertaining and attractive account of his journey,[1] and these letters prove, he could write wittily and well. Indeed, there were only two things wanting to his equipment as an artist: necessity and concentration. The Far East, as his delightful water-colours plainly show, attracted him enormously and, for a time, he indulged in a passion for Japanese servants. They certainly used to look very odd in the sort of glorified villas, such as Boldre Bridge House, that he used to hire in his beloved New Forest before he got Minsted Manor. And their oddity was not lessened when their narrow shoulders were clad in all the glory of the Hochberg livery of dark red and silver, their puny legs and calves seeming to be quite lost in plush breeches and white stockings. Fritz could never see that a trim parlourmaid or two would have matched the villa far better. Although very rich he never had any ready money. He would give gorgeous presents and forget to pay for them. Once he sent me from Alphonsine in Paris a dozen divine hats and a year or so later I had to pay for them myself. He would incur huge bills in London, Berlin, Paris, Dresden—wherever he happened to be—and have them sent to Halbau to his

[1] *An Eastern Voyage*, a journal of travels through the British Empire in the East and South, and Japan, by Count Fritz von Hochberg. 25 coloured and 48 black and white illustrations by the author. London, J. M. Dent, 1910; New York, E. P. Dutton.

Comptroller, Berthelmann, who used to become so distracted that he would start trying to tear out what little hair he had left. Then, when in the East, they had to keep sending him large sums of money all the time.

I have mentioned that he suffered from the Hochberg mania for building and this, in a way, brought about his death.

In 1921 he decided to build himself a house near Munich, partly, I think, to be close to me and partly because he adored Bavaria and its beautiful capital. The building was going on quite well when one day he insisted on climbing on the scaffolding to see something, missed his footing, and fell. He was taken to a nursing home, where he did well until some complications set in and he quite suddenly left us.

I have nothing but grateful kindly thoughts in my heart for Fritz.

5

Fritz and his brother Conny were wonderful friends, and were very similar in many ways. Like Fritz, Conny, as I have already said, loved England and lived there a great deal. He had for a time a place called Croydon Hall—I never quite knew where it was—and, when the war broke out, he, as I have already said, had a large place in Somersetshire which, with all its contents, was confiscated.

Bits of one letter from him will be enough to explain his point of view about life. It was written in 1908 from Schloss Dambrau, his home in Upper Silesia. The "English brothers" were of course himself and Fritz:

"My Dear Daisy:

"You are a brick and I am very proud of you and thank you so much for your dear kind letter, which gave me great pleasure. I am sorry I cannot join your party, but it is far too large and noble for me. I don't care for society a bit and go near it as little as possible. I hope you won't mind, but I really could not face it. Well, about the 'English brothers' you are quite right; but I don't think this English brother would make disagreeable comments about his German relations to foreigners and outsiders. That has been done. I don't mind very much because I don't care a bit what people say about me; such things really are not worth while bothering about; but I cannot feel very friendly towards people who gossip about me, and I make it a point not to force myself into their society. Besides, U. B. has an unkind provoking way with him and always tries to complete my education, which I think is rather too late at my age. However, it does not matter much; we have different interests, different friends, and look at life from an entirely different point of view; even our social position is somewhat different; and I know that he is rather narrow-minded and short-sighted and only understands his own point of view. All this considered, and having no intention or reason for quarrelling with him, I find it much better to see of him as little as possible, that being the best way to get on with him decently. I hope you won't be angry with me for telling you all this so frankly; I am so fond of you that I really should be sorry if you were. But honestly it is the best way, and I won't change it.

"I hope your cure is doing you good and that you will feel much better when you will be through it; but even then you ought to keep a little quiet and not do too much.

"With best love,

"Yours affect.,

"CONNY."

For some years Conny was a great invalid and bore almost continuous suffering with a quiet heroism and resignation that was at once pathetic and grand. A year or so ago in a Berlin nursing home death came and mercifully released him. His will was characteristic. He was not to be buried either at Klitschdorf or Fürstenstein, but in a Berlin cemetery. The service in the church and at the graveside was to be that of the Church of England, only English hymns were to be sung and a sermon in English was to be preached. . . . Poor Conny! I don't of course know if all this ensured him entrance into an English Protestant Heaven, but, if so, what a very odd place he must find it.

CHAPTER VI

ARE ROYALTIES DIFFERENT?

I

OF course they are; and equally, of course, they are not: like all members of a highly specialized hereditary craft—miners for example—they are in many ways unlike ordinary members of the community. To think or say that, as human beings, they differ in any fundamental way from the rest of us is clearly nonsense.

I suppose I have intimately known more than my share of Royalties and miners and, because I was close to them, yet not of their caste, I was always enabled to study them with a certain amount of detachment. Speaking generally, both miners and Royalties are aristocrats, that is, they are true to type and craft, and, in this sense, I like aristocrats.

Apart from Great Britain, where the general devotion to the Royal family is deeper and more intense than ever it has been, the idea of Royalty is in eclipse. But that is only temporary; it is a phase that has again and again appeared and disappeared. Royalty, as an institution, will again come into its own because the basic idea behind it satisfies an elemental need of human nature, and is, moreover, rooted deep in history. Like every other human institution it is continuously in process of change. It so happened that in Russia, Austria, Germany, and more particularly in Spain, this inevitable evolutionary process lost touch, at any rate temporarily, with the national march of evolution. In those countries, clinging over closely to the past, the Royal and monarchical ideal moved too slowly or, perhaps it would be truer to say, the people moved too fast: This only time can tell. Nevertheless, in its inability to move too rapidly, the Royal ideal was acting in accordance with one of its fundamental principles, which is stability.

Only in England has the evolution of the people, and that of their institutions, moved always in step, and that is because the normal Englishman is an orderly, law-abiding conservative animal, with a healthy inborn distrust of fanatics, doctrinaires and revolutionists—in fact of anyone who talks too loud, too long, too learnedly, or too often. But then all this unsettlement and revolutionary business that has been going on in Europe during the past twenty years took place in England hundreds of years ago.

Royalism, like government, is at once an art and a craft, but, like music, poetry, painting and literature, it is much more of an art than a craft. Naturally it has its own technique which some Royalties master with ease, some with difficulty. Just as in any other high-skilled and difficult profession success is conditioned by love of the game. A man who does not want to reign will never become a successful king, though he may be a good one. Mere goodness, however, is not a sufficient qualification for coal-mining or kingship.

2

I have said elsewhere that in my opinion there should be an age limit for Monarchs. Queen Victoria, the old Emperor Wilhelm the First of Germany and the Emperor Franz Joseph, from the point of view of their heirs, all reigned too long. As it happened, owing to his native resilience, this did not stultify King Edward the Seventh, but it did bring him to the throne too late, and gave Europe only ten years of his reign when it would clearly have been the better for at least twenty. The long reigns of Wilhelm the First and Franz Joseph, not only deprived their Heirs Apparent of all legitimate opportunity of showing their mettle while in their prime, but, worse still, brought their Heirs Presumptive to the throne long before they had been properly prepared and tested. This was, in the end, disastrous for Germany, Austria and for Europe. Even in an ordinary noble family it is, generally speaking, unfortunate when the heir succeeds too soon or too late: how much more so then when a great throne is in question.

If, because of circumstances, I came to know more of Wilhelm the Second as a Sovereign, and saw at closer quarters some of the excellences and defects of his technique as a constitutional ruler, I knew Edward the Seventh best as a man. From my childhood until his death he was my friend. King Edward's education, devised and directed by the Prince Consort, was German; he spoke German like a German. His favourite sister, with whom he exchanged a weekly letter as long as she lived, was German Empress: every one of his direct maternal ancestresses were Germans. He loved visiting Germany and adored Homburg and Kissingen. In fact he only gave up visiting Homburg when his nephew's tactlessness, combined with German pinpricks against England, made his presence there unwelcome. How absurd, then, to say that he was, or could be, anti-German! Like his mother, Queen Victoria, he loved and was rightly and legitimately proud of his German descent and connexions. The legend, still prevailing in Germany, that he was a sort of arbiter of Europe's fate is, of course, fantastic, indeed absurd. It was held even by so-called German statesmen like von Bülow and Bethmann-Hollweg, which only goes to prove that they had not the faintest notion of what the Sovereign's true place is in the British Constitution, nor had they even troubled to read such essential handbooks on the subject as Michael's *Englische Geschichte*,[1] or even an article in a good encyclopædia. The French, naturally enough, exploited the idea for their own ends, although they knew perfectly well that it was largely nonsense. The silly notion that the King was an

[1] Michael, Wolfgang: *Englische Geschichte im 18ten Jahrhundert*, Berlin, Vol. I, 1896; Vol. II, 1920; Vol. III, 1935.

enemy of the German people would not be worth a word were it not so mischievous. How could he be?

My own experience was that King Edward was not anti-anything—except perhaps anti-humbug. Like all who acquire their education and philosophy of life direct from life itself, he had no shibboleths, no theories, no panaceas, and few if any dogmas. It was his humanity, his versatility, his sense of humour that dominated his character and personality. He lived vividly, and living, learned from day to day. That was just what his nephew the German Emperor could not do. The King had all the best qualities of a good German; the Emperor some of the worst. German national weaknesses are apt to include an insufficient sense of humour, swagger, a tendency to bullying, an excessive belief in such things as discipline, repression and boastfulness. Above all—and it is an innate German characteristic—the Emperor was imbued with the two unalterable convictions! One is that the German *Wesen* is so superior to all others that it must become the salvation of the world: *Am deutschen Wesen wird die Welt genesen.*[1] The other is the everlasting German inferiority complex that keeps all the time looking out for snubs, slights and injuries where none are intended—the Emperor was always being offended about something! These two notions, although apparently contradictory, are of course in reality only the opposite sides of the same medal. Their obsession prevents the Germans from realizing the simple truth that other nations, whatever their hopes and ambitions might be, are much too occupied and worried by their own internal affairs to have either time or inclination to concoct far-reaching plans for the destruction of Germany, much less the money, power, armaments and energy required to carry them out.

The German obsession with such ideas as "encirclement," "rings of enemies," "campaigns of lying in the foreign press," "regaining her lost honour and prestige," and many similar

[1] By the German spirit or soul (or, more literally, essence) the world will be cured.

absurdities, are a bad inheritance from the old Imperial days and are still a powerful, indeed a determining factor, in the German mentality. They might not like to be told so, but many present-day leaders of German thought are as misguided and unrealistic as ever Wilhelm the Second was. Again the mystic element in the German temperament paralyses common sense, and leads them to mistake the shadow for the substance.

Then what is the sense of all this prating about Germany's lost honour and lost prestige? It is not true. She lost neither. She lost the Great War. But that is quite another story. No outside force can deprive a nation, or an individual for that matter, of their honour and prestige if these are based on reality and not on make-believe. The soul can be greater in defeat than in victory. It is ridiculous for Germany to deny that she was defeated and, in the same breath, cry out about her lost honour and the humiliations to which she has been subjected. Either she was defeated in all honour by superior force or she was not. If she was, then there is nothing to be ashamed of or to apologize for. If, on the other hand, the Allies bore her to the earth with shameful and humiliating terms and conditions, then, before the bar of justice and history, the shame and humiliation is theirs, not hers. I write this because, to my English mind, there is something abject in the way Germany goes on complaining about the manner in which she has been treated, almost as if she were a kitchen-maid punished for being sluttish, or a footman dismissed because he was discovered purloining the tea-spoons.

Altogether too many Germans carefully cultivate a little private plot of inferiority complexes of which, far from being ashamed, they are rather proud. In fact they will gladly wave their *Minkos* in your face on the very slightest provocation—*Minkos* being an indispensable diminutive for a word quite half a yard long.[1] When they do so it makes me blush for them and gives me cold shivers down my back, just as

[1] i.e. *Minderwertigkeitskomplexe.*

happens when a loved or admired relative or friend makes a bad *gaffe* in public.

King Edward, being brought up in sternly realistic England, had no inferiority complexes. The place of England and the British Empire was assured and unassailable; the King knew that without the slightest effort or insistence on his part that he was the first personage in any assembly anywhere he chose to go. He needed neither crowns, nor clanking swords, nor Horse or Foot Guards to remind people that he not only occupied the greatest throne in the world—ruling over one-fifth of the whole earth—but that, by virtue of his own personality, he was the first gentleman in Europe—or anywhere.

But as, in all probability, I am writing of King Edward for the last time, it is his unfailing friendliness and his warm, simple humanity that I prefer to emphasise and remember. His place in history is already assured, and, if it were not, mine is not the pen to assess it.

I have perhaps some special grounds for claiming liberty to make comparisons because it so happened that I have met and known many kings. Amongst sovereigns who became my friends is the gallant Alfonso the Thirteenth of Spain.[1] He had the unique distinction of being born a King, and the misfortune to become legally of age while still little more than a boy. True, for nearly twenty-seven years after his accession he had behind him the wise, sane, moderate advice of his wonderful mother, the unselfish and devoted Queen Maria Christina, Princess of the great Imperial House of Habsburg-Lorraine. Nevertheless, while still immature, King Alfonso had to pit his native boyish wisdom and courage against the wily, insincere, and too often corrupt, party politicians, of which Spain seems to breed more than her fair share. Perhaps those unlovely forces may have blunted the inherent generosity and trustfulness of the King's disposition and,

[1] B. May 17, 1886; acceded May, 1902; withdrew from Spain April, 1931; His Majesty has not abdicated.

to some extent, tarnished his early ideals. But he must possess quite unusual qualities to accomplish all he did in face of such endless difficulties. He successfully ruled turbulent and distracted Spain for almost thirty years, steered her with honour and profit through the Great War, manfully defended her neutrality and, by his fine work for the prisoners, wounded and missing of all the belligerents, won the admiration of all civilized people. The gratitude owed to him by the world for this service is, I fear, largely forgotten. But my friendship and admiration is for the man more even than for the King. Whether playing polo at Eaton Hall, Shelagh's country home in Cheshire, in London, in his own Capital, in Germany or in France—wherever I met him, I always found King Alfonso a true friend, a real gentleman and a first-class sportsman. A sportsman, that is, to whom nothing is sport unless it is accompanied by more than a spice of danger. What, by the way, could be more sporting, more dignified, more kingly, than the reserve and simplicity with which he has conducted himself since he voluntarily left Spain four years ago? And that last moving Proclamation addressed by him to the Spanish people is a piece of literature. It has the ring of great prose and is not unworthy of the Sovereign of the country that has the honour to claim Cervantes as its most glorious son.

King Alfonso has now to go about Europe even without a passport because his own country denies him the right to possess such a document and no other country is competent to issue him one. He was hurt to the quick when the Republican Government branded him as an outlaw, liable to be shot at sight by anyone should he put foot in Spain. But that unchivalrous action stained the politicians, not King Alfonso or the Spanish people, and I would remind His Majesty that it is in a way an expression of fear from his enemies. After all, the last European Sovereign considered important and dangerous enough to be proclaimed an outlaw was, I think, Napoleon the Great!

3

Leopold the Second of Belgium was a true Coburg. Though not a great man he was in many ways a great King. Belgium was too small for his energy and ambition, so he spread himself in the Congo, in some ways with unfortunate results. For two silly, sentimental feminine reasons I never liked him. He had a beard and, worse still, a long one, and he kept his nails too long—I mean, of course, his finger-nails because, fortunately, I never saw his toes, although many women of all ranks and conditions must, I understand, have done so! Once at a luncheon or dinner party at, I think, his huge ugly villa at Cap Ferrat, I saw him—I must admit very skilfully—peel grapes with those long finger-nails, and the sight so disgusted me that I always refused to meet him again. As he did so there was—or so it seemed to me—a look of satisfied cruelty on his face as if he were gleefully skinning alive the President and all the members of the Aborigines Protection Society.

Although his son, the present King Boris, then Crown Prince, was several times at Pless during the war, I never knew King Ferdinand of Bulgaria. This has always been to me a lasting source of regret, because I am convinced that he had a finer brain and greater intelligence than any of his contemporary brother Sovereigns. He was at once the fine flower of the two great families of Wettin and Bourbon.[1] The King is very fond of staying at the famous monastery of Ettal, a few miles from Garmisch-Partenkirchen where I so often reside. I have frequently seen the King in the streets of Partenkirchen, a rather shrunken figure, the parchment-like face, long Bourbon nose and keen eyes giving him the look of an untamed old eagle. Once I sat near him in a tea-room in the Ludwigstrasse and, as I watched him munching

[1] King Ferdinand of Bulgaria is the youngest son of Prince August of Saxe-Coburg-Gotha by Princess Clementine, d. of Louis Philippe, King of the French; b. 1861, elected Prince of Bulgaria 1887, King 1908; he abdicated in favour of his son Boris, the present King, in November, 1918.

Kuchen, wondered if anyone else present saw in that quiet figure the man who for over thirty years played with Emperors, Kings and statesmen as another man might play chess. Quite near the tea-rooms is a flower shop I often patronize and an even more characteristic sight was to see the King's motor-car outside its door. The buxom young assistant, prompted by her rather flustered mistress, would come out again and again bearing great bunches of daffodils, violets, mimosa, winter roses, flaming regal poinsettias for the King's choice. Clearly it was not enough for him to see them at a distance through the rather misty plate-glass window of the little village shop. He wanted to smell, touch . . . *taste* them. How well I understand that. The King would bury his nose in one after the other, indicate by a nod acceptance or rejection, peer into the shop window pointing to other flowers he wished brought out for his inspection and, his car full of lovely blossoms, eventually drive back to his monastic quarters at Ettal. The King adores flowers, rare jewels, works of art, rare and exotic literature and perfumes and . . . people with brains.

How the unknown and mysterious attracts women. Perhaps I find King Ferdinand of Bulgaria more fascinating than any Monarch I have ever met—just because I have never met him.

4

And now I want to show from a few of her own letters to me just what sort of a woman my friend Princess Victoria of Prussia really was; the second daughter of the Empress Friedrich could not have been quite an ordinary woman; and it is noteworthy that fifteen years after the death of the Empress, Vicky's admiration and longing for her mother should still be fresh and keen. All her life Vicky was starved for love and, sooner or later, a starved emotional life inevitably leads to disaster. Zoubkov represented the love she had never known and, like a famished being, she grabbed at it unquestioningly:

"*Schloss Friedrichshof, Cronberg, Taunus.*
"*May 8th,* 1916.

"DEAREST DAISY:

"Ever so many thanks for your dear kind letter, and the note from the *Lazarettzug* the other day. I couldn't answer it—not knowing your address! All that you write about—interests me greatly; glorious Partenkirchen must be—and now the sweet little blue room is empty. *How* often I think of those delightful hours—and all your kindness, etc.! Do hope the nursing doesn't tire you—admire your energy and pluck—you will surely be rewarded for it.

"Since Easter I have been staying with my sister here—in lovely Friedrichshof; it's beautiful at present—spring in all its glory—but Oh! how one pines for one's Mother dear—who built and created it; I shall remain on still—we ride and are much on the go. Can't possibly promise Daisy dear—if I can manage, Fürstenstein *will* be *delightful* and so good of you to ask me to come—it *must* come to pass once! The weather has been splendid—to-day pouring.

"With best love—ever yr affecate,
"VICTORIA."

This letter is absolutely characteristic. On July 9, 1916, her husband, Prince Adolphus of Schaumburg-Lippe, died and, like many another widow in similar circumstances, dear Vicky believed herself to be broken-hearted. She was, of course, nothing of the sort. They had no children, and they could not have had a great deal in common. Although its rulers were very rich, the Principality of Schaumburg-Lippe was of no importance, and Bückeburg, the little town where the ruling princes have their Schloss, is really only a large village. The castle itself is a quite beautiful baroque building in the individual North German style. It stands on the edge of the town in small but good gardens and, in the German fashion, there stretches round it for miles an open undulating tree-studded park. The whole landscape is sweet and winning rather than grand, reminiscent of the English home counties. A few of the rooms, showing in the doorways and decorations the work of Adriaen de Vries and other Dutch artists, are of unusual interest, but the others, as in most palaces, are merely dull and pompous. As for the Palais Schaumburg in Bonn, it was only a glorified suburban villa. Clearly, from the point of view of the Prussian Royal family, Vicky's marriage could not have been looked upon as a brilliant one. The stage was very small, and Vicky never had enough to occupy her unusual energies of which, like her eldest brother, she had a superabundance. Of course she should have married her one and only love, the handsome and gallant Alexander of Battenberg, who, for a time, ruled Bulgaria as its Prince.

Vicky's next two letters were written from *Seebad* Bansin on the Mecklenburg coast:

"*Sunday.*

"MY DEAREST DAISY,

"Thanks with all my soar (*sic*) heart for yr loving lines. I am absolutely prostrated—miserable and feel so far from well—they sent me here for a change, but it's no better. Shall *love* to see you—miss you as it is—had *quite* a secluded life all the afternoon on the beach in a chair. Come *when* you like—pray *alone;* at 5 I go upstairs for tea in my room!

"Tender love,

"Yr. affate. broken hearted,

"V."

"*On the beach, Bansin, Aug.* 15*th,* 1916.

"MY DEAREST DAISY,

"A 1000 thanks for yr very kind letter—and all dear words which comfort me—Yes! you understand, *what* great grief means—and Oh! the anguish at times—one pulls oneself together as best one can—so as not to be a burden to others—but life is bitter now—and the longing for one's dearest one, to return—hardly bearable. Miss you *very* much—what a great pity you couldn't stay on here—would have done you good! Am reclining on a chair—the weather sultry and warm—the waves rushing and rolling soothe the heartache a bit? Never mind—what people and the papers talk about—not worth while, it's *mostly* jealousy! Shall remain on a while here still—was terribly run down—getting stronger again! Hanna very glad her letter reached yr Mother! Baby came and said good-bye yesterday, sweet little fellow. The Fürst[1] sends many kind messages: God bless you,

"Ever yrs most affeate,

"VICTORIA."

Thinking that a sight of a friend might help her out of her fit of depression, and to give myself a very much needed change, I went to Bansin for a few days. While there I begged Vicky to return my visit at Berchtesgaden:

"*Palais Schaumburg, Bonn.*

"*November 12th,* 1916.

"MY DEAREST DAISY:

"So many thanks for your very kind letter. I was longing for news from you and somehow *felt* a letter was coming. *Do* hope you have had *good* news by now from home and need not worry or that there is any cause for anxiety left. Cheer up, don't fret, dear. It's *awfully* kind of you not to have forgotten about Berchtesgaden—am indeed looking forward to the time—*more* than I can say. Let's be together a long while—if I don't bore you. I can't say for certain yet when I shall be able to turn up—but shall *of course* let you know in due time—perhaps before New Year. Hanna can naturally live anywhere for the beginning. Unfortunately I don't know about the Fürst's plans either yet—he may be coming for Christmas—and I trust to manage a short stay at Berchtesgaden likewise. *When* do you go there? *Love* my room since you made it so homely and cosy. Very best love.

"Yours affectionately,

"VICTORIA."

The next letter, written in August, 1918, from Garmisch-Partenkirchen, must be the last one from Vicky quoted here:

[1] Her nephew Prince Adolf, b. 1883, the successor of her husband.

"*Garmisch,* 17, viii, 18.

"My Dearest Daisy,

"*So* awfully pleased to hear from you at last again—just recd. your very kind letter of the 13th from Fürstenstein, ever so many thanks in return! I often wondered where you might be—and *here* of all places. My thoughts are with you—and one longs for those delightful by-gone hours in the little blue cottage, etc.: perhaps they may return? You were so dear and good to me. The weather is change-able, but air splendid—and one loves the place; shall remain on till beginning of Sept.: and then, probably rush off to Lucerne to see my sister, if possible! Hanna is not married, left me, as her father wished to have her back again! Edina Montgelas has come instead—you remember her, I believe. So you are hard at work—splendid of you.

"Good-bye, Daisy dear—cheer up! Let's hope for a meeting again! Best love.

"Yr affectate,
"Victoria."

Hanna was my friend, Baroness Hanna Löwe, who, accompanied by her delightful father (always dressed like a Scot), came to see me many times during a recent visit to Partenkirchen. Hanna had been lady-in-waiting to Vicky for a long time; her successor was Countess Edina Montgelas, member of a noted Bavarian family. The sister Vicky refers to was of course the second-youngest, Sophie Queen of Greece, at that moment an exile in Switzerland with her husband and family.

5

Margaret, Princess Friedrich Karl of Hesse, is a very different type of woman from her elder sister, Victoria. While dear Vicky had in an exaggerated degree some of the worst faults of her brother the Emperor Wilhelm, Margaret inherited in full measure the finest characteristics of both the Emperor and the Empress Friedrich: an acute intelligence, courage, unselfishness, and a noble disinterestedness always ruled her whole being.

One or two of her letters will show how extraordinarily good a friend she was to me throughout the war. She was one of the principal intermediaries in getting my letters to England conveyed to "the other Daisy" in Sweden,[1] and she did all she could in 1918 to enable me to get permission to go to Sweden for a holiday. Her personal losses in the war were almost unbearable but, as it was all for the Fatherland, her high spirit never quailed. Fortunately she found in her husband, Prince Friedrich Karl of Hesse, a devoted, chivalrous companion and friend. Royalties do not often marry happily, but their married life was, and is, a beautiful thing to see. The following letter is particularly interesting as showing the German attitude towards France at the time. Friedrichshof is the imposing castle in the Taunus forest, some miles from Frankfort, built by the widowed Empress Friedrich and left by her to Margaret. It took many years to complete and the Empress derived great happiness from the task of designing and furnishing it, and laying out the lovely gardens:

"*Schloss Friedrichshof Cronberg, Taunus.*
"*April 29th,* 1917.

"MY DEAR DAISY:

"Thank you ever so much for your two kind letters and your telegram. I feel very anxious about Greece, but have no news. The last telegram, which came about ten days ago, said that the situation was becoming serious. Those wicked French are capable of any treachery down there and find the greatest pleasure in humiliating the King and tormenting his unfortunate country. It is only one way more of showing their hatred towards the Emperor, as his sister happens to be there.

[1] Princess Margaret of Great Britain and of Ireland (1882–1920), eldest d. of Field-Marshal His Royal Highness the Duke of Connaught, m. 1905 Gustaf Adolf Crown Prince of Sweden and had five children.

"Your letters sound so sad and I feel intensely for you. Don't lose heart, but go on doing good and living for your children. That always brings satisfaction and happiness in the end. A worldly life always means disappointment and ingratitude on all sides.

"Muriel Münster[1] was here for a day, but had to rush off to take leave of her second boy, who starts for the front to-day. Such a wrench for her. Spring at last seems to be coming to-day, and may it mean better times for us all. Cheer up, dear Daisy, and God help you. I often think of you.

"Love from Yrs afftly,

"MARGARET."

On June 12th King Constantine and Queen Sophie and their family were compelled by pressure from the Allies to leave Greece. It was, of course, not only a reverse for Germany, but a great blow to all the members of the Prussian Royal family. Nevertheless, in her letter telling me about it, Margaret, as usual, put me and my affairs first. Not one word about the part *my* country had played in bringing about what was to the writer a great personal tragedy:

"*Friedrichshof, June* 23, 1917.

"Many thanks, dear Daisy, for your last letter! I do hope you have had good news from home since. The enclosed has just arrived from Sweden. Do take care of yourself and try to get a thorough rest. Don't attempt to fight against the world, nor people, nor circumstances; it is no use and will only wear you out. Just wait till better times come, as surely they must some day.

"I have been through such anxiety about my poor sister, but now they are safe in Switzerland, thank God. But the injustice and wickedness of it all surpasses everything.

"Cheer up, dear Daisy, and make the best of things. Much love from Yrs afftly,

"MARGARET."

[1] Lady Muriel Hay (1863–1927), d. of 11th Earl of Kinnoul, m. in 1890 Alexander, 2nd Prince Münster (1858–1922).

From the moment I first put foot in Friedrichshof at the age of nineteen, I loved it and always found in it peace and a home: even a day spent there did me good—especially during the war.

"*Schloss Friedrichshof, August* 24, 1917.

"Very many thanks for your dear letter and for the illustrated papers which I looked at with great pleasure—excepting the pictures about the war, which I passed over as quickly as possible. They are too silly, misunderstood and exaggerated. Will truth and justice ever reign again? I hope so, and shall continue to think that in time all will improve and people in England will see *how* they have been misled.

"I'm so glad you had a fine day for being here, and felt a little peaceful. Wish I could do more for you, for I realize how hard and sad life is for you at this moment. But you must continue to be brave and above all think of getting strong, that is the only help to bear all that is sent. I have done all I could to get, and keep, my health in order; it is a duty towards those left to one, otherwise one becomes a burden to them.

"The fighting on all sides is too ghastly, but it looks more and more like a final struggle. May it bring on the end quicker than we think.

"Much love, dear Daisy, and thanks again from:

"Yrs affectly,

"MARGARET."

I don't quite know why it was that, during the war, any little action characteristic of ordinary *normal* life was so healing. Although such a gallant soldier, Prince Philipp,[1] Margaret's third son, had always a great love for everything beautiful. He knew all about my Silesian Lace School in Waldenburg, and in September, 1917, his mother wrote:

"My Philipp was here for a few days and left again to-day. He wished to be remembered to you and hoped that you got

[1] He and his twin brother Prince Wolfgang were b. Nov. 6, 1896; Prince Philipp m. in 1925 Princess Mafalda of Savoy, d. of the King of Italy.

the little pieces of lace he sent you long ago, which he thought might prove useful as patterns for your Lace School. They are old pieces."

A young soldier taking time during the war to send me patterns for such a delicate, lovely, fragile thing as lace seemed somehow a pledge that one day the world would be ordinary and peaceful again.

Princess Margaret and her husband got permission to visit Switzerland to see King Constantine, Queen Sophie and the Greek Royal family. This made me think that I also might go there. I even fruitlessly evoked the help of the Emperor Wilhelm. Upon writing to her of my great disappointment Margaret replied as follows:

"*Schloss Friedrichshof, Nov. 3rd,* 1917.

"Dear Daisy,

"Thank you so much for your last letter and for the illustrated paper, which I looked at with great interest and shall return as soon as possible. I do feel so for you with all the worry and bother about lawyers, etc. Everything has been forwarded, and the enclosed has arrived for you. I hear the other Daisy proposes you should go to Sweden for a thorough change, and it strikes me as if that would be just the thing for you. You ought to give your poor nerves and heart a rest, and get away from everything; you are sure to pick up then and return feeling stronger and happier. Do think it over. I am sure it will be easier to get a pass to Sweden than Switzerland. Switzerland is not the place for you; we of course enjoyed being with our dear ones, and it was a great comfort being able to meet, but we were glad to get back again. It is a disagreeable atmosphere, and a horrible set of people that meet there. I am sure you are as pleased as we are about our grand successes in Italy.[1] May it help to bring us nearer the longed-for end. Cheer up, dear Daisy, and do think about the proposed plan. The other D. is sure to look after you, and it will

[1] Oct. 24–28, great Austro-German attack took place on Italian front; the Italians retreated and 100,000 prisoners were said to be taken.

do you good to have other impressions and see other people. So glad somebody was nicer lately.

"In haste, with best love, yrs affly,

"MARGARET."

The next two letters have the historic interest that anything written during 1918 by responsible people in Germany now has; moreover, the first contains a touching reference to the *Rosenkavalier*:

"*Friedrichshof*, *March* 18*th*, 1918.

"DEAR DAISY,

"Thank you ever so much for several letters. I am so glad to be able to send you two, which arrived yesterday and to-day, and do hope they are the ones you are waiting for. It was dear of you to let me see those from my Philipp and the other D., and I read them with great interest and return them with many thanks. The death of dear, kind Fritz Strelitz also upset us terribly, we liked him so much, and it is terrible to think what he must have been through and how lonely he must have felt, before he took to such a step. No doubt, as you say, the idea of marriage frightened him. I think of you a great deal and hope we shall meet before long, and that you will also think of coming to these parts. We are having glorious spring weather. It is quite hot in the sun and one can sit outside. What will happen in the next few months? All is in God's hands and perhaps the longed-for end to this cruel, wicked war is nearer than we think, but the uncertainty weighs on one. May you have better news of your dear mother, and keep brave and patient, Daisy dear, until all your trials come to an end, which they will in time. I am working for you but there are still difficulties to be overcome.

"Love from yrs affate,

"MARGARET."

"*April* 12*th*, 1918.
"*Schloss Friedrichshof*.

"DEAR DAISY,

"Thank you for all your kind letters. I was so pleased to hear you had been to Vienna, and hoped it would have been a nice change, but I quite understand you feel up to nothing. These sad and cruel times take too much out of one. But don't lose courage and continue to be brave, as you have till now. There are still difficulties about your going to Sweden, luckily none that need distress you. I know for certain that people do not distrust you, nor doubt your loyalty to this country, so you need not worry nor feel hurt about that. But it seems not advisable to go to a neutral country at *this minute;*[1] it may be possible later on. So please be patient a little longer, poor Daisy. I know how cruel this will seem, but it is all for your good and you will be rewarded in the end. Things really seem coming to a climax in the West, and I think it would make the very worst impression if you urged things on, and insisted on going to a neutral country now. Perhaps you will soon be free to go where and do what you like, so take my advice, dear Daisy, and just wait. I am on the look out, and as soon as I see the right opportunity I shall let you know, and shall not give up working for you.

"Could you not come to Homburg and have the masseuse there, not to lose time? It is charming in the early spring, and very quiet there now, and we could meet now and then. How ghastly all this fighting. God grant it may lead to the longed-for end. It upsets me so to think that the fighting in the north of France is just round the place where my beloved second boy[2] is supposed to be resting. He was my ray of sunshine, the one I was quite wrapped up in, whom I miss day after day, as well as his brother. Never can I get over their loss.

"Good-bye, Daisy dear, and God bless and help you. Let us hope for a meeting soon, and please don't worry. I do so hope your mother will be able to give you good news of herself. Much love from

"Yrs affly,

"MARGARET."

[1] Haig's famous "Backs to the Wall" order was issued on April 12, 1918.

[2] Prince Maximilian, b. 1894, an airman, was killed in France in Oct., 1914; Prince Friedrich Wilhelm, b. 1893, was killed in Rumania in 1916.

I have the impression that English help was successfully invoked to discover Prince Maximilian's body but, as it could not be got to Germany, it was sent to England until after the war. I believe that the Prince now rests beside his eldest brother Prince Friedrich Wilhelm in the beautiful little private chapel at Friedrichshof.

6

I always liked and admired the Grand Duchess Anastasia,[1] mother of the Crown Princess Cecile of Germany. The daughter of the Grand Duke Michael Nicolaievitch, third son of the Tsar Nicholas the First, her birth and upbringing were not a very suitable preparation for life at a petty German Court. Her handsome husband, Friedrich Franz the Third, was one of the dearest men who ever lived but, compared to Russia, his Duchy of Mecklenburg-Schwerin was the size of a postage stamp. A personage of the first importance in her own vast country the Grand Duchess felt squeezed in by the absurd conventions of her German surroundings and naturally enough she did not like giving precedence to all sorts of persons who, in Russia, would have been nobodies. The consequences were that the Grand Duchess lived a great deal on the Riviera where she had an enormous villa and entertained a cosmopolitan society on a lavish scale. This did not endear her to the German Emperor and Empress, the Prussian Royal family, or the other German Royalties. However, one day Anastasia's elder daughter Alexandrine married the Crown Prince of Denmark,[2] and eventually became reigning Queen.

The following letter from Friedrich Franz IV., eldest son of the Grand Duchess, not only throws light on the charming personality of the writer, but shows that he was as fond of his cousin Adolphus Friedrich as the *Rosenkavalier* was of him:

[1] (1860–1922) m. 1879 Friedrich Franz III (1851–1897).

[2] Christian X, b. 1870; succeeded to the throne in 1912.

"*Neustrelitz, Nov. 2nd,* 1916.

"DEAR PRINCESS,

"Many hearty thanks for your kind letter. The address of my mother is: Territet, Grand Hotel; but if you have something to send to Mamma, perhaps a letter, which surely would give her great pleasure, I propose that you send it to me, as I have surer ways to send it than by post. I also was so happy to see you again after such a long time: I always hoped to meet you somehow but I did not know how to manage it; please accept my heartiest thanks for the freesias; what a touching and charming idea!

"I am sad that the visit here is over already; I always so enjoy being with my dear cousin, who is such a true friend to me; friendships in these sad times are more worth than any wealth of the world; can't you find a nice wife for the Gr. Duke; he must be so lonely here.

"Again many thanks,
"Your devoted,
"FRIEDRICH FRANZ."

The engagement of the Crown Prince Wilhelm to Cecile, the sister of the writer of the above letter, was, at first, most unpopular in Germany, and the German Press of the day was really shameless in the way it wrote and spoke about the bride-elect's mother. Admittedly the Grand Duchess was often indiscreet; but she was always a great lady, even if self-willed, erratic and unconventional. She was not made for narrow moulds and middle-class ideals and the Court of Wilhelm of Germany was, above all, middle-class.

I first met Cecile at Cannes in 1905 soon after her engagement to the Prussian Crown Prince was announced. I liked her instantly and, from that moment, we became real friends. I found her human and understanding and very tactful and intelligent. Her position as Crown Princess of the German Reich and of Prussia might well have justified her in treating me with reserve throughout the war. But far from it; she wrote me many letters, of which I will quote only two, one written early in the war and one late, just to show how loyal and unchanging she was. Both were written in English.

I know that we English are supposed to be more chivalrous, tolerant, broadminded and reasonable than any other nation. I sometimes doubt the existence of any of these qualities when I think of the hysterical war fever in appeasement of which we flung to the wolves such loyal and patriotic national figures as the brilliant and chivalrous sailor, Prince Louis of Battenberg, and the first-class statesman and organizer Lord Haldane; to the first we largely owed the preparedness and efficiency of the Navy; to the second that of the Army and, in particular—as Jack Cowans often told me—that of the Territorial Force. The full powers and ability of even such men as Lord Milner and Sir Eyre Crowe were to some extent neutralized by the mere suspicion of the presence of German blood in their veins. And did not poor dear Margot Asquith get into a ridiculous pother because she would not in August, 1914, instantly dismiss an old and faithful governess who was partly German and who, had she been inhumanly flung on the world, would have had to choose between the poor-house and a concentration camp? And did not Margot get into absolutely boiling water because, at the request of their parents whom she knew, she visited some German prisoners of war at Donnington Hall? I admire more than I can say that characteristic example of her fine courage and independence. These, and similar examples of British hysteria, reached Germany, of course, in a very much exaggerated form, were skilfully (and justifiably) exploited as welcome evidences of British funk, and again and again when cast in my teeth made me want to cry with shame or howl with impotent rage at my country's crass stupidity. Then think of the way the Speyers, the Schusters and many others were hounded down by the halfpenny papers to gratify the stupidity of the mob.

But I have wandered far from the Crown Princess Cecile—and yet, really, I haven't. What English Princess, I should like to know, would have dared to correspond in German with a German living in England during the war? Were there any German-born women walking freely about in England throughout the war? Here are the two letters; the first was written in 1914:

"*Berlin, Sep. 28th, Evening.*

"DEAREST PRINCESS DAISY,

"Coming into my room just this moment I discovered some lovely lilies, which looked like a fairy offering. I thought they had come to me as a God-send; *I love* lilies, and these are such a beautiful *unearthly* white. Then, looking down, I saw your note bringing me your good wishes. Oh, Daisy dear, it *is* kind of you! You have given me a *great* pleasure! Poor Princess Daisy! What you must be suffering just now knowing your countrymen in danger, and fighting your adopted country! I am so sorry for you; and I find it so sweet of you to think of me in this kind way—sending me those *lovely* flowers which I love so much!

"Very best love,
"From,
"CECILE.

"Excuse this scrawl—it is late."

The second letter was written in January, 1918:

"DEAR PRINCESS DAISY,

"Many thanks for your kind letter. I am so grieved for you, that your sorrow for your beloved father is still weighing heavily on you. But I think your work in Belgrade is the very best thing for your sad thoughts: it will keep them from wandering too much after what is lost. In thoughts and belief you are always united with your dear one above.

"My coming to Berchtesgaden has been postponed because one of my children has had measles. I am looking forward to the rest there, and intend living very quietly and retired. I think it is so plucky of you to go out to Belgrade again, and am sure you will find consolation in your work.

"Christa Salm was here before Christmas—*such* a dear.

"With every good wish for the New Year, and for your long journey, and your work down among the wounded, with best love, dear Princess Daisy,

"Your affectionate,

"CECILE."

I always greatly admired Cecile as a wife, a mother and a Crown Princess. The way she managed and kept Wilhelm, who, like his father, was none too easy, was a lesson in tact and forbearance from which I personally might well have profited more than I did. Since the revolution her skill in maintaining a difficult position without offending anyone has won the admiration of even rabid anti-monarchists. Quickly grasping the necessity for giving a new direction to the education of her boys, she had them all prepared to earn their own living as private persons. The Crown Prince (whom I always liked), being in exile on a beastly little island somewhere, Cecile successfully shouldered very heavy responsibilities to which she was quite unaccustomed. If the Hohenzollerns ever regain their throne—and I for one hope they do—Cecile will have to receive a considerable share of the credit. May she have her reward. Like Hindenburg himself I am an unrepentant monarchist, and don't in the least see why I should change my beliefs and principles just because other people have turned their coats.

7

In my two former books I said a good deal about the Crown Princess of Sweden, born Princess Margaret of Connaught [1]—but I could never say enough. She was the dearest, tenderest, most loyal of friends. I will quote a few of her many letters to me because they paint a much better portrait of her than I, with all my love, could ever do; in addition her letters remind us—and we are very apt to forget it—that the war caused food shortage and privations amongst the

[1] *See* p. 116.

THE CASTLE, PLESS: THE MAIN ENTRANCE

The Prince and the Princess on the Balcony

neutrals as well as amongst the belligerents. Throughout the war—as will already have been gathered by my readers—"the other Daisy" was indefatigable in trying to secure for me news of my English relations and friends, and in being the intermediary of letters between us. Her position as Crown Princess of a neutral country of course giving her great advantages and facilities. I did love her for thinking of heading her letter St. Patrick's Day!

"*March* 17*th, St. Patrick's Day,* 1918.

"DEAR DAISY,

"Many thanks for your letter. I'm so very glad to think that you are going to have a rest. I hope you will like coming here. Come as early as you can for Fr. Holmgren's sake, as she is due in Germany at some watering place end of May and it would be nice for you to be massaged by her. She will no doubt be able to find some little place for you to live in. I fear that to have your own household would in these days of bread cards, butter cards, etc., and rationing, be full of difficulties, but if we could find some little cottage near the water with a lady who could look after all that sort of thing it would be ideal. We shall do our best, that you may rest assured. I hope you will try and settle as soon as possible when you can get away, and as to whether you will bring your little boy or not, because it is no easy thing to get suitable rooms here in a hurry. Fröken Holmgren is in Germany at this moment if you could communicate with her. Your secretary at Charlottenburg knows her address. I hope you've got all the letters I've forwarded.

"Hoping this letter will find you well and with love:

"Believe me,

"Yours very sincerely,

"DAISY."

"*Stockholm, April* 10, 1918.

"DEAR DAISY,

"I hope you got my telegram saying your mother was at Newlands; you must be glad to think of her there. How are you getting on? I fear that there may be difficulties about your coming here now; they are beginning to make strict rules as to foreigners staying in Sweden on account of the want of food. I fear it may even be impossible—perhaps you'd better put it off for a little. I'm so sorry, but anyhow, you could try and meet Fröken Holmgren in Germany as she goes to her usual watering place in June and will be there all summer. A little massage would certainly do you good after your strenuous nursing.

"We are longing for the spring here but it doesn't come. That's the drawback to a Swedish spring; it takes so long to make up its mind to arrive, but when it really does so it is very lovely.

"We go to our country place for a week's rest and quiet on the 15th and go there for the whole summer by, I hope, the end of May.

"With love, believe me,
"Yours,
"D."

"*Sofiero, June 1st,* 1918.

"DEAR DAISY,

"Many thanks for your last letter from Serbia, dated May 17. I at once sent a wire to your mother but have, of course, not got an answer here as I gave her your address as Interpax, Berne.

"We have just got here to our country place; the weather is perfect, a blue sea and sky and the trees at their greenest. But rain is so badly wanted for the garden for vegetables and crops that one hardly feels one can enjoy the hot dry sunshine until we've had a little rain. The children love being here, of course, and running wild after nine months of town life."

The premature death of "the other Daisy" was indeed an irreparable loss to her family, every member of which was devoted to her, to Sweden and to Great Britain. As I write these lines I see that her delightful girl, Princess Ingrid, is to be married to the Crown Prince of Denmark, and I pray that their union may be rich in love and happiness.

8

I seem once to have been guilty of allowing the Empress Eugénie to go on for a whole week expecting me as a guest —and I never turned up. The Empress, characteristically, let me down with a very gentle rebuke.

"*Villa Cyrnos, Cap Martin, Alpes Maritime,*
"*February* 7, 1920.

"DEAR PRINCESS,

"I am extremely sorry not to be able to put you up at this moment. With a view to please you I have kept a room for you for a week, but in accordance with arrangements which I had previously made, the Princess de la Moskowa has just arrived for a month. If you would come one day to lunch I would love to see you; or, in a month's time, do come and spend some days.

"Yours affectionately,
"EUGÉNIE."

It was so quietly done that I quite loved her dear little letter. After all, she had occupied the Throne of France for eighteen years, and might well have resented such seeming discourtesy from a much younger woman. But she understood perfectly all I had been through during the war, how it had shattered my nerves and health; and, always—as the French people unchivalrously like to forget—she was unfailingly magnanimous.

Looking over my two previous books I am inclined to think that sometimes, especially in a few of my Diary extracts, I judged hastily and unfairly. Impatience was ever my besetting sin; and, while the Almighty himself is prepared to wait for it, Daisy, like many others, always wanted perfection, and wanted it *now*. Of course, as all who have read my books well know, I clearly saw and lamented my own imperfections, but somehow, as is not I believe unusual, they never seemed to me so disagreeable and irritating as some of the *perfections* of others can frequently be! I had, I felt, quite good excuses for most, if not indeed all, of my little failings.

One example of my over hasty judgment will serve: I now think that I never quite fairly estimated all the manifold difficulties the Empress Auguste Victoria of Germany faced and successfully overcame. The subconscious reason for this—as I belatedly see—was that I instinctively resented her obvious subservience to the Emperor. Of course I knew it was typically German and sweet and all that; nevertheless I thought it wrong. But what I forgot was that she had to live with Wilhelm the Second and I had not!

Of all the Royal families in Europe that of Bavaria is undoubtedly the most attractive, and, in the French sense, *sympathique*. Are Royalties different? Well, King Ludwig the Third, the last reigning Sovereign, was certainly different from any other king in Europe. First and last he was himself—a true Wittelsbach. Known lovingly to all Bavarians as "the Farmer King," he could be the most bourgeois figure imaginable with his ancient hats, concertina trousers and old loose coats, his impossible overcoats and exaggerated umbrellas. At the same time at Court ceremonials in full uniform with his upstanding figure, rugged features and white beard, he was a figure of genial yet commanding dignity. He is the hero of countless good stories.

The consort of King Ludwig the Third, born the Archduchess Maria Theresa of Austria-Este, was directly descended from Henrietta, the daughter of Charles the First of England and, therefore, the senior representative of the Royal House of Stuart; in fact, because there is no Salic Law in our country, the legitimist Queen of England. She was of a handsome and gracious presence, charitable and unselfish, and was as beloved as her husband in Bavaria. Her grandchildren, the children of her attractive eldest son the Crown Prince Rupprecht, frequently appear in the kilt of Royal Stuart hunting tartan, and assuredly none have a better right to do so.

I do not know well the Crown Prince Rupprecht nor his very distinguished-looking and charming wife, who was born

Princess Antoinette of Luxembourg, nor their six lovely children. Since the end of the war the Crown Prince has conducted himself with perfect tact and discretion. Seeming to live almost entirely the life of a country gentleman interested chiefly in sport and art, he is one of the best informed men of the day, and without question the most important and influential Royal personage in post-war Germany. His intellectual and artistic interests are wide, and it touched my heart that, when last in England in 1934, he and the Crown Princess took some trouble to go to unique Knole, the home of the Sackville branch of my family, and carefully inspect its countless perfect art treasures.

By far my best and most beloved friends in the Bavarian Royal family are Prince and Princess Ludwig Ferdinand and their only daughter Princess Pilar. Their younger son, Prince Adalbert, and his wife Princess Augusta, I am not fortunate enough to know so well, nor do I know so well as I should wish their two stalwart and handsome boys, Constantine and Alexander. A very close link between us is that Princess Ludwig Ferdinand, born the Infanta Paz of Spain, is an aunt of my dear friend King Alfonso the Thirteenth. Whether found at Nymphenburg, that magnificently designed summer palace on the outskirts of Munich with its imposing gardens and matchless Amalienburg, or in their old town house, the Palais Prince Ludwig Ferdinand overlooking the Wittelsbachplatz, the Ludwig Ferdinands, as they are affectionately known in Munich, are in every way delightful. The Prince is a fully qualified doctor and actively practised for years, mostly in the service of the poor and needy. It is not so well known that he is a skilful violinist and that for years he would on occasions join the orchestra of the Royal Theatre as a supernumerary first violin. He is a prolific composer but, like many artists, too much inclined to pass on to new experiments before polishing and perfecting the old or bothering about publication. Princess Ludwig Ferdinand once told me that wherever she went she had to drag a piano about with her if she was to succeed in keeping her husband content and happy. Here, dated May, 1915, is a passage dug out of my Diary:

"I was forgetting to record that I was three nights in Munich, and had two whole very nice days there. Princess Ludwig Ferdinand, sister of the late King of Spain and her daughter, Princess Pilar, came from Schloss Nymphenburg to have tea with me on the *Lazarett* train while it rested in Munich. Our head Doctor had invited to tea a lot of little Spanish boys who are in Munich under the guardianship of Princess Ludwig Ferdinand for the purpose of acquiring German and a German education, which after all is thoroughly sound and good. After tea we had the gramophone, but the records I bought in Metz were far, far better than those which my courier Seidel[1] bought for me in Breslau—at least so everyone said. I have not yet heard them all.

"Then I went to see a Frau von F. who wants to paint me for nothing (or so she says). She is a Hungarian, but I do not admire her art, as her figures look as if they were nothing but bones, and all the children she paints appear to squint. At any rate she seems very sad and declared that if I don't sit for her she will come to Fürstenstein to do me. But somehow I don't think I shall have the patience. Also, she talks far too much, so it would be no rest.

"The next day I went by myself to Nymphenburg. It was pouring wet, so we could not go out, but the fountains in the distance and all the statues were really lovely. I sang and made pretence. We made up verses about what we were going to do when the war was over, and I sang them. Then Prince Ludwig Ferdinand came in, and he really is full of music. It was extraordinary how he played. Giving him the titles, I got him to improvise on such subjects as 'Children going to School,' 'Coming out Again,' 'Attending a Wedding,' the 'Choir-singing in the Village Church,' 'Wedding Bells,' and so on. Then he played a 'Soldier in a Trench,' 'His Home-coming,' 'His Happiness,' 'Peace All Around Him,' then 'The Pain of Parting,' 'Going out again

[1] A manservant from Pless. Acted as courier to the Authoress throughout the war.

to the Front'—ending with the 'Roar of the Cannons.' This entranced us all so that it was after six o'clock before I realized that I must hurry back to Munich to receive Count Wolff-Metternich—long German Ambassador in London—who was coming specially from somewhere in the country to see me."

As all my old readers know, very high on my list of women friends stands Princess Pilar of Bavaria. From the moment I met her I liked her; that liking grew into a warm affection; it, in turn, into a deep admiration. The way Pilar has arranged her life since the Bavarian revolution evokes the highest praise. Like her brother, Prince Adalbert, immediately it was over she sent herself to the Munich University to continue her education; she undertook strenuously to improve her painting and drawing and has, happily, achieved considerable success as an artist and writer. She has exhibited in Munich repeatedly and once or twice in London. The travel book about her beloved Bavaria,[1] written in collaboration with my Editor, is, I think, enchanting, and deserves a great success. Three of her letters, all written during the war, will not only show how she is, but will show the development of our friendship:

"*Nymphenburg,* 28, v, 1916.

"My Dear Princess,

"You one time asked me for a photo that I never gave you. May I send it to you now and ask for one of yours in return? I would so much like to have one of you!

"This afternoon was so very nice. You were charming! I have just noticed that I have a crown stuck over my head on the paper border of the photograph. The invention is of the photographer and *not* of me.

"Much love.

"Pilar."

[1] *Bavaria The Incomparable:* An unpretentious Travel Book by Princess Pilar of Bavaria and Major Desmond Chapman-Huston. London, Cassell, 1934.

"*Nymphenburg*, 21, v, 1917.

"Dearest Daisy,

"Oh, don't be so sad! Don't worry about the things people say! We—my mother and I—know very well that you would have helped in raising funds here for the Red Cross Hospital in East Prussia if they would have let you. Hass was here to-day. He said that you were awfully nice to him, and that in order to make a 'Réclame' you even said you would give 1000 Marks for a noted impresario. Why, *more* you really could not do!

"But what I don't want is that you should be sad. The world is so lovely—all in bloom—all the birds singing—everything seems like a warm, soft love song—and why do people—people one has never done harm to—spoil one's happiness?

"Thanks so much for your nice greetings. I was so sorry the other day, when you were here, not to be able to take a walk with you; but we had been away all day, just come back, when you called up—and both my mother and myself had a very bad headache. That was why I did not appear!

"Don't worry!

"Much love—again thanks—your affectionate,

"Pilar."

"*am Chiemsee, Stock, Villa Rosen-Eck,*
"18, vii, 1918.

"Daisy—My Very Dearest,

"I cannot tell you *how* much happiness your last dear letter gave me. I am only sorry you are so sad. For I care for you very much—but I think you know that without my telling you. Did you never get my letters I wrote you to Belgrad? I have the feeling that the censor stopped them on the frontier or somewhere.

"It must have been so hard for you to have to leave your boy so soon again. My brother was here, too, and was also suddenly called back. Now he is in the midst of all the goings-on in the West. When will this war stop? Or will it ever end?

"I am glad that you come again to Munich and hope to be there by then. I think of returning towards the end of August. I am staying here with my Aunt Clara[1] in a dear tiny little villa and having a splendid time. Only it is terribly hot just now.

"Why must you return to Belgrad? You have done such a lot already—only you don't make so much fuss about it as others do. I like *your* ways better—I always did. I care for you very much. I have not forgotten you and I never will. Do come again to Munich, or some place near where we can meet.

"All my love to you! Your most affectionate

"PILAR."

Princess Pilar and I did not then realize that her brother and my son, while enjoying a brief holiday, had been suddenly recalled to the Western front because the German cause was in a desperate plight.

9

Pilar's name naturally brings me to that of her cousin Duke Luitpold in Bavaria.[2] Soldier, architect, artist, friend, I have spent many happy hours in his company, more particularly in the Bavarian mountains, because he is a climber, a sportsman and an excellent shot. The first letter from him I quote is undated, and was addressed to me at Fürstenstein. It was written from the Western front where the Duke was serving as a cavalry captain in the army of his cousin the Crown Prince Rupprecht:

"MY DEAR PRINCESS DAISY,

"I got your letter from Bansin yesterday—many thanks for it. I am sorry you are not well again for the moment —hope it is better now? What you wrote me about Pless was very interesting to me. I quite agree with you that

[1] Princess Clara of Bavaria, granddaughter of King Ludwig the First and youngest sister of Prince Ludwig Ferdinand.

[2] *See* p. 22 (footnote).

it will take alas! a long time until we get to the end of these sad times. All the same I am quite happy and very well. Quite a lot to do of course, but that's just what you want here. My position is very interesting as there is much change in what we have to do—inquiring from prisoners—going to the trenches to see the position—and a lot of sitting about in the office writing and telephoning. For the rest, here with the Staff it is quite a good life we lead—food and beds nearly as good as in peace. So I don't think I shall get ill any more so long as I don't get a harder post. I am sorry you can't tell me about your rooms, and about the King of Bav.? Why not?—— Please excuse hurried writing—but I haven't much time left. Best love to Lexel and all nice thoughts to you.

"Always sincerely yours,
"LUITPOLD in BAVARIA.

"I really can't send you a photograph *for the moment* as I haven't got any here! (nor at home to say the truth)."

The next is also from the Western front. The cousin to whom he refers is Duke Ludwig Wilhelm in Bavaria,[1] present head of the Ducal Line, and eldest son of the late Duke Karl Theodor (the oculist) whose widow, the delightful Duchess Karl Theodor, was born an Infanta of Portugal; Lory is his wife who was born a Princess of Sayn-Wittgenstein:

"*August 21st,* 1916.

"MY DEAR PRINCESS DAISY,

"Just a few lines to thank you for your nice letter. I was glad to have news from you, also I felt sorry for you, reading a few things you wrote about you and other people. You can always judge your friends by hearing what they say in your face, and what they say behind your back. True friends are very rare—those I mean who would be ashamed to talk in another way about you in your absence, as they would talk to yourself. I prefer sticking to those few I really can trust, as they trust me—than always searching for

[1] *See* p. 22 (footnote).

new ones. Deceptions are the usual results, if you expect too much of men. I too am very glad about dear Lory's and my cousin's engagement. I think the wedding will take place at Kreuth the end of Sept., and I hope then to have a few days for myself in the mountains. My cousin's house (the little one you know) where they are going to live and the garden are just finished now—full of flowers and fruits and really perfectly lovely. All the peasants know and love her since she was a child, and I am sure there couldn't have been a better Duchess neither for him nor for the country.

"I am quite well—but sometimes longing to do at last again some of the work I used to do in former times and finish my house and garden, and many things that have been retarded for months, if not for years, through this sad war-time.

"Good-bye now, dear Princess Daisy, and all nice thoughts to you.

"Yrs always very sincerely,
"L. B."

Duke Luitpold is bitten with the Wittelsbach mania for building, and before the war had started to make a most imposing castle in the Byzantine manner on a lovely spur of the mountains overhanging Tegernsee. After the war came the inflation and, as a result, the house, I am sorry to say, remains unfinished to this day.

The next letter is from Duke Ludwig Wilhelm himself. I take a slightly malicious joy in quoting it because the Duke gives me a good scolding—which I richly deserved:

"*Egern am Tegernsee, Mai* 11*th*, 1915.

"DEAR PRINCESS DAISY,

"Just got your furious letter you sent to Biederstein. I am so sorry, but still I can't help smiling. I do not quite understand the letter for there must have been *one* misunderstanding: I never told you 'such an untruth.' The message I sent to the Continental by telephone was that I ***wouldn't go out*** to Tegernsee the same afternoon, but only the morning after, as I had something more to do in Munich. When I first telephoned that I would take you for a drive at 2.30 I really absolutely intended to do so and the motor and everything were already ordered for that time. But at lunch-time my friends from here telephoned in that it was no use to come out as it had been raining so much in the mountains that we couldn't play tennis in the afternoon, as we wanted to. When my companions heard this (I had them for lunch) they all rushed at me to stay for the evening and go to the theatre with them, and not to drive out to the mountains and just sit there in the rain for nothing. So I telephoned to the Continental I wouldn't go as I knew it couldn't matter very much to you, as you had your own car still here in case you wanted to go home to Partenkirchen. Somewhat rude perhaps—may be—but you have told me so often you didn't care for formal politeness! I knew you would have done exactly the same thing with me if you suddenly had wanted very much to change your plans—as I know from experience at Partenkirchen. So I can't see why you are so very cross—you have done too often the same thing with others. I know you like very much to make other people do just what you want to do—unfortunately I am very much *like you* in that point. But all the same I think we could be quite good friends as this is not the *only* point in which we meet, but have got the same feelings in other ideas too. I can only imagine one thing as a reason for your furious letter that jumped on me like a waterfall: that the people in the hotel have told you I had been forced to leave for Tegernsee at once?—and that you were highly astonished to see me arrive at Nymphenburg with a lot of people afterwards? . . . I know I am an awfully naughty boy and ought to say: 'Dear Princess Daisy, please excuse me and don't be cross any more.' But all the same I can't help grinning a little at the idea that you would have done exactly the same thing to me if you had wanted to. Yes—you would have done it, don't you think so? I am not going to finish this letter as you are nice enough to come here in two hours and I am so pleased to see you soon.

"Au revoir.

"Yr awfully naughty boy but devoted servant (sometimes at least) who kisses your hand all the same.

"*Later:* As you didn't come I am posting the letter all the same. . . . I am quite glad if other people do what they just want to do—only 'sometimes' I do the same. Now please do laugh, as I couldn't help doing.

"I am, kissing your hand once more as,

"Your Highness's obedient servant,

"L. W."

"(Excuse hurried writing.)"

CHAPTER VII

A GALLANT AUSTRIAN SOLDIER

COUNT Alfons Clary, whom we all called Alphy, the eldest son of Siegfried, Prince of Clary and Aldringen, is an Austrian noble of the highest rank, an hereditary member of the Austrian House of Lords. The family place is Schloss Teplitz in Bohemia and they have, or had, houses in Prague, Vienna and Venice; Venice, I think, because the family was, very long ago, a Florentine one. They became Barons in Bohemia three hundred years ago and Princes of the Holy Roman Empire soon after.

Alphy was a student of law, banking and diplomacy when I first knew him; when war came he proved to be a gay, hefty, charming, brave and efficient cavalry officer. We became great true friends and kept up an intimate correspondence for many years; because there was some sort of a marriage connexion between our two families he always called me "Cousin Daisy." Thank God he came through safely and, since his father's death a year or two ago, has been the head of his ancient and distinguished House.

If Prince Eitel Fritz of Prussia may be taken as a typical Prussian soldier of the best type, then Alphy was without question his gallant Austrian counterpart. I have before me a reproduction in colours of an equestrian portrait of him painted in 1915 by W. Kossack, who was, I think, a Hungarian painter. Alphy, mounted on a splendid bay charger, has his back half towards the spectator, his head with its smart red forage cap, turned half round, shows clearly the well-cut features; the blue, red-braided tunic with its black astrakhan collar, and the red breeches, show off the slim, cavalry figure to advantage. It reminds me of the old lovely, pre-war uniform of the Cherry Pickers.[1] Alphy's sister, Elisabeth Alexandrine, whom we often called Elisalex, was one of my true friends; she had married in 1904 a Belgian nobleman, Henri Comte de Baillet Latour. During the war she lived a great deal at Welbeck with the Portlands, who are devoted to her.

Knowing that each one might be the last, it was during the war that we all first started religiously preserving the letters of our soldier friends; therefore, I can only find a few of Alphy's pre-war letters. I clearly remember them reaching me at a time when I was seedy and depressed. The first came when I was taking a cure at Bad Orb in the Taunus Forest some time after Bolko's birth; the second one when I was at Cannes doing what the doctors so oddly call an "after cure." Graphic and characteristic, here they are:

"*Brussels, Aug. 19th,* 1912.

"'PRINCESS DAISY' dear, I like your signing your letters thus, because it really is a little bit similar to a fairy tale, but then you *are* a Princess in a fairy tale; sometimes one wonders if you can be real—you are certainly too good and beautiful for this beastly earth, and you have the wonderful gift of always saying and doing the right thing to make people feel that you understand them, and even your presence is sometimes like *eine moralische Liebkosung*—a moral caress.

"I can't thank you enough for having been so kind to me this summer and I wish that I could ever pay it back to you! I'm sorry to hear that you are not well; how I hope that your cure and all the quietness of Orb will do you good and that I'll find you quite well again at Lancut in October—it is such a long time till then, and I'm afraid I've no hope of seeing you before, as I remain here in Brussels till the end of August and then go to Bohemia—Schloss Teplitz. I always wonder why you call me Alfred? It's certainly a very nice name, but it happens not to be mine —which is Alfons.

[1] The nickname of the 11th (Prince Albert's Own) Hussars, given because it was the only regiment in the British Army to wear crimson overalls.

"I'm not going to talk of your not being well to people; they are so not-understanding, and then they are all so selfish. They want other people to be well because then they are more fun, and so they force it, and don't want to allow them to be ill. That's so horribly human. I'm quite alone here in Brussels, my father and mother are in England, and both sisters gone, and I am having a very quiet life, playing golf and studying.

"Did you ever hear of me doing anything else?

"This time it is preparing myself for my bank, where I'm going in November. I rather like being alone; it makes one think of better things than pleasure and worldliness, and makes me read serious books; but if nobody comes to shake me up a bit I'll grow into quite an old man, and you'll not know me again when we meet. I'd hate that.

"I can't tell you how I am looking forward to seeing you this autumn, and then again in the winter in Berlin. If only I could, how I would like to come to Orb now and see you, and try to amuse you a little, but I can't go away from here. Elisalex is going to Friedrichshof to the Hesses; I wish I was with her as it is quiet near Frankfort I think.

"The weather here is like the worst in Scotland, quite too wretched and *so* cold.

"Thank you once more so much for your nice letter which gave me the greatest pleasure; I *do* like hearing from you, and I hope your next news will be much better. I kiss your hands—in thought—dearest Princess Daisy.

"Your very devoted
"A. CLARY."

"*Brussels, August 31st,* 1912.

"MY DEAR PRINCESS DAISY,

"I was really quite miserable when I read your letter because when I thought of your cure at Orb I was sure you would come back well from there and that you would have an autumn to yourself without any doctors. And to hear how that brute of a doctor nearly did you the most awful harm. I am glad that the other man gave him a *mauvais quart d'heure*. But I'm glad to hear that you really have nothing wrong with your heart (how could you with a heart so nice and beautiful and full of kind thoughts for all your neighbours—as the Commandment has it!) Of course you must be careful this autumn and not tire yourself out like last year and not go to Lancut—how I hate the idea of not meeting you there. All the beautiful plans are falling down hopelessly, but I'm so happy because you say that I may come to Fürstenstein all the same. That at least is a nice thing to look forward to. But I *wish* I could come to Cannes now—but first of all it is horribly far from here and then I'm leaving in quite a few days for Teplitz in Bohemia and then for Vienna and perhaps Hungary, and on Oct. 1st I'm going to Lancut on the way to my Radziwill relations at Antoniny. If you so kindly sometimes send me news they will always find me if sent to Teplitz-Schoenau, Bohemia, and will delight me. I can only think with the greatest *envie* of Cannes now, of all the sun and nice flowers; it *is* so horrid here, cold and rain, and I feel glad to be leaving soon. I'm working to try to understand a little bit of banking before I get to Hamburg and the only fun I get is golf and now and then some beautiful rides in the Forêt de Soignes, which is near here and quite charming; beautiful old trees and bits of scenery.

"You wrote about something lovely to show me—oh, *do* write and tell me what it is, alas! I shall not be able to see it. Your letter was so nice and I liked it best because there was so much of yourself in it! I'm well and happy (that is, relatively), because I'm afraid you are right in what you say, that I feel things too much to be really happy—I mind small things so intensely—'the small sounds of life.' That is a charming and excellent expression, to quote you. But is it possible ever to be quite true to oneself? I somehow feel that it would be too dangerous! I would not dare because it would mean dragging down every curtain. The one thing I really mind terribly is when friends get to be untrue. The finding them out and the horrid feeling of having given so much of our life and thought and heart to some person who did not really care—it is such waste—but one always does it again because it's so nice, and then one always hopes that it will be different next time.

"It's very good to be alone sometimes; it gives one time to think over so many things. You have such a wonderful way of understanding people and of always saying or writing the right thing—which they just want.

"Elisalex is staying in the country near Antwerp at her place Château Donck but leaving for Vienna on the 8th of September, when we all meet for the Congress.[1] Her address there is Herrengasse 9, Palais Clary.

"I hope my letter will find you quite happy in Cannes, enjoying the sun and the bathing and feeling well again. I am really looking forward to see you in October! I kiss your hands, dear Princess Daisy.

"Ever your very devoted

"ALPHY."

"*Karmelitergasse, Prag.*

"*June 3rd,* 1914.

"I wanted to write to you yesterday, beloved friend, but I could not sit down and tell you how utterly upset and sad I was to have left you; those two days with you passed like a dream and I only realized, when in the train, that I had really left and that *the* days I had been looking forward to since months, the days of happiness I had been dreaming of, had really passed, and that it was again months I would have to wait till I could see you again. I was so happy every minute at Pless, so happy that it hurts to think back, because it's terrible to miss one's happiness again.

"I wonder why you have such a marvellous gift to make people forget everything around them, and to make them feel that nothing else on earth is of any value but you alone? I am dreaming back to Pless, and I feel that I want to be there again; I feel most of all that I want *you* again to live happily.

"But months must pass—they will, thank God, pass quickly if I work hard—and then in September I may come again, and we shall once more be quite happy and play like two children again; we will punt and run about laughing and, beloved friend, the happiest moments will be when neither people, preoccupations or duties come between us.

[1] The twenty-third International Eucharistic Congress, Vienna, 11th to 20th September, 1912; the great procession took place Sunday, September 15th.

"Think of me sometimes, but think of me as a *very* lonely person, quite alone, and struggling against all the dark shadows.

"I had a *horrible* journey. I missed my train at Seidenberg at 7 a.m. and had to sit there two hours, only getting here at 1 p.m., after fourteen hours' beastly journey instead of nine. But in my day's sadness that fitted in quite well.

"I have tears in my eyes as I write this, my very dear friend, and I thank you from the bottom of my heart for your kindness and the blessed happiness you have given me. May all earth's loveliness caress you.

"A."

Alphy's next letter, though also written in June, 1914, is really a war one. The great oncoming blackness soaks through it and, even now in long retrospect, makes the heart sink. It also shows how terribly bitter were the feelings aroused in Austria-Hungary against Servia. That bitterness still, alas! remains. His strong personal feeling is to some extent accounted for by the fact that Alphy's great-grandmother was Countess Aloise von Chotek, and he was therefore a relation of the Duchess of Hohenberg, the morganatic wife of the Archduke Franz Ferdinand.

"*Karmelitergasse, Prag,*
"*June 29th,* 1914.

"Oh Daisy,—I am writing to you with my most aching heart and tears in my eyes, tears of sorrow, or terrible rage and fury.

"Oh, the misery of it, he our future, our leader, who was to be the strong man, he to whom we all looked to in the future as our saviour out of all the long past years of ineptitude: he is not there any more. They have slaughtered him and her too, his wife, whose life was only love, who followed him whenever danger was near, and she died trying to protect him with her body. They lived a life, a noble life of love, and to think of those three little children waiting, waiting for their parents to come home again, they who had every happiness of family life; now they are *quite* alone, no one to take care of them, no one to love and protect them against the hardness of life, that they must feel so soon.

"How can one bear such felony, and must not every civilized creature on earth stand up and pray for damnation and God's fire of vengeance on that vile murderous country —Servia. They slaughtered their King and Queen already —but to send their men into *our* country and kill our leader— oh, they knew where to set their deadly weapon, they knew the point where they would hurt Austria most.

"Franz Ferdinand and Sophie died like heroes—after the first bomb was thrown they went smiling on, and they *knew* that there was danger and murder everywhere round —but they braved it out, and pluckily showed themselves to their people without any guard, without any safety. They could not think *that King Peter of Servia had bought men to murder them*. Oh, and I want to cry that out in civilized England, that there was a conspiracy leading to *Belgrad,* because we cannot possibly entertain the idea that any Austrian could act so vilely.

"We are all in such utter misery—and oh, think of our beloved old Emperor who—eighty-seven years of age— after having lost his wife, his only son and his brother the Emperor Maximilian in such a terrible way, now also has to lose his Heir in a similar tragic fashion. We all see red here, and what we *long* for is to kill every damned Servian alive—if you see Prince Paul of Servia, spit in his face from me, please.

"I can't say any more.

"A."

The next letter does much, in my opinion, to explain the Austrian attitude towards the events of July and August, 1914; moreover, it really does a great deal to excuse Austria and to make plain why the Austro-Hungarian Government could hardly, in the circumstances, have succeeded in averting war:

"*Karmelitergasse, Prag.*

"*July 23rd,* 1914.

"Thank you ever so much for your note and wire, beloved friend; it is not easy to write a letter with any sense just at present, because we are all spending horrid days waiting, and nobody knows what for. I hope it will be *war,* because we cannot go on living with an abscess on our side, stinging and poisoning us day by day; it is better to cut it open right away and see if we can get over the operation.

"To talk of the future seems rash just now, when the peace of our country, perhaps of Europe, is hanging on the edge of a hair. We must either crush Servia utterly, or we must get sufficient guarantees that the great movement of 'Greater Servia' is to be extinguished for good; any third possibility means a complete fiasco of our politics, shows an impossible weakness—the beginning of the end of Austria. We still have an Army we can boast of; we have a lot of strong men who love their country and who will die for it. We have lost our great leader who was a man of peace. The next man will have to be a man of *war,* if he wants to escape being slaughtered. Will you believe that Servians have tried to kill the new Heir to the Throne already! Will you believe that an attempt was made at the life of a great general of the *Etat Major?* Can life be possible under such circumstances, and must not Servia be punished? Please read *The Daily Graphic.* There are always very excellent leading articles about Austria. Let Russia come on. They *knew* of the planned *attentat* of Sarajevo, and their Minister in Belgrad, Hartwig, came to tell our Minister there that he regretted all that had happened and, uttering the words, he dropped down dead. There is a story like that in the Bible—Ananias. God punishes lies—if they are too wicked.

If nothing happens, if we are destined to finish our life in dishonest peace, eating and sleeping like degenerate brutes, if love of money is stronger than love of our country—well, as I say, if nothing happens, then I shall be here till mid-August, then soldiering at Cracow, and hope to see you at Pless.

"In all this trouble it will be sweet to see you again, darling friend.

"Think of Austria, please, with every sympathy and do not let anyone misrepresent us.

"Good-bye—I could not come to England anyway just now, would not leave my country before all trouble is over.

"Bless you, beloved!

"Alphy."

The next letter is, alas! the first of thousands I received between August, 1914, and November the eleventh, 1918. Thank God I did not foresee this or I should immediately have gone mad! We sometimes speak of the darkness of the future; but how often it is a merciful darkness, hiding from us terrors and duties and responsibilities we dare not face could they be foreseen:

"*Aug. 11th,* 1914.

"DAISY—dearest friend, just a hurried little line to say good-bye before leaving for camp—and to say that if I never return I want to thank you for your friendship, Cousin Daisy—I want to tell you that I loved the many hours spent with you; they are like a ray of sunshine that comes with me to the end. God bless you for your dear self and your sweetness, and help you to carry every burden in life easily. If ever you have time, write to me '1 *Korpskommando Feldpost No.* 112' *Ordonnanzofficier Leutnant Graf* Clary; it will be nice to hear from you. If I come back—in spring—it will be as a victor—because we *will* win this war. I love to fight for my country; but I would *love* to sit and punt with you, dear.

"God bless you, beloved friend, and make you happy.

"Au revoir.

"A."

Alphy's remaining letters I give just as they came. They tell their own story and need no comments of mine:

"*Dec. 31st,* 1914.

"BELOVED FRIEND,

"Before this grey old year is finished I want to tell you how my last thoughts in 1914 are for you, as my first will be for you to-morrow. You know so well how wonderfully happy I was during the, alas! very few days I was allowed to spend with you, and how I thank you from the bottom of my heart for your friendship.

"I wish that 1915 may bring you every possible blessing, every wish of yours, and most of all peace and happiness.

How very wonderful if we really could meet again in summer and punt together down the little river near Pless. It all seems so far off, like wonderful stories and fairy tales. If I look at life's big picture book and skip 1914, even amidst all the terrible misery and sorrow, I feel that the days with you are like rays of sunshine, giving one hope and strength to carry on. I wrote to you some time ago and gave the letter to a man who ran down to Vienna, quite a long fat letter; I wonder if you got it. It was to thank you for the nice pictures of yourself with your wounded friends. I love the little pictures and I envy the soldiers. It is so terrible to think of all our dear friends here and in England, who are dead already.

"This is just a little line with a funny little picture of myself in winter uniform!

"God bless you, cousin Daisy. There is no other friend like you on earth.

"ALPHY."

"*March 26th,* 1915.

"DAISY,

"I want to thank you a million times for your letter. Oh, the wonderful pleasure it gave me. I have only five spare minutes, so this is no answer; it's but a few words of fondest thanks—a nearly empty envelope—which my thought full of love and infinite friendship will fill. I loved the little photo and the locket; it's so sweet of you to think of me, but you need not send a forget-me-not—because my thoughts seldom leave you!

"I was only two days at Cracow, and I'm afraid I shall not get away again for a very long time, but if I do, I shall let you know, and try to run down to Pless to see you.

"God bless you, Cousin Daisy dear,

"A.

"I never got the little parcel you spoke of—alas!"

"*June 7th,* 1915.

"I am writing to you quickly to tell you that I have just got your letter of June 1st. Oh, Cousin Daisy darling, it made me *so* sad to hear that you are not well; how I hope and pray that it may all soon be better, and life easier for you. I wrote to you some time ago to answer a letter you wrote in April; I can't understand that you never got it.

"I never got the things you sent, which is not astonishing considering that I've been shooting about all over the country lately, changing my *Feldpost* numbers several times. Now it's the same old one again. I've been very busy for the last month. We did some tremendous work to get the enemy out of Galicia; now it's quieter again and I've got spare moments to think it all over, and I feel very upset about Italy.

"No words can describe the felony of the Government there, and I sincerely pity the poor people; they are being driven into war by some ruthless men without morals of any kind, who have sold themselves to the *Entente* for gold. But they will be fearfully punished, I am certain, and I think the moment is very near when we shall have peace here in the East. It's horrible to think of war in Italy. Everyone who has seen a real modern battle must shudder when he thinks of all that can happen in Milan or Ferrara, even in Venice perhaps. What idiots these people are to let themselves be driven into such misery by quite a few men. Sonnino, Tittoni, Salandra, d'Annunzio, and a little group of Generals have decided Italy's fate.

"People in England will of course be very glad that they have succeeded in buying Italy, but King George must surely feel a bit disgusted when he'll be obliged to kiss Vittorio Emmanuele. I have very scarce news from England, no letters from Elisalex since weeks, and none from other people. It's nearly impossible to write to them because too many things have happened, such odd queer things, that cannot be left unspoken between friends.

"How terribly you must feel all that, dearest friend, the more so as I am sure there is nobody to make it easier for you, no one to help you, and only beastly unkind rudeness from every side. I would simply love to see you again, if only for a day, and tell you once more that nothing on earth could alter our friendship and that the happiest moments for me will always be those near you *et à vos services*.

"It is just a year ago that I was at Pless and that we motored over to Fürstenstein, just a year ago that we punted merrily along the little river like children and talked about life, and love afterwards, like old Greek philosophers; I can never get my thoughts away from those two days. They were so very wonderful and I was never so happy as then, each moment has remained quite vividly painted in my memory. But such days will all come again I am certain; next spring we shall all be happy once more; we will draw a veil over all the misery of two years and pretend that it is all the same, that nothing has happened between the then and the now. And perhaps you'll manage to forget some of the beastly injustices. You know I can never imagine how it is possible for anyone to be otherwise than kind to you, because to me you are the incarnation of Beauty, of Charm and of Love. You are like sunshine and when I think of you I feel like an *auréole* around you all that is marvellous. But even if it makes me very sad to hear them, I like to know of your sorrows, I like you to tell me everything, because I love the thought that you trust me like a real and absolutely safe friend.

"I never got that book, *Kisses and Other Nonsense,* which is very sad, because it would have been quite nice to re-read the very words we together then read.

"There are such lots of things I am wanting to say, things that are not easily said in open letters apropos of your wire from Elisalex and such things. But, of course, you know that I understand you perfectly. Alas! I can get no leave—perhaps next winter, if war really does last as long as that.

"Will you remember *tous les mots tendres et doux que je t'ai dit* and will you re-say them again to yourself and try to think that I am beside you saying them to you—via Potsdam. God bless you, dearest of friends, quite specially.

"*À toi pour la vie,*

"ALPHY.

"Ifo Potocki kisses your hand!"

"*Aug. 30th,* 1915.

"My Dearest Friend,

"I got both your letters at Teplitz—the one Osy[1] brought from Berlin I showed to Lilli[2]—and she was very much touched by the kind words you say about herself. You know I told her again and again how very wonderful you are, and how I have always considered you my very best friend, and always shall go on doing so, and I hope to see you *very* often after the war. I'm sure we have quite charming times to look forward to at Pless and Fürstenstein, or wherever you'll live the life that is worthy of you—that is a sunny life, quite free and untouched by anything that is not beautiful: we shall always remain the very best of friends—that I feel, and I shall always look forward with joy to any meeting with you.

"I truly think that a real unselfish friendship is the greatest gift of God and it's something very, very beautiful and pure. But then everything connected with you cannot but be beautiful and pure—I know your soul I think, and I love it so very much, because knowing you has given me back everything that is good in life. Think and believe: nothing can ever undo the link between our two souls. And I can never forget the charming time—you are so right to say that even now I have it sometimes.

"My thoughts drift back so often to the exquisite days at Potsdam and, quite specially to Pless, when we lived like two children, so wonderfully gay and happy. You have the gift of making people happy—and if you are quite sad, if life is quite hard to you, then you need only remember that fact to help you on—that all your life was one long chain of unselfish deeds to help others, to make other people happy. Such women were made Saints in the far-off Middle Ages, and their pictures and statues were put in churches. I have put a statue of you in the chapel of my heart long, long ago, and it will always remain there. No, I will not bury your little picture; the little locket with the Daisy inside

[1] Princess of Löwenstein-Wertheim-Rosenberg, b. Countess Josephine Kinsky, aunt of the writer.

[2] Countess Ludwine von Eltz von Stromberg, whom the writer married Jan. 5, 1916.

never leaves me (nor your picture either); it lives in my portfolio and every time I open it my eyes meet yours and I smile at it and say good-day to you; then my most tender thoughts drift to you full of sweet memories.

"I wonder if Osy told you everything about Lilli? She is really the greatest little darling you can imagine and I'm so sure you'll love her when you meet her; she is so clever, and we have quite the same ideas of life and everything. God really has been very kind to let me find such a treasure. Mother *adores* her already, which is a great joy to me. I only had a few days at home, and it was beastly to leave Teplitz again with no hope of coming back for ever so many months.

"I'm very busy just now; we are doing pretty hard work, but I hope getting nearer the end and definite victory.

"And now I want to thank you, my dearest and *only* real friend, for your wishes, and I want to tell you that you can always consider me as your most devoted and true friend. God bless you, Cousin Daisy darling, and may He make you happy and give you back all the good you have done to others.

"Ever yours,

"A. CLARY."

"*Aug.* 22, 1916.

"YOU DARLING FRIEND,

"I was so glad to get your letter to hear that you are well; and to see your writing alone is a pleasure and joy for me. But first of all I want to tell you how I thank God that He saved you from drowning; you say that you wondered why He wanted you to go on living. I think I can give you the answer: because we want you to live, we, your friends, who always think of you with such infinite tenderness. We want you because, in future, when we come back from this ghastly life out here, we want your sunny beauty to give us back our former happiness. I think of you so often, and my thoughts drift back so very often to those golden days of happiness, days that were so full of sun and joy, and bliss, as if life had wanted to show us once more how marvellous it could be, before making us suffer. Our friendship is too great, too deep, for anything to be able to change it, and I am longing for the day when I can see you again, when I can sit with you and tell you of all my great impressions of the war. We shall be sad, very sad at the beginning, because we'll have to talk of all our dear friends who are gone.

"I have just heard of Emmanuel's[1] death; it's too sad for words—poor, poor Archduchess Christa. I always feel that we shall all have a reward afterwards for the hardships of this life, and the summer and autumn of our life will be quite beautiful.

"I am putting a great, great mass of love and tenderness into this letter. I want you to feel it and when opening the envelope I hope you'll feel many quick and tender little kisses on your fingers.

"God bless you, dearest friend,

"Ever yours,

"ALPHY."

"*Lancut, Hungary, December 25th,* 1916.

"MY DEAREST FRIEND,

"I want to send you just a few words to wish you a very happy Xmas and New Year, and may 1917 bring you every possible happiness, everything you wish. That's what I pray for. My thoughts are with you so often, so very often, nearly always, and I'm a little bit sad not to have had any news from you for such a long time. I am staying at Wolbrom now for a short time at the Head-quarters of my Regiment, and after Jan. 20th I shall be out again in the trenches. I left my old *Korpskommando* and am going out this time really into the trenches, which delights me.

"We came over here for Xmas, which was quite delightful; only Betka and Alfi Potocki are here—how often my thoughts are with you here in Lancut, dear, and what longing I have to see you again. Perhaps 1917 will at last bring us *ein Wiedersehen*. May God bless you till then and make you happy and let your thoughts sometimes drift away to your truest and ever devoted friend. I kiss your hand very tenderly, dearest friend, and am for ever yours.

"ALPHY."

"I am sending this from Wolbrom—hoping you may get it sooner."

[1] *See* p. 62 (footnote).

"*Wolbrom, Jan. 8th,* 1917.

"Ever so many thanks, Cousin Daisy darling, for your good wishes and that nice little picture of yours—what joy to see your face again; oh, *how* I wish I could really see it once more. I sometimes have such a longing to see you again—when will it all be over? Your letter only came here yesterday, as my address had changed again. Did you get my letter from Lancut? I am staying here till the end of January and then I'm going to rejoin my Regiment in the trenches. I'm, of course, delighted. I have been longing for it for a long time.

"I pray that God may bring us all safely home and give us *ein Wiedersehen.* Know that my most loving thoughts are always with you, *bien chère amie.*

"A."

"*May 1st,* 1917.

"I'm sending you a little line, dearest friend, just to thank you ever so much for your letter from Munich of Feb. 22nd, which only reached me a few days ago, as it was sent to the old address, which I left many months ago, and so it travelled about for ever so long, but did reach me at last. I *was* so glad, as I have had no news from you for such a long time, which made me very sad. I'm so glad to hear that you are better and I hope I'll find you quite well when we meet again. How delightful it will be to see you again, to talk to you, you dearest of all friends; I wish it could be at Pless. I think so very often back to those delightful days in June, '14, the last happy days before the war—blissful, quiet hours. You are never out of my thoughts or prayers, and all these three years of war I always have your little photo in my pocket book.

"I'm with my Regiment now, out in the trenches, and I love my new life and feel very content. I'm well and very fit and ever so much happier than as an A.D.C.

"I'm sending you a snapshot, done a few months ago. I hope you'll like it. Mother is very well. I've good news from her often—and Lilli is going to have a baby in September—think of the joy. I *do* hope it will be a boy.[1] Do write

[1] It was: Count Hieronymus, b. Aug. 27, 1917.

sometimes, Cousin Daisy darling, and may God bless you and help you in every way.

"I kiss your hands very tenderly,

"Ever your devoted,

"ALPHY."

"*June 8th,* 1917.

"Cousin Daisy dear, I just want to send you a little note written on my knees in the trenches, to thank you ever so much for your dear note which gave me no end of pleasure. It was so delightful and there was a real ray of sunshine in it, when you wrote about the punting in Pless with the baby! I simply *heard* you talk when reading those words, and it was so delightful—a flashlight of the happy, glorious past. I've had a letter from Elisalex of May 7th, *such* joy; poor dear, she was ill again, but, thank God, is well and always with the Portlands, who are perfect angels to her, such staunch, loyal friends.

"I wonder if you realize what a glorious man our beloved young Emperor Karl is? You would if you had heard his words when he spoke about 'peace without hatred.' He does everything he can to do away with that ghastly hatred between the countries.

"Bless you, dearest of friends,

"Ever yours,

"A. CLARY."

CHAPTER VIII

THE FOUR LAST WESTERN EMPERORS

I

WHEN my husband started altering Fürstenstein in 1912, rebuilding large portions of it, and enlarging a house already enormous, I was decidedly against the plan, having a strong intuition that it was somehow unlucky. The older parts of the Schloss date back to the end of the thirteenth century and, as it already contained I don't know how many rooms, no one could understand why Hans Heinrich wanted such extensive alterations. The story goes that on someone in Berlin asking someone from Silesia why Hans was rebuilding the Schloss, he was told:

"Well, you see, it's like this. Many of the public rooms in the mediæval part of Fürstenstein have low, narrow stone doorways through which three persons cannot pass side by side. If the three Emperors happened to be staying there together, it would be very inconvenient and raise all sorts of awkward questions of precedence. Pless thought that the simplest way out of the difficulty was to have the Schloss rebuilt."

And he did! The decision, whatever the grounds on which it was made, was characteristic of Hans Heinrich; he always does things in a big way! The castle, enlarged and magnificent, is there. But no one can afford to live in it. He himself has a suite of rooms in one of the lovely old ranges of stabling with their stone dormers which line each side of the avenue that leads up to the great library—which, by the way, is a large handsome building completely detached from the house, and containing a famous collection of books—numbering "umpteen" thousand.

Yes; Fürstenstein is there. But where are the three Emperors?

The doorways need not have been so very wide, and certainly need not have been high, to allow Franz Joseph, Wilhelm the Second, and Nicholas the Second to enter or leave a room abreast. Nor was my fourth Western Emperor, the unlucky Karl of Austria-Hungary, either tall or broad. Although Nicholas the First and his Prussian Consort stayed at Fürstenstein, Nicholas the Second was never at either Fürstenstein or Pless. He and the Tsarina were at Breslau in 1896 as the guests of the German Emperor and Empress, for the unveiling of a statue to the Emperor Wilhelm the First, but that was the nearest the Tsar ever got to Hans Heinrich's widened doorways. Moreover, it was the only occasion on which I saw "Willy and Nicky" together; and I only once saw Franz Joseph and Willy together, and that was when I was in Vienna in 1906.

I really should have enjoyed seeing the three Emperors under the same roof had Hans Heinrich ever succeeded in getting them there. I'll swear that the nearest they would ever have got to each other would have been when they passed side by side through a doorway at a formal moment. The temperamental, personal, dynastic and political differences between them were unbridgable. Franz Joseph, cool, reserved, thinking and feeling entirely in terms of the eighteenth century; Wilhelm, effusive, voluble, always striving for effect; Nicholas, saying nothing, doing nothing, feeling everything.

All three rulers were unlucky, and Nicholas, with whom I will begin, the unluckiest of all. Unfortunately, mere goodness is not a sufficient qualification for kingship; otherwise Nicholas the Second would have been one of the most, instead of one of the least, successful of modern rulers. In every sense of the word he was, as a man, far finer than either Franz Joseph or Wilhelm. His Peace Rescript alone proves this. It was he, not President Wilson or the victorious Allies of 1918, who really started the League of Nations, although it is now fashionable to ignore it. In fact, a better or more high-minded man I never met. He was gentle, considerate, charming, well informed, conscientious, hard-working, a perfect husband and father, utterly and unselfishly devoted to the interests of Russia, and to the Russian peoples, whom he deeply loved. But he was incapable of ruthlessness and without ruthlessness the Russians cannot be governed. Fundamentally an Eastern people, made up of many divergent racial strains, primitive, passionate, childlike, unstable—apparently they only understand the knout, and think and act only in terms of violence. This is a truth the sentimentalists of Western Europe refuse to swallow. We, especially in England, have become so chicken-hearted that we have forgotten that pain, hardship, and struggle are inherent in the universe, that they are the source of all progress and achievement, and that, when all is said and done, life and death are but little things. Russia, being the most western of Asiatic peoples, and not, as is commonly taken for granted, the most eastern of European peoples, understands perfectly and accepts the idea of Fate. A passionate, emotional people, the Russians were no more shocked by the brutal assassination of the Imperial Family than they are by the proven horrors of the Bolshevik régime: Both, as they see it, were necessary; therefore both were unquestioningly accepted.

One of the many curious, indeed inexplicable, elements in the character of the Romanovs is that, although in reality a German family—completely taking colour from their surroundings—they became more fatalistic and acquiescing than the rudest Russian of the steppes. How often in the twenty years before the war have I prayed those of the Russian Grand Dukes who gave me their friendship, to shoulder their proper burden and bear themselves against the coming revolution like men. Some of them could not, others would not, do so.

I do not, of course, claim that I personally knew the Tsar well; but I met him several times, was intimate with several members of his family, as well as with many personages who were in close touch with him; I got many vivid side-lights on his character and personality from such men as my dear friend, the late Gottfried Hohenlohe-Schillingsfürst—who for several years served in the Austrian Embassy in St. Petersburg. Soon after he took up his new post he wrote me as follows:

"*St. Petersburg, July 19th,* 1905.

"I think you are already back in Fürstenstein and so I will send you these lines—to tell you that I am still alive for the present. What it *will* be in times to come—heaven knows. I live in Tsarskoe Selo, where the Grand Duke Vladimir, who is really awfully kind to me, has given me some rooms to stay for the summer, so that I visit the Embassy only once or twice a week when I have to come up to town on business. It is very pleasant and nice to spend the summer in good fresh air, and to have the splendid Imperial parks to ride in on horseback or on a bicycle.

"I should like so much to see you and to tell you all about what has happened here since I last did so. I see it all from a front row stall, as I live with all those people who are most closely affected by the dreadful events. But as I am sure this letter *will* be opened, I must content myself by saying that the outlook is, if possible, still gloomier than I thought it was when we talked about it a month ago. . . . It is just possible that I could get away for a week or so (without special leave) and manage to spend a day or two at Fürstenstein. One wants some fresh air if one has to live in such an atmosphere as this—where one never knows what the following day will bring.

"Carl Fürstenberg[1] has just been appointed to here, which pleases me greatly as I like him and his wife *very* much; he is such a good fellow, far more so than his noisy and rather stupid brother Max.[2]

[1] Prince Karl Emil, b. 1867 at Prague, m. 1902 Countess Maria Festetics von Tolna.

[2] Prince Maximilian Fürstenberg, b. 1863, m. 1889 Countess Irma von Schönborn-Buchheim. He was one of the favourites of the Emperor Wilhelm the Second and entertained sumptuously at his castle of Donaueschingen in Baden. His wife was a sister of Prince Gottfried's brother's wife.

"And now good-bye, *dear* old friend; I hope you sometimes think of me, even if it is not in the same way (!) as I think very often of you.

"Many very nice thoughts from your old

"GOTTFRIED."

Gottfried had arrived in Russia a few months after "Red Sunday,"[1] as it came to be called, because some hundreds of people were shot in the streets. How trivial the event compared with the scores of thousands that have been massacred since—with hardly a protest from the outside world! In February the Grand Duke Serge,[2] whose lovely wife—the elder sister of the Tsarina—I knew well, had been assassinated and, in May, Admiral Togo had not only defeated the Russian Fleet, but had captured Admiral Rozhdestventsky. I will say no more about the Russo-Japanese War now because I mean to return to the subject. Here is Gottfried's next letter:

"*St. Ptsbg, November 9th,* 1905.

"My dear, old friend [in fact I am old (of course without the dear) as it is my 38th birthday to-day]—well, my dear, I was very, very glad to hear from you, as I really began to think you had quite forgotten that I still exist! How long I shall be upon this earth—*that* is another question, as things here don't make one very confident and cheerful!

"It is really the most extraordinary time I have ever been through. It is not amusing; no, but interesting, and though I prefer a quiet time when I can follow my own interests, still it is rather curious to have seen what is happening here. I really *have* seen very extraordinary things in all directions. We are much too old friends for me to inflict upon you silly love phrases, but I must say 'honestly and truly' that I *long* for the moment when I can tell you everything that I have gone through here: all the great

[1] Jan. 9 to 22, 1905, when many thousands of working men, led by Father Gapon, marched with Ikons to the Winter Palace to "speak to their Tsar."

[2] 1857–1905, uncle of Nicholas II, he had married Elisabeth of Hesse (1864–1918).

events that have changed, and will change still more the face of the world; and then all the personal things which I am sure will amuse you!

"The other day I found in an old diary of mine some short notes, amongst them an account of the soirée at the Meiningens' and the amateur theatricals at Breslau. Do you remember? It is some years ago and what on earth has not changed since? I felt quite funny when I read it, and at the same time happy that we have remained such good friends—at least I have. . . .

"Please write me all your plans; if by chance there is not another Strike for some time, I should like *so much* to get away for a few days to see you somewhere. . . .

"I must hurry up as we have now a Postal Strike, so I must send this letter by the Embassy courier. . . .

"May Fürstenberg has arrived to-day. I received her at the Embassy and went with them to their rooms, but as they began at once to kiss each other in *such* a way, I immediately effaced myself and as Charles has not appeared since—well, I always understood that union is strength, and I think they acted according to that principle. *Du reste c'est bien égal si c'est jour ou nuit* for that sort of performance.

"Always yrs.,
"G. H."

Gottfried's next letter now reads strangely ironic when we remember that in October the Tsar had signed a Constitution that was known as the "Russian Magna Carta." How clearly that bears out the saying that it is men, not measures, that matter.

"*December,* 1905.

"Well, I am awfully sorry that I have to stay on here, and dare not leave even for a few days as only the devil knows if one could get back in time; the trains run for two days, and then often not for a week. . . . I have not the faintest doubt but that it will come to the *very* worst if the Government continues to look on, and to try to *calm* and *quiet down* the revolution. It is very sad; but there is nothing else to do except to try to squash it with those troops that are still loyal. If one cannot do that, well, then it is the end of everything . . . as things are getting worse and worse every day and, at last, everybody *has* to become a *revolutionnaire* when he sees that, under the present soi-disant 'Government,' he and his family and all the land he owns is handed over to the mob.

"I was received by the Emperor yesterday and talked with him about all this. I cannot write it all now as I must hurry up with my letter, but I will tell you everything when we meet again. . . ."

On January 3rd over one thousand people were shot in Moscow alone and on the 30th Gottfried wrote from St. Petersburg. The letter throws a flood of light on the Russian mentality. Perhaps it even serves to explain, if not to excuse, the Bolshevik policy of regular purges and chronic persecutions. It's a terrible thought; but, possibly, as I have already suggested, *that* is the only method by which the Russians can be got to work continuously and constructively:

"Dear Old Friend,

"I am so sorry that I still cannot leave, but I have to stay on, and cannot make out yet when at last I shall be able to do so. At any rate I shall do my best to come and see you at Fürstenstein before you leave for the Riviera in the middle of March. . . . Here there is not very much new.

"At *last* the Government have decided to show the 'mailed fist,' and order and calm were re-established without great difficulty. That would be all right, but it does not mean everything, as there will be a lot to do *after* order and calm are reigning again. And I must say I don't believe that people here will be able to reorganize everything that requires it.

"They are so lazy that so soon as they have made *one* effort, as now, they will want a rest; and that will be just long enough to give time for all the *révolutionnaires* to recover and begin again. So I repeat—I don't see the end of it all and I am afraid that the worst has still to come!

"It is not over-amusing here, but still we have some fun, especially in going out snow-shoeing. We have a Club in Finland, half an hour by rail from here, and we go there twice or three times a week. There are several ladies, too, and you have no idea how funny it is to see all the falls! How I wish you could be here, you would enjoy it immensely.

"In the evenings we play Bridge: Do you remember how cross you were with me once, when we played a three with John Henry[1] in Fürstenstein?

"I send you, dear friend, a charming pig, which I hope will bring you very, very good luck for 1906.

"Good-bye and don't quite forget me, *dear* old friend.

"Always yrs.,

"G. HOHENLOHE."

In May, 1906, Count Witte,[2] the Russian Finance Minister, resigned; in July the Tsar dissolved the Duma, convoking a new one for March, 1907; in August, Stolypin's [3] life was attempted, and a Strike broke out in St. Petersburg; on September 15th Gottfried wrote:

"*Tsarskoe Selo, Sept.* 15*th,* 1906.

"DEAR OLD FRIEND,

"Many thanks for your telegram which I have just got; as I never received your letter I thought that mine had perhaps been lost.

"It is so beastly dull here that I hope I can manage to come soon for a few days to Fürstenstein just to see *you* and have a change. At any rate I come at the end of October.

"The Grand Duke Boris, in the end, did not go to the Manœuvres and he was very sorry because he had been looking forward to visiting Fürstenstein. If you would make him awfully happy send him a telegram and ask him to shoot at Fürstenstein in October. He simply longs for

[1] i.e. Hans Heinrich (the Prince of Pless).

[2] Witte, Sergius Count de (1840–1915), Minister of Finance 1893–1903; negotiated the Russo-Japanese Peace; Premier, Oct., 1905, to May, 1906.

[3] Stolypin, Peter (1863–1911), Premier 1906, till his assassination, Sept., 1911.

it; the Grand Duchess Vladimir was much touched that you asked the Grand Duchess Ellen[1] to Fürstenstein for a shoot, at least Ellen writes so from Athens. Boris is such a nice boy that he really wouldn't be a bore.

"How are you, dear old friend; I am still alive, but one really does not know from one day to the next if one won't be blown up!

"I hope I shall still get your letter, as I really want to hear from you sometimes. The little Christa Salm wrote me the other day; she enjoyed Cowes awfully and said: '*Bei weitem die schönste Frau, von allen die da waren, war Daisy Pless*.[2] I was quite glad to hear it. . . . It looks terribly gloomy here; I can't write you everything, but awful events might happen before long. . ."

"Awful events might happen before long." Upon reading that, I got little Dollie to look at Haydn's *Dictionary of Dates* to see what did happen. Pages and pages were filled with long lists of "frightfulnesses," so awful that I could not read them, though I find it fascinating (and I hope my readers will also) that Gottfried was then looking at those events from one end of a telescope, and we are now doing so from the other.

That was twelve or thirteen years before the actual downfall of Russia in the autumn of 1917. And it is clear that, even then, the very foundations of the Empire were undermined.

In so far as the Tsar and Tsarina were concerned, I have always felt that the inner cause of their failure to have the slightest effect on what was happening in their country was that they were both born mystics. That was why they magnetized each other from the first moment they met, and it was the basis of a lifelong love between them which was unbreakable and imperishable simply because it was at once sensuous and spiritual. The terrible power of this union was such that inevitably it caused them to withdraw themselves,

[1] The Grand Duchess m. in 1902 Prince Nicholas of Greece; their youngest daughter, Princess Marina, became Duchess of Kent in Nov., 1934.

[2] By far the most beautiful woman present was Daisy Pless.

first of all, step by step from the other members of the Imperial family, from the aristocracy, and, finally, from the official and governing classes.

This would not perhaps have mattered so much had the Tsar possessed a strong will and a capacity for leadership. The masses of the Russian people could quite easily have comprehended—and would have gladly followed—a mystical Emperor enthroned and enshrined, provided only that he came down from heaven often enough to give them a lead. Their nature needed, and their history taught them to expect, such leadership. Was their Sovereign not at one and the same time the Tsar of all the Russias, the Great White Tsar, and the Little Father? Was he not indeed to his peoples almost as much as God himself could be? The monarchical ideal is, of course, basically mystical; but the Romanovs instead of wisely utilizing their excessively mystical inheritance, allowed it to become an obsession.

Nicholas the Second occupied a terrible, perhaps impossible, position, and any chance he ever had of filling it successfully was finally lost the day his eyes first met the lovely deep blue, sombre eyes of Queen Victoria's granddaughter, Alix of Hesse. Nicholas won the love of this strange girl, who always looked as if fated—as if born—for a tragic destiny. They achieved the seemingly impossible task of making a home, a real home, within a Russian Imperial palace. They fought for each other and for their children against all that came and kept each other to the terrible, foreordained end . . . but the price they had to pay was the utter destruction of Holy Russia.

The lesson it would seem is this: Mystics are dangerous people, and should be confined to cloisters, because they are the human transmitters of spiritual forces and powers man is, as yet at all events, quite incapable of comprehending or using. Above all, they are a danger on a throne and, if the throne be that of a mystical people such as the Russian, they inevitably bring utter disaster to themselves and to those whom they rule.

It is not without significance that the world has always segregated or destroyed its mystics and, perhaps, for its own safety, will always have to do so. In a materialistic civilization they are a terrible danger. . . .

A glance at history proves that when the true mystic comes, he, or she, must destroy or be destroyed. I don't know anything about the ancients, though I suspect that Homer was a mystic. But Christ and Paul and Peter and John, Saint John of the Cross, Santa Teresa, Saint Francis, Saint Joan and Savonarola; Charlemagne, with his vision of a United States of Europe; Charles the Fifth, with a not dissimilar vision; Napoleon, who inherited both these dreams; Nicholas the Second, whose Peace Proposals, already mentioned, prove that he, and he alone, was the author of what we call the League of Nations; then, on a smaller stage, Cavour working through to a United Italy; Disraeli, with his dreams of a great free British Empire; Bismarck and his plans for a United Germany. These were mystics and they fell.

In our own day and generation we have had amongst us the authentic mystics, those who see visions and dream dreams, Lenin and Stalin, Pilsudski and Gandhi, Mustapha Kemel and Mussolini. Hitler.

Yes, indeed, mystics are very dangerous and unaccountable people!

2

As I have said the Romanovs were far more German than Russian; their cradle was Schleswig-Holstein: Catherine the Great, the most "typical Russian" of them all, was, of course, pure German. But this fanatical mysticism of which I speak is almost as markedly a German, as it is a Russian, characteristic. In Russia since the Revolution it has found expression in the canonization and worship of Lenin; the distorted belief in the vital necessity for agony, suffering, poverty, death. The willing sacrifice of countless lives and the almost glad acceptance of the unbearable, almost unbelievable, misery of millions on behalf of some far-off, mystical good.

In Russia, the Jews have with passionate brutality used this holy ideal for their own unholy ends. They have crucified, are crucifying, the Russian peoples as their ancestors crucified the Christ. They have destroyed the soul of Russia to give it . . . a machine. And the machine, when they have succeeded in erecting it, does not, as a rule, work!

Have the inhabitants of the City of London, Mayfair, Westminster, and Belgravia ever reflected as to what would happen to their wives, daughters and cherished possessions if for one brief forty-eight hours the protecting arm of the civil and military power were paralysed and the East End, with its alien mobs, were allowed to pour into the West End to pillage, pollute and destroy? If Great Britain were *in extremis*, as Germany was in 1918, would these elements prove stable, law-abiding, loyal? European history of the past twenty years does not go to prove that they would.

France, I honestly believe, is financially far too much in the hands of aliens, and there are indications that they are quite prepared to let revolution loose in that country when and where it suits them. They showed their power in the abortive revolution of January and February, 1934, over the Stavisky affair. The United States, too, has great need to watch its large and powerful alien population. If it does not curb and control them they will get out of hand and cause national trouble.

And why, oh, why, has my country let the minds, emotions and morals of its men, women and children be poisoned for all these years by the low, base Jewish profiteers who are, in the United States and to some extent in England, behind the kinema! For five-and-twenty years they have not only mentally poisoned the people of Great Britain, but those of the whole Empire. They have almost destroyed the immense prestige of England once enjoyed in India, the Dominions and the Colonies, and lowered it throughout China, Japan, and the whole civilized world. It is significant that one of the first things done by the Government of the Irish Free State, and by Hitler, was to control the films.

3

I have been close to the continental Jewish peril for over forty years. Fürstenstein, in Upper Silesia, is only about one hundred miles from the old Polish border, and Pless itself was in German Poland. In both places we were the centre of great coalfields, those of Pless being the richest in Eastern Europe. As long as ever I remember there was Socialist and Communistic agitation amongst the miners in both places and, almost invariably, it was propagated and organized by low-class Jews.

There has been a great outcry all over the world, and especially in England, about the recent treatment of the Jews in Germany. I pass no judgment on that because, as a great Jew said long ago, "Although all things are lawful, all things are not expedient." But had England been as close to the Jewish peril from Russia as Germany has been during the fourteen years following the 1918 revolution, would she look upon the Jewish peril with such complacency? If the British Government had had to face a similar position to that of Germany during the revolution, I think that, like the Germans, they would have said: If these people are such a danger and such an evil the only thing to do is to dig them out root and branch. Of course there would have been many injustices in such a summary process, many hard, even pitiable, cases, much to cause regret. But, as the English themselves say: "Hard cases make bad law."

Although I may seem to have travelled a long way from Russian mysticism and the downfall of the Tsars, I have, in reality, come to my next point by the one direct and pitiably tragic path.

Russian mysticism and German mysticism are akin. It is this fundamental fact that made Bolshevism such a real peril in Germany—a peril by no means as yet entirely averted. It is because the German is at heart a mystic that the British and French have such difficulty in understanding him. To the German, ideals and abstractions are real, vital, living things: his nature requires intensely and passionately an ideal to live up to and a leader to follow. The inevitable outcome of this is Nordicism—or whatever you call it—and . . . Adolf Hitler. The Emperor and each one of the German Kings and Princes let fall in the gutter their mystical Royal mantles. Hitler found them there and, symbolically speaking, picked them up and put them on. The nation accepted and followed Hitler because it needed him. It was he, and he alone, who held high the light. True, he promised them economic salvation if they would follow him but, in the same breath, he demanded from a spent and disillusioned people further, more intense and more prolonged sacrifices: Tightened belts; long marches; discipline; hard bodies and stout hearts; brotherhood; self-sacrifice; heroism; equality. These were the banners he boldly displayed, and it was these that called the young men to his side. The name Hitler stood for heroism, therefore all Germany shouted *Heil!*

Is this a trivial thing? Why carp at and belittle a task such as no single man in history has yet accomplished? That was not, in times past, the English way. When any man, even our bitterest enemy, put up a good fight, we stood still and acclaimed him.

All my life long I have asked for, and pleaded for, a good understanding between England and Germany: Again I plead for it now.

4

Of the Emperor Wilhelm the Second of Germany I have said so much in my two previous volumes that I will add little here. Like the Tsar Nicholas the Second, he was a mystic, but of an altogether different type. His mysticism was typically German and Western in that, instead of—like that of Russia—causing him to feel vividly that he was an infinitesimal, but integral, part of the great body mystical, as all true mystics should feel, it only served to set him in his own mind above, and apart from, all other men. Of course there is a sense in which, historically speaking, kings and rulers always have been uplifted and apart and, to my mind, if in modern times Sovereigns allow this ancient tradition entirely to die, they will fatally undermine one of the basic principles and appeals of monarchy. The fact that to-day this world-old, instinctive respect for the kingly office tends to take the form of prestige rather than that of veneration, does not make it any less powerful or intangible.

It is easy enough to jeer at the divine right of kings, which was a powerful tradition in Prussia, and one in which Wilhelm the Second, and most of the members of the House of Hohenzollern firmly believed. But is it in any way a more ridiculous doctrine than that of its opposite, the so-called "divine rights of man"? To take only the Hohenzollerns. They have, after all, by long service to the Prussian people in the highest and most arduous office in the State, proved that the kingly ideal can enrich and ennoble the lives of the people. Whatever might have happened otherwise, it is historically correct to say that, without the Hohenzollerns, and, in particular, without Frederick the Great, there would have been no Prussia and, therefore, no modern German Empire. For centuries the Hohenzollerns gave their chiefs and heroes to the Prussian people, represented that people before the world, acted as their spokesmen, leaders and defenders. That office is at once kingly, valiant and priestly. Like all sacred and representational offices, its mere exercise confers not only dignity and importance, but also a measure of sanctity, on all those who exercise it. Wilhelm the Second inherited all this, and was fully, and rightfully, conscious of the fact. It is merely senseless to deny this because, as the Empress Eugénie once said to me: "You cannot unwrite history."

But, to return for a moment to the complementary doctrine of the "rights of man." I have always wanted to know from whom those rights derive. Far more nebulous than that of the divine right of kings which, after all, has a source and a pedigree, these proletarian rights must, one supposes, originate somewhere, because out of nothing nothing comes. For the most part they are vociferously advocated by Communists, Socialists, Atheists, and a particularly vocal brand of the internationalized intelligentsia, none of whom admits either the existence of a Heavenly Father, or the capacity or right to inherit anything from an earthly one. Where, then, I ask again, do these "rights of man" originate? Who first won them? From whence or where? What exactly are they? How are they transmitted? To whom? How are they to be recognized, justly apportioned, enjoyed?

Talk about the mystical elements in religions—why, such elements are as concrete as the Himalayas compared to the turgid mysticism embodied in the so-called principles of this economic dogma! (But this is only one of Daisy's asides.)

Wilhelm the Second was inspired by a genuine devotion to what he believed to be the best interests of the German peoples. In many ways he was an idealist, and he was a genuine lover of, and believer in, peace. Deny it now though they may, he was a representative German; throughout his reign the only people who disapproved of him were the Socialists. Fate laid on his somewhat narrow shoulders a task for which he was not big enough, and he therefore failed. But has no other ruler or statesman in history ever made mistakes or failures? Do party politicians never fail?

I am one of those who firmly believe that in advising the Emperor to abdicate, Prince Max of Baden and Hindenburg were acting disinterestedly and patriotically, carrying out a most heart-breaking and humiliating duty. In the circumstances of the moment no other course was possible, because the Allies flatly declined to treat with the Emperor. Had the Emperor been better advised, less reluctant to quit his post, a truly representative Regency Council could have been established; the Emperor and Crown Prince could have magnanimously stood aside, the Crown Prince's eldest son Wilhelm been proclaimed Emperor and King and, with a long minority in front of the young Prince, the Allies could not have refused to treat with the Regency Council. In fact, the Council would have been in an impregnable position had it been shown—and it could have been shown—that, in addition to all the forms of legality, it represented the will of the German peoples.

Led by Prince Max of Baden as Imperial Chancellor, with Ebert, the Socialist shoemaker from Heidelberg, as its temporary figurehead, all the German Kings and Princes would have rallied round the Council of Regency and both Germany and the monarchical principle would have been saved—and, in all probability, Austria as well.

As always happens in such circumstances, delay, uncertainties, selfishness, disunity and sheer stubbornness and shortsightedness played into the hands of the extremists and, as it so often does, stupidity won. But that crass stupidity was not to be found in Germany alone. It took a much grosser, because less excusable, form amongst the Allies who, like a Communist rabble, declared that, before they began to build, they must first destroy. I am as convinced to-day as I was in November, 1918, that had the Hohenzollerns remained in their rightful places, Europe would have been saved nine-tenths of its post-war miseries. You cannot destroy elements that have been for more or less a thousand years part of the very foundations of European civilization without ensuring disaster.

That those assembled at Versailles in 1919 and 1920 were merely politicians and not statesmen is proved by one simple, indisputable fact. They were actuated by personal feelings and prejudices, not by unassailable principles and cold reason. Each one of them, Wilson in the United States, Lloyd George in England, Clemenceau in France, Venizelos in Greece, Sonnino in Italy—had their ears to the ground listening to the mob, instead of their eyes serenely and firmly fixed on the goddess of reason and the Muse of history. Such a debasing attitude is only fit for demagogues fighting for the spoils of victory; it inevitably induces spiritual and mental vertigo; it would be an impossible attitude in statesmen fighting only for right against wrong under the white banner of justice and truth. Looking down, all that the Recording Angel could see of these so-called statesmen was their behinds!

The day the Allies received in the lovely forest of Compiègne, as the true representatives of the German peoples a hastily improvised mob of nonentities, was the day they struck an irreparable blow at the stability and order of Europe. Of course they declared with all sorts of noble and heroic posturings, that they were receiving the "new Germany" and would never receive the old. Well, I wish them joy of that "new Germany." They had it, and its immediate progeny, for something like twenty years, and they don't seem to have loved the outcome as much as all that.

No; it was not the loss of the war, nor Socialism or revolution that destroyed Germany: It was the immoderation of some of the victors. Those who had lost least demanded most.

The bitterness and irony of this entered deeply, if largely subconsciously, into the hearts of the German peoples, corroded their very souls, and the soul of Europe, and that virus, alas! will not be extirpated for generations to come.

5

Surely the naked and unpalatable truth is that in Europe in 1918 there was hardly a glimmering of statesmanship. Prince Max of Baden, Lord Lansdowne, Smuts, perhaps Austen Chamberlain. Balfour could have done much at Versailles and, apparently, did nothing! Who else? But Lansdowne was too old, Balfour also, and Smuts could not be expected fully to comprehend the age-old complexities of Europe. Lloyd George was, and is, much too astute and clever a politician ever to become a statesman, even an elder—that is to say a worn-out one. An extinct volcano if you like. But I never heard of volcanoes erupting anything good. The truth is that there is no relationship between the qualities of the successful politician and the successful statesman; the former are temporal and ephemeral; the latter spiritual and permanent. If a politician displays any of the characteristic qualities of statesmanship it is, as a rule, only by accident. Men did not in the time of Christ, and do not now, gather grapes of thorns nor figs of thistles. The fact that the mob still suffers from the delusion that it can be done is at the root of the universally acknowledged failure of democracy, and the cause of the rise and progress of Communism, Socialism and Dictatorships.

Clemenceau inherited to a fanatical degree the antediluvian dogma that France is Europe. He held it more tenaciously, narrowly and illogically than any one of the hundred kings who governed France for a thousand years. As a descendant of Thomas, second Baron West, who was amongst those Englishmen that gave France a good licking at Crécy, and as one of a family that sent several of its members to fight at Waterloo, I cannot, and never will, subscribe to the doctrine of French predominance in Europe. France (like other nations) has great, very great qualities, but she has also great, indeed very great, defects. Her extreme logic leads her to adopt, and maintain, the most absurdly illogical positions, positions quite unjustifiable and untenable. Why, for example, should the safety of France be the most vitally important thing in Europe? It is important—but not more important than that of, say, Poland or Italy or Germany, or even poor old England—that hewer of wood and drawer of water (and payer of bills) for all the rest of Europe. Then France is frantically ungrateful and incurably suspicious. To hear some French people talk you would think that there were at most only one hundred British soldiers in France between 1914 and 1918, and that they spent all their spare time in the brothels of Paris while carrying on their nefarious business of secretly planning the downfall of France and its annexation by the British Empire. In lesser ways, too, the French are impossible. Their rapacity and greed have driven the Americans and English out of France. With the most charmingly insincere manners they will cheat and lie and overcharge and beg—yes, beg—until they make one's very heart sick. Their ideals are the ideals of the *petite bourgeoisie*, selfish, narrow-hearted, ungenerous, penurious. They have no leaders, and financially they are corrupt from top to bottom. Their somewhat sordid peasant virtues enable them to survive, but they have no future. Their undoubtedly glorious contribution to European civilization is of the past. Napoleon was the last Frenchman—and he was an Italian.

It is time someone plainly said that had it not been for England, France would have disappeared from the face of Europe during the Great War, and Wilhelm the Second, taking a hint from his grandfather, might have been crowned King of France at Versailles! For mind you, had Germany won, there would have been no sentimental nonsense about self-determination, the rights of the conquered, and so on. There would have been none of Louis Philippe's fatal truckling to the populace by adopting the style of "King of the French." Wilhelm the Second would have been *de facto*, if not *de jure*, King of France, and no cheap electioneering posturings about it. Moreover, instead of living discredited and forgotten in exile at Doorn, the Germans would have deified him and placed him beside, perhaps above, Frederick the Great or even Charlemagne himself!

No man will have the courage to say this plainly, therefore a woman must. Which, perhaps, leads to the old conundrum: Where does courage end and foolhardiness begin?

6

One of the major mistakes of the Emperor Wilhelm the Second was that he failed to keep in touch with his eldest son the Crown Prince, and, through him, with the younger generations. Of course it is traditional that Sovereigns and their Heirs are invariably at loggerheads; Wilhelm the Second himself was always in opposition to his father the Emperor Friedrich, and therefore could hardly complain when his chickens came home to roost. The relationship is, of course, an extraordinarily difficult and delicate one, and but few princes succeed in solving it so successfully as Edward the Seventh did during his long years as Prince of Wales. It must be almost impossible to adjust one's mind and conduct with nicety to the fact that one is the second person in the realm, and yet that personally, politically, and perhaps even socially, one is of no importance whatsoever! Then, apart from the fact that his father is also his Sovereign, how difficult it is at all times for high-spirited youth to avoid criticizing its elders. History is full of the antagonisms and enmities between kings and their eldest sons and, even now, it is doubtful if this fundamental antagonism has at all Courts been successfully resolved. Rumour has it that the Crown Prince of Italy does not always see eye to eye with his father.

I knew the German Crown Prince well from the time when he was a boy of twenty, and always recognized that, beneath his youthful pranks and high spirits, he had plenty of brains. Those who considered him a fool only labelled themselves by that name. Since the German revolution he has survived a delicate, even dangerous, series of crises with extraordinary tact and success. He has managed all those years to sit on the fence with every outward appearance of satisfaction and enjoyment, and anyone who has tried it knows how difficult a feat that is. Moreover, as the Emperor was at Doorn, it was largely owing to his adroit handling that the Hohenzollerns managed to retain most of their wealth; and now, as always, wealth is power. He has overcome a somewhat inordinate passion for pretty women; curbed a dangerous tendency—inherited from his father—to talk too much and make tactless remarks. He has even succeeded in becoming to some extent popular amongst the younger men in Bavaria, a country that has always disliked the Hohenzollerns, although it is the cradle of their House. Only once of late years, so far as I know, has the Crown Prince been guilty of an unfortunate remark. When the Nationalist Socialist Government sent a soldier from somewhere to be *Statthalter* or Governor of Bavaria, the Crown Prince is reported to have said: "Thank God! That's the end of the Wittelsbacher." It was an extremely tactless and stupid thing to say, because a child could have foreseen that it was only the prelude to the appointment of a *Statthalter* of Prussia, and that, if the

Crown Prince's *mot* was true, would, presumably, be the end of the Hohenzollerns. The ancient jealousy of Prussia for Bavaria was always idiotic, because Bavaria was, in fact, or could easily have been induced to become, not the rival and enemy of Prussia, but her prop and ally. It should always have been clear to the Hohenzollerns that the day monarchism was destroyed in Bavaria and South Germany, that day it began to perish in Prussia.

7

What would have happened had the Emperor stood firm and refused to follow the advice of von Hindenburg and Colonel Heye on November 9, 1918? What would Germany have done? What would the Allies have done? Germany, as I have already said, would have rallied round its Emperor. The Germans have always been faithful to their leaders. The resistance to the Communists, rebels and defeatists would have had a focus, a rallying point.

I know many true Germans thought the Emperor should, at all costs, have remained. My dear sister-in-law, Lulu Solms, who was for so long First Lady to the Empress, wrote me on November 7, 1918, from Klitschdorff, their Silesian home. I had just let her know that I had escaped from the revolutionary outbreaks in Belgrade and Budapest, and was safely at Partenkirchen in Bavaria. Here is her letter:

"Bravo! Daisy, well done!

"I must say myself I thought *perhaps* you wouldn't mind being made a prisoner by the *Entente*. I beg your pardon for the thought, or suspicion, and am very glad that you came back; and how right you are, for the sake of your boys—the difference it will make in their lives later on to know that their mother was true.

"About the Emperor—I hope and pray he will be firm, and won't abdicate; they *were* quite resolved to be firm, and the Empress told me to say everywhere that she stands firm. The only thing I am afraid of is that if they tell him that he hinders the peace, then, what is he to do? It is difficult. For the rest, I am persuaded that if he abdicates everything falls to pieces.

"One must pray and hope.

"The people want him to stay, only the quite bad want him to go, and I believe the majority are good and sensible. One can't conceive of anything else.

"Best love to Fritz; I will write him one of these days; Rosy[1] with her six children is here.

"Thank you for your letters; thank God you got out of the Belgrade muddle in time.

"Bless you,
"Yours,
"LOUISE."

Less than a week after Lulu wrote that the Emperor was in Holland; the poor Empress was at the Neues Palais at Potsdam with the Crown Princess, the other Princesses, and their children. The Palais was under the protection of the Workmen's and Soldiers' Council. The Empress personally received a representative of the Council, thanked him, and through him the others, and placed herself under their further protection.

On December 3 (1918), at Partenkirchen, I wrote in my Diary as follows:

"The country has dismissed its Emperor. Poor man, he had no one brave enough to advise him courageously. I wanted to write to him, but it all happened as I was escaping from revolutionary Belgrade only to meet another revolution in Munich! Oh, if the Emperor had taken off his crown and given it back to his people with the words: 'I shall only bring more trouble to you all by remaining here; I wished you always what was best, and my whole ambition was for my country. The crown became too illustrious, and brought me envy. So, with prayers for all your future, and longing for a better understanding in the world, I leave you!'

"He was my friend, and knew well what those miserable war years brought to me; but he has gone; and *Vater,* my dear *Schwieger Vater* has also gone. . . . I am alone.

[1] e.d. of my sister-in-law, she m. in 1903 Otto, 3rd Prince of Salm-Horstmar.

"Personally I have nothing left but bitter memories of Germany. I gladly take off my princely crown and retire to a dear green island, or to my hills in France. . . . My boys, naturally, will marry Germans, and their wives will not welcome an English mother-in-law."

8

I only saw the Emperor Franz Joseph a few times, but he was to me, more than anyone I ever met, embodied history. Marie Antoinette was only thirty-odd years in her unknown, heroic grave when he was born; therefore, as a child, he must have often heard her terrible story retold by those who knew it at first hand. He knew and remembered the Eaglet—Napoleon the Second—who had sat on his knee and whose dead young face he had looked upon—in death far more Habsburg than Bonaparte—as the death mask proves. It is even said that the Archduchess Sophie, mother of Franz Joseph, inspired a romantic devotion in the heart of Napoleon's only legitimate son, such as is often aroused in the imagination of a romantic boy by a mature and accomplished woman.

Franz Joseph also was a mystic and a fatalist; more, he was a *dévot* who sacrificed his whole life to the fulfilment of the exacting and endless duties of his exalted office, never forgetting for a second that he was an Apostolic and anointed King.

I often speculated as to what exactly were his relationships with the lovely Empress Elizabeth. That they were to the end close friends is proved by the fact that the Empress magnanimously received and showed friendship to Frau Schratt, the Vienna actress,who was the Emperor's *chère amie* and confidante for many years.

Very small and slight, the Emperor had great charm and dignity, his utter simplicity giving him a natural distinction that no assumption of regality could have conferrred. As I have already mentioned, I only once saw him and the German Emperor together, and the Habsburg made the Hohenzollern look pretentious and tawdry. Franz Joseph was one of the last *grands seigneurs*.

The Emperor Karl of Austria I only met a few times. When his uncle, the Archduke Franz Ferdinand, the Heir Apparent, morganatically married my friend Sophie Chotek, in 1900, Karl became for all true Royalists and legitimists, Heir Presumptive. But there was always something a little equivocal in Karl's position in Austria. It was well known that the Emperor Franz Joseph would never recognize Sophie as a possible occupant of the dual thrones of Austria and Hungary, nor agree to one of her children becoming his successor. On the other hand, Franz Ferdinand was ambitious, stubborn and very much in love with his wife. He was opposed to the policy of his uncle the Emperor and, having a considerable following of his own, could easily count on any number of lawyers who were prepared to maintain that, whatever the historic and legal position might be in Austria, he was quite free, when the moment arrived, to have Sophie crowned Queen of Hungary, and her sons accepted as in the legitimate line of succession to the Hungarian Throne. To do Sophie justice I must say that I believe she cherished no political or dynastic ambitions. Her mother being a Kinsky, she was on both sides of a very good, but not great, Austrian noble family, had been lady-in-waiting to the Archduchess Friedrich, and, in the face of tremendous obstacles, had married the man she sincerely loved, and was a most devoted wife and mother. Four of her sisters were comfortably and happily married; her family, so far as I know, contented and unambitious.

However, fate unravelled that particular dynastic knot at Sarajevo in June, 1914, at the price of setting most of the world on fire.

I never discussed politics with the Archduke Franz Ferdinand. His personal position in Austria, and the relationships between Germany and Austria were too delicate to permit of that. He was a heavy, rather plethoric man in body, a determined rather than a skilled and adaptable sportsman, and my woman's intuition told me that his mind was not unlike his body. Like most of the Habsburgs he was stubborn. I doubt if he possessed either the pliancy, the vision, the patience or the powers of leadership that were essential to any man who hoped to build a new modern Austrian Empire on the old Habsburg inheritance.

Franz Ferdinand's nephew, Karl, was a very different type of man. He inherited from his father, the Archduke Otto, personality, good looks, charm, and from his mother (born Princess Maria Josefa of Saxony) integrity, a fine sense of duty, intelligence, and a love of the simple, beautiful things of life. He was deeply in love with his wife, the handsome Zita of Bourbon-Parma, and devoted to his large, healthy, ever-increasing family. His love of Austria and Hungary and his unselfish devotion to the best interests of his peoples were unquestionable. A hater of war as an instrument of policy he longed for peace; from the moment he ascended the throne fought for it and, with it, the opportunity of rebuilding anew the Austrian Empire on a sound, modern policy of self-determination, collaboration and give-and-take. However, he was too young and inexperienced. He succeeded at an impossibly difficult hour in the history of Europe. He did not know, was not in sympathy with, the old-fashioned advisers of Franz Joseph, and, in the midst of war, he had neither time nor opportunity to seek out and gather round him new, trusted, modern-minded men, in touch with the ever-shifting policies and quicksands of the Europe of 1916.

There are those who said that Karl was too much under the influence of his wife. But that was mere gossip and, anyhow, they always say that a ruler is under the influence of some woman or another. I am as fully convinced to-day as I always was that the 1916 peace efforts of the Emperor Karl were inspired and, had they succeeded, they would not only have saved the Austrian and German Empires from destruction, but they would have saved Europe and the world from the evil fate on the brink of which we are still trembling.

One day the task the Emperor Karl heroically began in such hopeless conditions must be resumed and successfully completed by his son the Archduke Otto. When that happens the gallant young Karl will be historically justified.

CHAPTER IX

A PRUSSIAN SOLDIER PRINCE

I

OF all the six sons of the Emperor Wilhelm the Second I knew most intimately and liked best the second, Prince Eitel Friedrich. It was not, I think, that we met so often, but, especially during the war, we kept up an active correspondence. We are so constituted that to some people we can best show our true selves in personal intercourse; to others on paper.

Outside Germany (perhaps sometimes inside also) it is too often erroneously supposed that to be a Prussian, a Prussian Prince and a Prussian soldier is to be all that is narrow, arrogant and ruthless. The best answer to that false assumption is to present a true picture of one who was all three, one who, it might be supposed, would naturally exhibit all the worst characteristics. Yet what stands revealed in this self-portrait, painted without any thought of posing, any idea of publication, written simply and directly with friendliness?

What do we find?

A man strangely chivalrous to a foreign woman who fell under suspicion in his country in the early days of a long and bitter war; the son of the Sovereign, yet not afraid to take the side of the alien accused of being a traitor and a spy. A simple soldier preferring the austerities, even the rigours of camp life to the pomp and luxury of palaces. A good fighter, yet hating all the beastliness and waste of war; a loyal patriot, who could yet grieve for the despoiling of the enemy country; a man who in the midst of carnage turned for comfort, warmth, companionship and understanding to his dog and horse, to the little flowers that courageously thrust their smiling faces upwards from the shell-riven craters of the battlefield.

If I asked for his permission to show forth this man in all his fineness he would probably refuse. But for the sake of our common humanity, for the sake of Germany and Prussia, in honour of all good soldiers, and clean fighting in every country, it is right to let it be known that this Hohenzollern Prince, whose example was followed by many thousands throughout the war, was an honourable soldier and a great Prussian gentleman.

Early in December, 1913, the Prince seems to have been with us at Fürstenstein and shortly afterwards wrote me as follows from Potsdam:

"*Villa Ingenheim, Wildpark.*
"*December* 11, 1913.

"My Dear Princess of Pless:

"So many thanks for your kind letter and the very pretty picture. I find it very nice and not at all flattering. It's really like you.

"We had very bad weather in Öls—rain and snow. Now Wilhelm[1] is with you. I was so sorry that we just missed each other at Primkenau.[2] We had a few very nice days there. Now Christmas is coming and you will have to be very busy to get all you want done in time. It's rather a joke to go buying things, but we have very little spare time as the royal service takes up so much of it. Did you sing again since the other night in Fürstenstein? It was so nice and *gemütlich* in the low rooms; one had the feeling one was on board a ship. And that's just the thing I love. Where will you stay for Christmas? And have you good news of your poor little baby?

"Well, I have to say good-bye now, dear Princess, kissing your hand I remain, with best wishes for a Merry Christmas and a Happy New Year,

"Always yours,
"Eitel Fritz P.v.P."

[1] The Crown Prince Wilhelm spent Christmas, 1913, at Pless. *See* p. 62.

[2] The country house in Silesia of Ernst Günther, Duke of Schleswig-Holstein; his elder sister, Princess Auguste Victoria (1858–1921), became German Empress in 1888; a younger sister Luise Sophie m. 1889 Prince Friedrich Leopold of Prussia (1865–1931) and is the authoress of *Behind the Scenes at the Prussian Court.*

Some people found Prince Eitel Fritz brusque and overmuch the soldier. I never did because, as that letter shows, underneath his big, hearty exterior he had a keen feeling for the softer, finer things of life. It's always a little tragic, even for a man, when our appearance belies our true nature.

I particularly appreciated the Prince's friendship because, from the very outbreak of the war, it was staunch and true: when, towards the end, he was able to give me priceless comfort by looking after Hansel when the lad went to serve under him on the Western front, he did so most generously. Some of my readers will perhaps remember that in the autumn of 1914 I committed my unforgivable indiscretion by visiting the British prisoners of war in the Döberitz internment camp near Berlin, and one of the consequences of which was my subsequent banishment to Bavaria[1]—after, of course, a stout resistance on my part. I wrote and told the Prince of what had happened about Döberitz and this is what he replied. I will not correct his amusing English spelling:

"MY DEAR PRINZESS,

"Many thanks for your kind letter I gott yesterday; I was so happy to gett it and to see that you are well. I can understand your feelings quite well and can't blame you for anything you did. I find it disgraceful that . . . did not rush to you and help you in your difficult position. Of course, you made some mistakes and perhaps it would have been better had you not visited the prisoners. Especially if one is a stranger, one must be doubly careful. Nevertheless I always have believed in you and been convinced that you never did anything wrong; therefore I can write quite planely what I think about it because I write the truth and don't want to blame you in any way. What you did was perhaps *unvorsichtig,* I don't know the proper word in English, not careful enough perhaps, but never anything bad, or something that gave the people the right to treat you as they have done. But who could have wired you about it I do not know! It's such a bother if people interfere where

[1] *See Daisy Princess of Pless*, London, 1929, John Murray, pp. 293 *et seq.*

they have absolutely no right to do so. In such difficult times as these I think people ought to hold close together and help each other as we help each other in the trenches—when death is nearer than life and you pray your last prayers thinking you will never see the night. Then every *Kamerad* is a brother and we have all the one idea which is to hold fast and to win with God for king and fatherland. And so it ought to be also at home, all going one way, and not as it often is, one despising or injuring the other. That's the finest part of the whole war—that you and your men feel absolutely one. It matters not if I fall; another man will come and take my place the next minute and will fill it just as well as I, yess, shurely much better; and you and your soldiers face the same danger, the same pain, the same pleasure, and the same thankfulness to your Lord for health and victory. All our little sorrows are so poor compared to the big danger in which the fatherland stands. Of course I would love to come home and feel in a good sort of way; it would be the greatest joy if this awful war would stop soon, but, first, the rascals who were so vile to make us this hideous war have to be beaten so that in the next hundred years they won't have the courage to try again. And then I would love to see you again, dear friend, and help you as far as I could with my poor abilities. . . . How beautiful is the feeling when one knows that at home a woman is longing for you and praying for you, but who never makes you week or sorry as she realizes that you are only doing your duty in fighting for the fatherland. Then, for the women at home, to know that they have a soldier in the war who does his task well, and who is liked by his people, and who thinks—although the enemy throws 6000 shells on his head inside four hours—of his dear sweet wife at home for whom also he gladly goes through all that. But God will give us the victory and will punish that wrong Island. We passed through a very serious time during the last four weeks, but the boys were such heroes and did their duty beautifully. I was quite alone with my Brigade and gott a special job—Reconnaissance—for that is what the Brigade have been doing during the last month. Even so heaps of the dear fellows had to die, or gott wounded, and that's always so hard a thing to bear. Well, dear friend, I have to finish this letter. Please don't mark all the wrong words, but its meant well, also if it's not spelt correctly. So I hope after the war we will see each other again, and I can help you if necessary, and we shall have a nice tea in your little wood cottage and will forget this awful war. Please write if you gott this letter as we are always uncertain if our letters arrive.

"To-day a beautiful day and we had a fine walk and ride through the woods. These are the days of the rest, the awful days of bloody work come again soon enough.

"I still often think of the nice songs you sang in the small little rooms in Fürstenstein which were so *gemütlich* quite like a ship's cabine. You remember still our trip in the motor boat. And you hurt your bad leg and von Oppen and I had to carry you back. Poor Oppen is dead already a long time; he was the first officer of the Regiment to fall. He has now many followers.

"Well now I have to say good by, dear friend.

"Kissing your hand, I remain always yours very truly,

"EITEL FRIEDRICH."

In the spring of 1915 the Prince's Division was moved to Galicia and he wrote me in May from a position on the San near Jaroslav:

"MY DEAR PRINCESS DAYSY,

"To-day I wright during the thunder of the cannons and the bursting of the enemy's shells. . . . We have had a hard time this last fortnight. Fighting and marching every day in awful heet on very difficult roads, but we hunted the enemy in front of us for over a hundert kilometer and made several thousand prisoners. The thirst was very hard as we could only get a sort of coffee from the *Feldküche*. But nobody grumbles; all are glad that we are going forward, and my beautiful soldiers take all fatigues on them. I am quite well, rather stung by insects, burnt like a chestnut, and feel quite well. Of course the hope to come once home after all that you have gone through is big: especially when it's such a nice season like now, you long for your nice quiet garden with all the flowers, etc. But you have to be hard against yourself as well as against the others, to pull through. Well, you wrote you would have liked to have gone with me alone without old Seebuch; of course it would have been much nicer and I don't know wy you were shy of me. I am no wilde man, only very shy too in strange company. I heard that my father comes to Pless and perhaps you will see him there. Perhaps Mamma comes to see him there one day, then you would have a good opportunity to speak to her quite planeley. I said to good General v. Gontard that if he met you he was to be nice to you. G. is a man whom you can believe in as well as in yourself. He is my best friend. He will be very nice to you. I told him that I felt they have been doing wrong to you, and he promised me to help. He can help you in all things, even in the house and if there are still things to be arranged. Of course I did not tell him anything about . . . . ; I just said I felt they did wrong to you and he should see if he could not help. That was the best thing I could do for you. So goodby dear Princess. Many thanks for your last letter. I got it sitting in a trench before Jaroslav. I have to go a killing people and seeing dear fellows been wounded. When will that have an end! I remain, dear friend, kissing your hand, always yours truly,

"EITEL FRITZ."

English people will remember the importance attributed to the fall of Przemysl on March 22, 1915. The Prince was in the German advance:

"*Kloster Lazy near Przemysl,* 6. vi. 15.

"MY DEAR FRIEND,

"Many thanks for your dear letter from Pless I gott yesterday. I am so glad that you like my letters and that I help you a little bit to pass heavy hours in which a friendly word helps more often than heaps of other things. How nice for you to have visited Fürstenstein and also the charming little wood cottage where we spent such a nice quiet half an hour. Of course I would have given those two brave foresters my hand, and my wife would do the same. Do they not shed their blood for us? That we give our hands to them is really the very least we can do. Especially so when they are one's own people. I give every soldier who is wounded my hand. But you must not spoil the wounded too much with beer and books and teas and all sorts of cosinesses that they are not accustomed to. If you do they find it always very difficult to come back to the hard life at the front, and sometimes spend more time at home than is right or necessary. This is a thing we found out already. But otherwise our people are beautiful. You always write that I am such an example; but I don't do anything more than the rest of my people, and anyhow it's only my duty I am doing. You think much too well of me. I am a simple soldier like every other one. And now about the Kodak. Many thanks, but I already have one and two would be too much. For the bottle of champain which shall arrive I am very thankful as we are very close with wine. If you could send now and then some bottles of champain I would be very thankful. We are still in position near the big fortress of Przemysl which surrendered the other day, so I believe we will be soon going on working against these *Moskalis*. But even if the world should be full of Devils we must winn. These false doggs the Italians—and the Rumanians—you never know for quite shure when they will begin. It's a hard, very hard task but we must pull it through.

"Well, dear friend, you can be shure that I only think the best of you and hope that you, dear Daysy, will not have too much trouble. How I would like to be near you, and be a nice little help for you, and then we would go down to your nice little house and you would sing some beautiful songs in the solitude of these fine woods. But these are pictures of a dreamland that arise in my imagination. I am still sitting in the midst of uproar of cannons and bursting of shells, and the picture my mind is painting is so far off. But nevertheless I kiss in thoughts your dear white hand, and am always your true friend.

"FRITZ."

"10. vii. 15.

"MY DEAR PRINCESS DAISY,

"So many thanks for your dear letter from Pless just before going to Bansin. I was very glad to gett it and still don't find it funny or akward in your writing me. He who sayes that is an idiot. On the contrary, I find it very nice that you write me when you have a spare moment, and am ever so thankful for your nice letters, as I feel that it is a pleasure to you to write to me and to give way to your feelings to somebody whom you know is a good friend of yours, and who understands your feeling so well, and who has great pitty for you. You know you can trust me in everything, that I am a silent good friend (like a book) to whom you can speak about everything. You know that I am very devoted to you and would like to help you. But alas! when sitting here in Russia near the enemy, the shells bursting all around, it's very difficult. But if God let's me come back safely I will speak about all that at once to my mother, and I am shure there will be found out some mistakes, and also that unworthy way of treating you in Silesia will be at an end. . . . You dear friend, how I pitty you.

"How nice of you, dear Prinzess Daysy, to think of me sitting in your little house and sending the four-leaf shamrock. Also for the bottle of champain I gott the other day, many thanks. It's so dreadfully warm and dusty here that we are more or less alwayes thirsty. The heat these last weeks was quite abnormal and the strain on officers and men marching and fighting day after day in this dead heat was prodigious. But, nevertheless, our splendid soldiers worked on alwayes with good spirit. It's grand to see the beautiful men doing their duty. I live mostly in a tent in which I have a small camp bed which can close up like a handbag. Of course there is not much comfort on it, but it's much better than nothing. The flies are very disagreeable. They sit on your nose, or buzz on your naked arms just when you want to go asleep; then you wave your hand—but they are soon back again. Well, I am hunting for a ladyes vale to put over my face as keeping the blanket over the head the whole time is so very warm.

"Now we had three dayes rest. The Russians lie opposite to us about three klm. from my village. Their first line trenches are of course hardly 1 km. away, so we get, mornings and evenings, the shells into our breakfast and supper.

A Prussian Soldier Prince

A Gallant Austrian Soldier

That's not quite the thing to make the place cosy, but you gett accustomed to much. As a soldier and a man you must bear difficulties and risk your life for King and fatherland. What is your little being in komparrison to our great country?

"Well, dear friend, I have to shut up now and say good bye. You see the lettter has gott already longer than three words, and I hope you are not angry about it. You may not look at my spelling but that's all the same, I have not the time to think if this stupid word is written with or without an h. I hope you will answer soon. It's so nice to gett letters during the war and to forget for a short time this terrible fighting. Write about everything that interests you. Theater, Dresses, Books, Invites, Seabathing, your Neighbours, Horses, or anything—only not about the war. As we have to think of it the whole day. How splendid it must be now on the seaside. I whished I could bathe now in the beautiful salt water.

"Many thanks too for your telegram. Who told you that it was my birthday? You did not know it, did you?

"Kissing your hand, I remain dear Prinzess Daysy,

"Yours truly,
"E. Fritz."

A last vignette from the Eastern Front:

"12. viii. 15.

"My Dear Princess Daysy,

"Ever so many thanks for your dear kind letter I gott yesterday. Of course I gott your two pieces of chiffon, and I hope that in the meantime you gott my letter thanking you for your so kind parcel with the fly killing paper, the oils, etc. I use them always when I have just a spare moment to lie down during the daytime, and it is a really splendid thing to have it over the face as you go mad in smashing your face during the mosquito hunt. And the bottle with the *Salmiakgeist* [ammonia] was also very good as I was stung by a bee, just on the nose, yesterday morning. I put a little drop of the stuff on it. It was so strong that the water came to my eyes, but it helped directly. I am sitting here on a fearfully strong Russian position we conquered this morning. They are extraordinarily celever in building these forterresee-like positions. But ower beautiful men gott into them nevertheless. We gott on a good bitt since I wrote last time. But it's a very hard task against so many.

"The view from this spot where I am sitting is splendid. You look over fare meadowes with trees standing here and there, quite like a big English park. There are a great deal of lakes and moors and some big forests. Therefore it is not quite so easy getting through this country. Well, that we gott Warschau[1] is splendid, and God will help us further.

"That you saw the Emperor made me so happy, and I sent directly a card saying so; I hope you gott it. It must have been funny to be invited in your owne house, but nice for you to see everything, and see my dear General von Gontard. I am devoted to him, he is my very best friend as well as *Kamerad*. I was shure you would like him and am very glad that I was right in it. How amusing that motor tripp must have been when the Artillerie General arrived.

"Are you now quite back at Fürstenstein and will you stay there or do you return to Bansin once more. I write to Fürstenstein as I am not shure. My last letter I sent to Villa Buchenhof. How nice your garden at Fürstenstein must be now, also your small rose garden, you know you showed it to me. And all the flowers in the houses. It's one of the things you miss the most—never to see a nice well-kept garden or a nice flowery border. Everything burnt. The soil dirty and covered with old straw. It's not a great pleasure, and you long for a quiet little spot of green grass with the sweet smell of the flowers which they have after sunset before going to sleep. That's one of the hardships of war, as I love all nature, flowers, trees and beasts—so I miss it doubly.

"I have a small little bay horse *Schecke* [piebald] quite brown and vite like a Chesnot. It's so nice and tame like a big dog and comes with me into the house; the other day it slept beside one of my officers. And it has such a nice

[1] Aug. 4, 1915, Warsaw fell, after the Russian evacuation.

high voice. You have to have some creature to spoil, else you feel too lonely. Of course good old *Görtz*, my black dog that you saw in Fürstenstein when I stayed there, is always with me.

"Now about your boy. Please do not send him out too early as the war may go on still very long and it's too fatiguing for a young chap. He can gett something with the heart or lungs before he is any use; wilst if he vates still a little bit until he is really quite strong and firm, and has learnt at home what is absolutely necessary for a boy who getts into such a big position, then he can come out. But I can understand that you as Mother are proud of such a nice boy and want to give also your part for the war, but it has no sence if he is young, 18 years is the best but not younger. But do write about it, dear Princess Daysy, to good old Gontard; he is the man who will give you the best advice, and has such a big experience as he had brought up all of us, and he will write to you what is really the best, without jealousness or envy. Alas! dear friend, you will find both so long as the world exists and we can't change it. I personally can't understand that a man can be so inferior as to be jealous. Dear Pr. Daysy please don't be angry, but today I am quite an idiot in spelling; that comes from the noise of the bursting shells near you, so that you look always about.

"I sleep in the tennt on my small field bed. It's rather cold during the night already and in the morning everything is wett and cold from the dew. It's not just the most agreeable thing to dive into a damp cold shirt and the feet plunge coming out of the nice cosy bed into the wet grass, but you get accustomed to everything and these are so small chagrins that you don't think about it. I am thankful to God and Gontard that he has brought me up in such a sensible way that I can support all that. But sometimes you do wish to have the feet under a nice table with a vite linen on it, or to sleep in a nice bed without hearing always with one ear what is going on outdoors.

"How I wish to walk with you dear Prinzess Daysy through your beautiful woods near Fürstenstein, or have a nice little supper in that cosy old stable where we lived for the

Fasanenjagd [pheasant shoot]—or hear you singing at the piano.

"The music is also a thing you miss so much. The other day I lay beside a church and a very intelligent little officer of the Hussars went in and played the violin accompanied by the organ in the dark old church. You felt you were alone with the old Polish [undecipherable] and then to hear the *Largo* and the *Träumerei* and several other pieces—it was really a great pleasure. But dear friend, I have written already enough and I think I bore you with all this.

"So good-bye dear friend. Don't worry too much about what people say, but do the right thing you feel you have to do, and you will always do the best.

"Always yours, kissing in friendship,

"Yours truly,

"E. FRITZ."

Three weeks later the Prince was back on the Western Front, and wrote:

"*Strassburg*, 6.9.15.

"MY DEAR PRINCESS DAISY,

"So many thanks for your dear letter I got yesterday and which made me very happy. As in this awful war time to know you can help a little bit to make somebody happy for a few minutes is, for a man who has only to think of killing other people, really a relief. Of course, dear friend, you can write to me as much as you like; I will always be very glad to get a letter of yours. You know the letters are only for me, I don't speak to anyone about them, and I burn them, so you can write whatever you want. I am only sorry not being able to answer in a proper way, but I suppose you, dear Princess, can understand even if a word is missing or wrongly spelt, as I have no time to look for a dictionary.

"Yes, I can understand your grief and sorrow, and I wish I could be near you to console you and make you happy again, as I believe in you, and don't think that you could have done anything wrong. I would take your hand dressed in a dainty glove between my two brown hands and say, now my dear friend, forget your sorrows and be happy again. I wish we could make nice walks together in those beautiful woods near the little *Teehaus* where we were together after the *Fasanenjagd* with Count Seebach.[1]

"I had to go through an awful time in the Champagne were we were attacked day and night and the whole earth shook the whole time. It was no pleasure party, but we pulled it through nevertheless and, although they poured 100,000 *Granaten* [shells] during several hours a day for many days on our poor heads (all American ammunition—that's the shame) they didn't succeed in breaking through; but sometimes you thought you were going mad, and then to keep cool and give your orders quietly was not quite easy. But what you do yourself is nothing, comparatively, to what is done by our beautiful men. They are all heroes and I beg God often enough to spare them; but of course the losses are big and that's always for my heart the worst part, all the dear fellows knocked out. The danger and the fatigues are nothing besides that. Now we have a little bit of rest, and so I can write this letter.

"I hope you are quite well dearest friend, and keep your head up. It must be awful to have no help from those who ought to be your shield and protector. And you are so fair in not writing names. Well, you know you can write to me whatever you like and pour out your heart; It goes into a shut box and so far as I can I will try to bring some happy thoughts and ideas to you, to make you happy for the few minutes you are reading these lines. I remain dear friend,"

"Yrs.
"E. Fritz."

Addresse
Oberst Eitel Fritz P. v. P. *Stab* 1.*G.I.D.*
Kommandantur 1.Garde I.D. *G. K.*

I have told in my first book of how disgracefully the military authorities treated Professor von Küster, who was unceremoniously removed from his post in charge of the first Red Cross Train on which I served. Frau von Küster implored me to try to obtain redress for her husband, so I wrote to and bothered everyone I knew, including, of course, Prince Eitel Fritz. Here is his answer:

[1] Intendant of the Dresden Royal Opera House.

"16.1.16.

"DEAR PRINZESS DAYSY:

"Many thanks for your nice letter I gott yesterday with the card of you standing in front of the train. To beginn with the buziness. As Grandmaster of the St. John's Order I will ask why the Professor v. Kürster is taken away from the *Lazarettzug* Y. Then they must give a reason and I will write it to you. As I am going to have a Chapter of the Order in January I can enquire directly, but there must have been a real reason, else they could not remove a Professor like that *sans façon*.

"How interesting your walk up to the old Serbian Fortress of the time of the Turks. The mud must be rather deep just there, but also here we have enough of it. Well, the crossing of the Danube in the winter when it is in flood must be splendid, especially during the night whilst there is moonlight. It's so misterious, the flowing forward of a dark water in the white light of the moon.

"I was on Xmas night and new year's night out in the trenches, and especially the Xmas night was very thrilling, to walk about 50–100 m. from the enemy in the moonlight and see the nice English boys having their little trees in their earth wholes, and singing the Xmas chorals, and they were so nice and thankful. On Xmas eve I had a heap of things to do. To arrange the presents for all the soldiers of the Staff, those in the Hospital, and then for the officers of the Staff. Then we were also in the church, and that was the worst moment. You had time to think about things, the church was dark and only the two Xmas trees were burning and the dear old Xmas songs rang through that little French village church, and you had to bite the teeth rather hard not to begin to weap like a little girl! But it was the second Xmas far away from home, and I find Xmas just the day when you have to be at home with the family. All other days of the year are not so important as that one day. The feeling of home and house has its culmination on Xmas eve, and there is a big blank if you can't be at home on that day. Also on New Year's evening we were again in the little church and our song *Deutschland, Deutschland über alles* sounded so impressively and so hopefully. Service to the Fatherland is now Divine service. And the good Lord will help us in the New Year; and I have the safe feeling that He will be with me also, although I am not worth it at all. He was so marciful during this last dreadful year, and held his shielding arm over me in so many critical moments that I humbly trust He will do it also in the coming year. How often my men thought I was killed or wounded; how often the man beside me fell; a shell tore in pieces a friend just in front of me; a bullet shot went through the window in front of which I was standing; but God held His arm above me else I would have been already buried under the cool green grass. But I finish with these gloomy thoughts.

"I wish for you, dear friend, strength to pull through all difficulties, and self-control to keep quiet and true, so that you may find the best always. So, good-bye dear Prinzess, it's very late and I must go to bed.

"Always yours,
"E. FRITZ."

I like enormously the soldier's simple faith and satisfying creed. It is the power of this direct, unselfish faith, and its appeal to what is good, fine and disinterested in the human heart, that, pacifists foolishly belittle, even deride:

"4.6.16.

"MY DEAR PRINZESS DAYSY,

"Many thanks for your dear letter I gott yesterday evening, and also the last one with the letter of Frau v. Küster. It's a most difficult thing. I tryed my very best, but up to the moment have had no chance of helping him. I have spent hours in reading the letter and have not yet given up utterly the hope of being able to help him. . . .

"Well now you too are in France, but very far off still from where we are. You are near Metz, and we fight up here near Noyon, only about sixty miles from Paris. From a hill near by you can see the *Eifelturm* and *Sacré Cœur*. I have a little garden round the house with nice big trees and a little *Gemüsegarten* [vegetable garden] in which I have worked nearly every afternoon for the past half a year. We have already had *Salat*, *Spinat*, *Radieschen*, *Sauerampher*, and strawberries out of our little garden, and hope to get soon peas, artichokes, and so on. The house is an old dirty sort of chateau with no style at all. It lies only four kilometres behind the foremost line and often enough the shells burst quite near.

"The other night we had an attack by the aeroplanes and it was rather disagreeable. Twenty bombs round the house, all windows broken, and you had to run down into the cellar only with night-shirt[1] on and a cloak thrown over you. And just when I went to bed again another bomb fell on us. That's really disagreeable because you get uncertain when the next will come. At night you are absolutely helpless against them.

"There is much shooting about here, so when I have a spare hour in the evening, I go a little further away in the woods or on a mountain where you have a little, but fine *Aussicht* [view]. And there we make a little fire and cook some potatoes and eat *Salat*, *Komissbrot*[2] and just a slice of cold meat—and imagine that we are at home and making a trip by motor-boat—until the pounding of the cannons or the sound of the propellor of an aeroplane tells you that you are dreaming. You are lying on French soil, in the biggest war ever been fought, going on only three or five miles off.

"Yes of course I love nature, flowers and trees and even here on my table stands a big bunch of marguerites—don't you call them also Daysys? On the meadows here there are thousands of them. I always find every plant has its soul and its little will by itself; it grows a little bit ahead of the next one, and tries to be a little personage for itself. And to lie quietly in the green and hear the birds sing and see all the different beetles hum about, and the nightingale sing its melancholy song, and the animals come out of their secret places, and the light and colours changing are so beautiful that it is like a big page in the book of nature.

"But alas! here is not much peace . . . the whole day you hear the smashing noise of the shells entering the ground,

[1] Pyjamas did not come into general use in Germany until after the war!

[2] Black rye bread as served to the German soldier and sailor—very good indeed.

disturbing men and beasts and nature, and it looks as if the green meadow was wounded where the fresh green is broken by the holes made by the *Granaten*. I find people can disappoint you but never nature, and you are in the best school if you try to enter into the wisdom of God's artist hand which has formed all that. But that goes on too far.

"How nice it would be to walk under those shady trees near your little wooden house and sit there quietly, not disturbed by this awful war or by noisy people who have no idea of nature, and to speak with your dear friend about the wood, the flowers and the little pond. Well, we have to hope that after the war there will be at least once an opportunity to visit that fine wood again, and I will come very willingly, but I fear there will pass still some time, and thousands more shells will burst before that will happen. And nobody can know if his own fate is not at an end in the next minute.

"Look here, dear Prinzess Daysy, I go out so often in the morning into the trenches and there the bullets whistle past, and the pitsch-putsch just beside you, is so close that it could just as well have smashed your leg. Some shells burst the other day just ten inches from me; I jumped under a little shelter, and there the fragments came down. Then you thank the good Lord that the French soldier did not aim a little to the side! And then again you know that you are protected by Him. But of course only so long as His wisdom finds it well. You cannot say how long and then—farewell house and wife and everything. You must be ready to enter heaven any moment.

"And this feeling grows as the war goes on; and you get rather serious about it, and then you try to do as much good and give as much help as you can as long as you are still on this earth. You do your duty as well as you can so that you need not be so much ashamed when you have to appear before the face of the good Lord. And then you think that all our little quarrels and anxieties are so small and *unbedeutend* [trifling] that you try to get over them.

"And somehow I think this wish is also with you dear Prinzess. Don't bother about so many things; try to do the right and then you will have the best reward in your own self control and serenity. Well, I must beg your pardon, dear friend, for writing such a long letter, and it gets more like a sermon than like a letter to a dear friend to whom I would send some lines to cheer her up. I am no clergyman—not at all, and that you know well, nor can I explain things as I should like to do, nor is my English good enough to express my thoughts as I am only a simple soldier fighting with all my heart for my Fatherland, facing since twenty-three months every day the death. You get the eyes truly opened by such an experience. I hope I have not hurt you or bored you? You can send some day an answer how you think about that.

"In thoughts I take your hand and kissing it say good-bye dear Prinzess Daisy, don't bother too much what other people say—I am sure you are trying your best.

"Always yours truly,

"FRITZ."

And how the serving soldiers of all nations asked for full descriptions of home and trivial things. The silly letters we wrote somehow assuaged their fathomless nostalgia. They, in turn, more than repaid us if they could tell of some loved one serving near them whom they had seen, as the Prince in his next letter does about Hansel:

"18.5.1917.

"MY DEAR PRINCESS DAISY:

"Many thanks for your letter from the mountains. How beautiful it must be in the early spring in the valley of Berchtesgaden with the Watzmann[1] and Untersberg still covered with snow, and then, when the sun is setting, everything looks like burnished gold! I should prefer being there to being in this awful war. We are just coming out of the battle near Reims. It was a very hard struggle against masses of enemies, but our beautiful men stood the fire like heroes and no Frenchmen broke through. Also my quarters were shot at nearly every day and we got bombed from the air, and our own ammunition went up with an

[1] 8,900 ft. Highest peak of the eastern end of the Bavarian Alps and only 1,000 ft. lower than the Zugspitze, the highest mountain in Germany, at the western end.

enormous uproar, so it was no health resort—but God protected us and we all came out safely.

"Hansel is quite well. He is growing always stronger and still taller. The day before yesterday we had a Parade in front of the Crown Prince. He said to Hansel: 'You are getting taller every day.' Then H. marched past with the Hussars. His signalling course he passed very well, and one of these days he will get the Iron Cross for bravery and coolness, as he really helped us. He is in very good hands as Mirbach[1] is a splendid man and a gentleman who is very good in bringing up young officers. The *Regimentsführer* Graf Bredow[2] is a splendid soldier and the Adjutant, Count Hohenthal, is also a first class fellow. So Hansel could not be with nicer people. In fact, all that we can do will be done to make a good soldier and an honourable officer out of your dear son.

"I am glad I can write this to you, dear friend, as I know how you love your children and how a mother is proud if her child is making progress. So, dear Princess Daisy, you have all reason to be proud of this nice boy, and I only hope that he will remain what he is now and that time won't spoil him. Of course the danger begins when we are back in garrison in the big towns. With much money and an old name there is always danger, but so far as I know, Hansel has enough grit to resist.

"So I congratulate you as mother and kiss your hand because your boy won the Iron Cross. I thought this good news would help you over times when you feel unhappy and unsatisfied. Try to find your happiness and satisfaction in your dear boys, in bringing them up as good men who know how to work by themselves without twenty servants hanging around them.

"Hansel has learned out here that I am quite like you; I like best being alone with Lotta,[3] without a *Hofmarshall*

[1] General von Mirbach, then commanding the 1st German Guards' Division, in which Prince Hansel of Pless was serving.

[2] The Regimental Leader, Colonel Graf Gisbert von Bredow (1859-1924).

[3] Prince Eitel Friedrich married in 1906 Duchess Sophie Charlotte of Oldenburg; the marriage was dissolved in 1926.

or Adjutant—only the men who are absolutely required in the house, garden and stables.

"How splendid the woods near Fürstenstein must be now in Spring! Your little *Teehaus*—shall we ever again have a nice cup of tea there together near the Lake under those old trees!

"Well, good-bye dear friend! I hope I can send Hansel for a short time on leave this summer, that he can rest and sleep, for we never know how long this war will go on.

"I remain—kissing your hand dear Pr. Daisy,

"Always yours,

"E. FRITZ."

The next letter must complete the sketch I have tried to make of a simple German soldier. A great and chivalrous gentleman, the Prince ever acted the part of a father to my seventeen-year old eldest son, then facing not only the physical, but the even more deadly, spiritual, dangers of war. I often noticed in the letters of English soldiers, who were prisoners of war in Germany, such as Robin Grey, Ivan Hay, Reggie Fellowes and Rupert Keppel, how they loved to find in the German landscape bits of scenery that reminded them of home—not necessarily of where they happened to reside—but their ancestral countryside. The Prince's reference to Brandenburg has this significance because the Hohenzollerns ruled in Brandenburg for hundreds of years before Frederick the First [1] became King of Prussia in the beginning of the eighteenth century.

"6.7.1917.

"MY DEAR PRINCESS DAYSY,

"To-day only a card to tell you how sad I am that you have lost your dear father. Daughters are specially attached to their father, more than boyes are, who always love more their mother. That's nearly always the case. I can very

[1] (1667–1713) Elector of Brandenburg; crowned first King of Prussia Jan. 18, 1701; his 2nd wife was Sophia Charlotte, sister of the Elector of Hanover, afterwards George I of England; they were the grandparents of Frederick the Great.

well understand you not being able to see strange people after getting this awfully sad message. I hope you will be strong enough to pull through, and don't get too miserable about it, but it must have been an awful blow to you dear Prinzess, so I kiss your hand as sharing your sorrow.

"I am glad Hansel was so nice to you; I spoke very seriously to him before leaving me and I think he understood he should try to help you, and be a prop to you. I also spoke about other things, the life of young men on leave, and girls; I spoke to him as you asked me to do so. I hope he will take heed of it all his life. For the next few days' fighting I have taken him on my staff. There he will see a lot, and learn much, and is, so far as I can protect him, safer than in the trenches. I am sitting in a peasant's little house, just a small room with a stable and a bit of an orchard behind it. The weather changes often; we had a week of rain and now it's good weather again. The landscape is rather nice: woods and hills as in Brandenburg.

"I have finished the book of *Elizabeth and her German Garden* and did like it exceedingly. Do you know the Marchioness of Valmond? She must be a dear, but clever young woman. Only the Germans she does not like very much. I am reading now *Unter Blutbuchen* (Under Copper Beeches), rather nicely written, a Westphalian book. Well, I have to shut the letter as we have to go to the front. Still am telling you dear Prinzess, how sorry I am about your loss. I remain,

"Sincerely yours,

"FRITZ."

CHAPTER X

RETURN TO ENGLAND

ONE of the most hateful things about the hateful business of war is the way it shows people up. People in whom one had hitherto implicitly believed sometimes turned out to be pinchbeck, or even cardboard.

I have been thinking over those who rallied round me when I returned to England in that gloomy spring of 1919. Of course I leave out my sister Shelagh, my brother George,[1] Patsy, Aunt Min and the Wyndham family. Outside these there were not too many. And here I am going to say something the English do not believe and will not like. On the whole I am inclined to think that the Germans of my own class were more broadminded and more tolerant, more understanding and sympathetic towards my unenviable position than those of my own class in England. Naturally, I put aside in both countries the mob and the popular Press that panders to them; they will always be extreme and malignant and are in no sense truly representative.

I only ask one question. Was there any German-born woman living in England throughout the war who was comforted and supported to an equal degree by the Sovereign and most important members of the British Royal Family? Of course there was not. Not that the British Royalties were, or are, one whit less loyal to their friends than the Germans, but for the simple reason that the British public, and the Press which echoes them, would not have understood or tolerated for one moment similar loyalties. I write this now after twenty years, not to stir up strife and bitterness,

[1] Major George Frederick Myddleton Cornwallis-West, late Scots Guards, b. 1874, of Llanarmon Towers, Denbighshire, m. 1900 Jeannie (d. 1921), w. of Lord Randolph Churchill, 2nd, Beatrice Stella, w. of Patrick Campbell.

but to vindicate the Germans, who are so often maligned about such matters, and to invite the English to take down from its dusty shelf their vaunted spirit of sportsmanship and carefully overlook it to see if some of its fairness is not a little tarnished by reason of the fact that it is nowadays too much taken for granted. The living reality has, perhaps, become largely a convention.

Then, apart from the various German Royal Families and other prominent personages who might quite legitimately have pleaded that their positions necessitated a considerable amount of reserve towards myself and others similarly situated, just look how splendid practically every member of my German family was to me. In the present inflamed state of public opinion in Europe such things cannot be repeated too often.

Well, there was no wild rush of people to welcome me when I arrived in England after the war. A dear old friend, a railway porter at Southampton, recognized me and with exquisite tact addressed me in the old way as "Miss Daisy." Could any Ambassador anywhere have surpassed that? Unfortunately—and that was very far from his kindly intention—it made me cry. As soon as I got to London I drove direct to Ken Wood, to dear Nancy Leeds. She was by that time Princess Christopher of Greece and, as the Greek royal family had no House laws preventing it, a real Royal Highness. I found her just the same warm-hearted Nancy whom they all said had been a typewriter in her youth but about which—even if she were—I did not care a hang! The Empress Eugénie at once invited me to Farnborough Hill and I went there for a longish visit soon after Aunt Min's[1] death. I speak elsewhere of how Soveral immediately called on me; and nobody could have been nicer and kinder than Maud Cunard, which was all the more remarkable as we did not know one another very well before the war. Queen Alexandra at once sent for me and received me at Marlborough House and behaved like a mother, a sister and a Queen all in one.

[1] See page 31 ante and footnote.

It is very difficult for a woman to be quite fair to a man who "makes love" to her, whether with or without her consent. I have been looking over what I wrote in my previous volumes about the late Marquès de Soveral, who was for so many years Portuguese Minister in London and one of the most prominent figures in late Victorian and Edwardian society. A bachelor, a great favourite with King Edward the Seventh and Queen Alexandra, reasonably well off, a good talker, he went everywhere and knew everyone.

His two greatest faults were that he overrated his own diplomatic power and influence and that he was, in the delicious Victorian phrase, a professional lady-killer. I always understood that a certain number of women thought him irresistible, but I found that side of him annoying, not to say disgusting. He was altogether too Latin in his attitude and methods, but that no doubt appealed to women whose motto is easy come easy go. Then I had a shrewd suspicion that his love affairs were to some extent diplomatic. Most wayfaring men can quite easily fall in love with "a little milliner," a chorus girl or anything of that sort. But Soveral liked the objects of his temporary affairs to be well placed socially. He always pretended to make a great fuss of me. Perhaps, being as black as a half-caste negro, he really did admire my blonde appearance; nevertheless, he was not unaware of the fact that I was a good deal behind the scenes in Berlin—where he had once for some years been Attaché and therefore considered himself an authority on German affairs. In England he, of course, knew that I was perfectly at home. The Portuguese Minister in London tried to make up in influence what he lacked in power, and he was so assiduous, tactful and ubiquitous that, over a long period of years, he succeeded. No one was more a *persona grata* in Edwardian society. If poor dear Wolff-Metternich had possessed half of Soveral's energy and pushfulness the German Embassy might have exercised a real influence in pre-war London.

Soveral never forgot that a Portuguese Princess had been Queen of England; or that the fact that he was the diplomatic representative in London of England's oldest Ally of itself gave him a certain unique prestige.

Amongst the few old friends who rallied round me when I returned to London in the spring of 1919 after the war Soveral must have a prominent and honourable place. I was ensconced quietly at Brown's Hotel, with only a lady's maid, when accompanied by the Marquis Imperiali, the Italian Ambassador, he immediately called on me. To bring with him the Ambassador of one of England's Allies in the war was a superbly tactful gesture characteristic of the man. Not only did Soveral call, but he offered to do anything in the world he could to help me.

There is no characteristic I admire more than loyalty, and, without question, Soveral was always a good friend to England. Moreover, he was tenaciously loyal and faithful to his country and his Sovereign. King Carlos the First [1] trusted him implicitly. The King's brutal murder and that of his son is an indelible stain on the Portuguese people. To the tragic and bereft Queen Amélie, and her second son, King Manuel, Soveral was unalterably faithful and devoted. Let a letter Her Majesty wrote me at the time of Soveral's death be his epitaph. He could not have a finer one:

3.11.'23.
"Château de Bellevue, Le Chesnay-Versailles,
"S. et O.

"Dear Princess of Pless,

"Your kind letter touched me deeply, and I would have written sooner had not a severe chill kept me in bed and in my room for several days, and left me very tired indeed.

"Life has been so hard, and for all of us, during these last years, and I do sympathize with you in the loss of those dear to you. I know only too well!

"The loss of such a dear friend as Soveral is terrible; all his life was devoted to us, and I can hardly realize the awful truth! The only, but supreme consolation, is the conviction that he is happy, and we must not be selfish!

[1] Carlos I. (1863–1908), m. 1886 Princesse Amélie de France, d. of the Comte de Paris, and great-granddaughter of Louis Philippe.

You know also how he loved England, and what a true and loyal friend he was. He very often spoke of you, and of having seen you again in London!

"My dear Princess, with renewed expression of my heartiest thanks, believe me,

"Yours very affectionately,

"AMÉLIE."

The point is that each one of those I have mentioned were foreigners . . . not English. I leave it at that.

2

I cannot now remember quite how it happened, but somewhere or somehow I met Margot Oxford soon after my arrival and, quite needless to say, she was as friendly and cordial as she had ever been. I wonder if by any chance she remembers one of our earliest meetings, when she was still unique Margot Tennant. We were both staying in the Pytchley country for hunting. Meeting in some house for luncheon we went upstairs together to wash our hands, and Margot remarked quite casually:

"You know what I'm going to do, don't you, Daisy?"

"No."

"I am going to marry a Prime Minister."

"How awful—what do you mean? What is he like, Margot?"

"He is a brilliant man with five children."

"What! He has been married before?"

"Yes—but that does not matter. He is very clever."

I thought how very boring the words "Prime Minister" sounded, particularly for Margot who was at that time mad on horses and gave up her life to them. Nor could I understand marrying a man who had another woman's children. I was young then and very simple.

As I write I can see Margot exactly as she was in those days and how marvellous she looked when mounted. Off a horse she never seemed to me quite the same woman, though she was, of course, always ready to exchange swift, witty chaff, make a joke, and keep everyone alive. There was a time—or so the story went—when she wished to have an intimate conversation with the German Emperor during one of his visits to London. So she pretended her horse was running away with her in the Row, very nearly bumped into him, and apologized. He had at any rate seen at close quarters a pair of eyes alive with intelligence and a good seat on a horse. But I think the acquaintance somehow failed to materialize into friendship.

Margot was, and is, one of those intense, vivid women whom you can love or detest. Some people did detest her, but only the cheaper sort who are either too stupid or too conventional to see that one woman like Margot is worth a million bores. Of course she could be devastatingly rude —but what other weapon ever proves effectual with a really crashing bore? It was a weapon I personally never had the courage or skill to use, though I often wished I had. That awful heart-sinking moment when you see the worst bore in London bearing down on you with an inane, determined grin and you wait like a lamb before the slaughter for the deadly, inevitable "I'm afraid, dear Princess, you have quite forgotten me" and—not in the least like a lamb but like a stupid old sheep—you hastily put on your party face and answer lyingly, "Oh, of course not . . . er——" instead of truthfully exclaiming "I'm afraid I have. Quite." And passing on like a real woman. There is, however, a degree of truth in the answer, because in his own dreadful way the creature is quite unforgettable. There used to be some two hundred and fifty such detrimentals in the London of my day, and I am quite sure that if I were to return again to-morrow I should find them there still. Of their numerous feminine counterparts it is unnecessary to speak. One woman always knows how to be icily rude to another without saying a word.

If I should by any chance have forgotten a single one of the old friends who gathered round me upon my return to

England I hereby humbly beg their forgiveness. Aunt Min had just died; Patsy was mortally ill; I had to go into a nursing home. The world was still upside down . . . and so was Daisy. But I can never forget Winnie Portland, or how dear and sweet she was to me. Here is a characteristic note from her in which there is a reference to Resy Clary,[1] the beloved mother of Elisalex, Sophy and Alphy:

"*Welbeck, Worksop, Notts.*
"*Nov. 3rd,* 1919.

"Dearest Daisy,

"I am writing in the train, going to Welbeck (and two functions in Nottingham and Mansfield). So am starting at ten-thirty, too early to go and say good-bye to you. I hope to see you when you come back; let me know. I loved the dear letters from the person I adore best in the *whole world* of all my relations or friends—Resy—she is a real treasure and like no one else. Portland and I love her equally—and our *one* hope is to look on her beloved face again—soon! I hope you will soon be feeling strong and well—I am *so* sorry for all your worries.

"Yrs affectly,
"Winnie P."

3

Amongst the men friends who rallied round me when I first returned to London I particularly remember Harry Stonor and Jack Cowans. Harry, who never seems to grow old, is as kind and helpful as ever; beloved Jack left us very soon after the end of the war.

How many women were in love with Jack Cowans? Dozens. A friend of mine describing Jack's state funeral in Westminster Cathedral told me that considering the corpse—as they say in Ireland—it was the most extraordinary scene imaginable. The spectacle of Jack, who hadn't a spark of

[1] Countess Therese Kinsky (1867–1930) m. 1885 Siegfried, 6th Prince of Clary and Aldringen (1848–1929).

conventional religion in his whole make-up, being, so to speak, enskied with all the pomp of the Catholic Church, must indeed have been amazing. But my friend said that the most striking, indeed original, feature, was what he was ironically pleased to call the vestal virgins. There they sat, so to speak, row on row, draped in the utmost black . . . elegant, French, woebegone in the most picturesque manner. Jack's had-beens, might-have-beens and hoped-to-bes drawn momentarily together, one must assume, by a common sorrow. How Jack would have revelled in it all! Now that there is no one alive whom it might hurt I may tell a true story.

As everyone knows, Monte Carlo is about the size of a pocket-handkerchief. There is, literally, no place to walk—which is one of my many excuses for hating it. The consequence is that it is impossible to go out without everybody meeting everybody. One reason why everybody sins, as it were, on the housetops in the Principality is because there is nowhere else where one could find space enough for the purpose. Living there in sin has therefore not even the merit of being scandalous as it is all, so to speak, open and above-board! Well, dear Jack always kept on the best of terms with all his lady-loves, and they all went on loving him, even if they could not quite bring themselves to love one another—although I have heard that to be one of Jack's relinquisheds was, in its way, quite a real bond amongst themselves.

Bored with a boring Monte Carlo life a certain woman who shall be nameless went for the treadmill walk along the front, round the Casino, up the Grande Place, along the Boulevard Grimaldi, or whatever it is called, and back to the Hotel de Paris. Reaching her apartment where the rest of the party were playing Bridge this conversation took place:

"Hope you enjoyed your walk, darling?"

"Well, I didn't."

"Why not?"

"Because there is no place to walk—and, anyhow, one never does enjoy anything in this beastly hole!"

"Whom did you see?"

"Oh! nobody—everybody——"

"Everybody?"

"Yes. Of course I saw everybody. It's as inevitable as death. I saw the reigning Lady Cowans, the Dowager Lady Cowans, the ex-Lady Cowans, the deputy Lady Cowans—and all their understudies!"

That may seem exaggerated—but, really, it hardly was.

The stories that used to go around about Jack's *affaires* were legion, and almost all of them were lies. In the summer of 1903 I was present at a luncheon party given by Mrs. Sassoon. The daughter of Baron Gusatve de Rothschild, Aline Sassoon, was rich, clever and eclectic. Therefore her parties were always delightful. I only remember the presence of Julia Maguire,[1] Violet Rutland, and Lady Charles Beresford.[2] Lady Charles who, poor dear, was not very brilliant, would insist on retailing at length the life story of a certain Baroness de Zero. This lady, the legend went, was the daughter of an Italian Princess who was compelled to hide her once lovely face from society long before death hid it from the world. The Baron, whose pockets were as empty as his title, was accommodating or, as they now say, broad-minded. Some people in London received the lady; Jack met and admired her; the Baron and Baroness somehow appeared at an unimportant function at Buckingham Palace and even claimed to have been informally presented to the Queen. The Baroness then secretly put about the story, that in reality, she was a daughter of the Tsar—which Tsar she was extremely careful never to specify; sometimes she forgot about the Tsar and declared that Jack was her father!

Now the Baroness, on the most charitable of assumptions, was by no means young and, when dismantled for sleeping purposes, could hardly have looked five years younger than Jack. I am no good at arithmetic, but I have some imagination, and I nearly cried with laughter at Mrs. Sassoon's

[1] d. of 3rd Viscount Peel; m. in 1895 J. R. Maguire, M.P. (1855–1925).

[2] Mina, d. of Richard Gardner, M.P.; m. in 1878 the late Admiral Lord Charles Beresford, 2nd s. of 4th Marquess of Waterford.

luncheon table as I made a mental picture of poor old Jack at the mature age of five or six escaping from the clutches of his dour north-country nurse and having a fruitful *affaire* with an Italian Princess. I was at one time or another shown at least a dozen women who were said to be Jack's daughters—he never seemed to be able to manage to produce a son. Jack, in fact, according to gossip, was almost a match for Augustus the Strong of Saxony—a true German hero—who had hundreds of children,[1] yet still managed to have time to make Dresden the most beautiful city in Germany and, between times, be King of Poland. In fact, ubiquitously constructive!

Jack had some true women friends, he had numberless *affaires*, but he had no true loves. Essentially he was lonely and, like all loveless people, he sought to mitigate his isolation as best he could. People who know what heart-loneliness is will understand and make allowances for this. Jack was a matchless friend, a loyal comrade; if he found a pretty woman was accommodating, well, he could not be ungallant, could he? But if a woman was straight, honestly out only for friendship and companionship, no conventional Galahad could be half so chivalrous and unselfish as Jack so often proved himself to be. I once asked him why he seemed to want to protect in his fatherly way every attractive girl he came across, and he said he expected it was because he had no girls of his own and would have loved to have had at least a dozen. On another occasion I asked him how he who knew every lovely, elegant woman in London could waste his time with pretty amateur cocottes from the musical comedies. He said: "Well you see, Daisy dear, they are restful. One needn't bother. If they give little they demand little—a good dinner somewhere in public where they can be seen, a jewelled gewgaw or a beaded bag!"

During the war—as I heard afterwards—Jack was much criticized for appearing frequently in public with such "little

[1] 1670–1733, Elector of Saxony and King of Poland; the Princess exaggerates. King Augustus the Strong was only *known* to be the father of 194 children. George Sand was his great-granddaughter and inherited some of his redundant sexual energy.

bits of *lingerie*." This criticism mostly came from people who had never in their lives accomplished anything and who were long past loving anybody. Throughout the war Jack was carrying in his smiling, apparently light-hearted way one of the most stupendous tasks of its kind in all history. He brought food from the ends of the earth across perilous seas and, as a result of his foresight, energy and unique organizing skill, not one of England's five million soldiers—not a single English child—ever went hungry. If an hour or two at the Carlton Grill eating with a little lady who was "doing her bit for the fighting men," helped Jack to carry on, why I for one would have lined Whitehall with what he used to call "little bits" just to please him.

Jack's powers of organization were simply miraculous. He got the original British Expeditionary Force over to France before Germany, with all her remarkable skill in obtaining information, even knew it had started. His calmness and equability, as this little tribute tries to show, never once deserted him. I find amongst his letters in his own writing the following bit of doggerel. It is so characteristic that I must quote it. I don't know who wrote it but it was no doubt inspired by the story of Drake continuing to play bowls on Plymouth Hoe while the Spanish Armada streamed landwards like a conquering host:

When the Germans landed
I was playing golf—
All the soldiers ran away,
All the ships were stranded—
And the thought of England's shame
Completely put me off my game!

The critics forgot that for over four years from nine in the morning till eleven or twelve o'clock at night Jack was in his room at the War Office. He was the only soldier who served on the Army Council from before the outbreak of the war until after the Armistice. One way or another each of them went down under the strain. Jack survived—because he relaxed. But, in the end, it killed him. He gave his life like any Tommy in a front-line trench.

Of course we heard in Berlin exaggerated accounts of Jack's little wartime flapper parties, and what they stood for depressed Germans dreadfully. If that was the way the British Quartermaster-General went on things could not be so very desperate in England and, even if Whitehall, Westminster Abbey, Buckingham Palace, Victoria and Charing Cross stations and Woolwich Arsenal had been blown up by Zeppelins, clearly the Carlton and Savoy Hotels remained. If Great Britain and the British Empire never clearly realized how much Jack did to make the Allies victorious, there were no illusions about it in Germany. From the end of 1915 onward Germany became certain that food would win or lose the war and, as it went on, there were not a few in high places who thought that if only Germany had a Jack Cowans victory would be certain.

The little things that have altered history are a subject of endless fascination. A year or two before the war Jack had the winning ticket for the Calcutta Sweep and, upon someone asking him for a few spare ones, sold it! In 1911 he was terribly disappointed because he was not made Adjutant-General in India. Had he won the Sweep he would, he declared, have left the Army: Had he been tied up in India, we might not have won the war so easily—if at all. I always recall these two incidents when inclined (as I frequently am) to take the government of the world into my personal keeping!

Of course, it is absurd to speak of any one person, more particularly, any one politician, as being responsible for winning the war, but if such a claim could seriously be sustained for one moment, the only two names that could possibly be considered would be those of King George the Fifth and Jack Cowans. The King inspired his peoples with his own calm, quiet serenity and his faith in ultimate victory. Jack fed the fighting men faultlessly.

What were the secrets of Jack's social and professional successes? He was no Apollo, he was (in truth) no Don Juan, and he was not a great man or even a great soldier. There were scores of bigger men in the British Army at the same time, and not one of them did a bigger job or was so consistently successful. Why was this?

Well, I think the basis of his all-round success was similar to that of Nelson—humanness. There are probably all sorts of grand names for it but I don't know what they are, nor am I going to look them up in a dictionary because that would only be information—not knowledge. The greatest of Sailors and Jack possessed to an extraordinary degree that peculiarly English quality of being human, understanding and sympathetic which seems to be denied to so many good Frenchmen and Germans. I cannot quite explain it any more than I can explain electricity or wireless, but I can recognize it as easily as I can see a lighted reading-lamp or hear Dr. Goebbels when he makes a speech on the radio—as occasionally he can be coaxed to do.

Now this gift of being human is, let me repeat, largely British. Apart from it they are rather a stupid people. It is the real foundation of all their greatness and success. Education seems to tend to destroy it. The French and Germans, for example, are far better educated than the English, but they are not, and never will be, equally successful. This gift of success has nothing whatever to do with the ability to pass examinations, write long muddled philosophical treatises like the Germans, or short, concise, perfectly logical ones like the French.

Either Nelson or Jack would have died rather than read a play by Shakespeare—in fact, would have died had they been compelled to read, say, *Timon of Athens*—not that the fact is so remarkable because to read *Timon* would kill almost anyone! Nevertheless, Shakespeare would have loved both the Admiral and the Quartermaster-General and again and again, by anticipation, put both of them in his plays. No! I'm not going to say just where because, in fact, I don't know; I only know that he really did so. Nobody—let alone Shakespeare—who wrote a real English play could avoid putting them in because both were full, all-round typical men and typical Englishmen, yet entirely individual, original and authentic.

Just as Falstaff, when dying, babbled o'green fields, so did Jack. Always, as I have said, lonely, he was alone down on the Riviera when he realized that death was close at hand. The green pastures he caught glimpses of were those of our Christian paradise and he sent for a Catholic priest who saw to it that the gates to the meadow were opened and Jack let in. And few could have a better right because, whatever his failings, he was neither mean nor spiteful, a liar or a pharisee, a slanderer or a cheat. I cannot tell how it was with him at the end or exactly why he became a Catholic. He was faced with an unknown journey on an unknown road to an unknown destination and I can well imagine him, as was his habit, sending for the nearest expert and taking his advice, because, like all big men, Jack could take and follow advice. And, as always, he would want the whole thing done concisely on, as he used to say, half a sheet of notepaper. He had a tidy mind. He possessed two dominant qualities that endeared him to many women: he wasted no time and he was never ambiguous. Unlike most male flirts, he never attempted to mix love and friendship. In the passionate sense he might not want a woman very long but, while he did so, he wanted her at once and ardently. If, on the other hand, he became her friend he remained her friend. I loved this quality in him as I love it in all men.

To such a temperament as Jack's, Protestantism is innately antipathetic. . . . Perhaps at the end he felt that the Virgin Mary (unlike any Protestant saint) would smilingly and gladly draw aside the black curtain at his coming and that when she did so it would be found to be lined with blue.

4

One of the real pleasures of writing books of reminiscences is that it often brings one again into contact with old friends with whom one had lost touch; the other—and I have stressed this before—is the many new friends one makes by means of their letters. To give some idea of how interesting such letters can be—at any rate to those to whom they are addressed—I will quote one or two that give glimpses of Patsy and of my own early days. Admiral Mark Kerr, a lifelong friend, says:

". . . I think I knew your mother better than I did you. I remember well the first time we met; it was at a Review at Portsmouth when I was staying with the Saxe-Weimars;[1] Augusta was a first cousin of my mother's. Your book is full of interest and has brought back many memories to me. I first met you when you were only a child; after that I cannot remember, but we used to meet at Trentham or Dunrobin. Later on at Joe Laycock's . . . I knew the Emperor well, and was in attendance on him for some time. We used to correspond on the subject of Nelson principally. I was also in attendance on his mother and knew the whole family at different times. I saw your son at the polo ground at Cannes last March. I was with Princess Nicholas of Greece and Princess Marina her daughter. . . . I defended King Constantine in my book and in the Press and had a good many bricks in consequence . . . so I can understand better than most how very much you must have suffered from your fearless outspokenness. . . ."

Dear old Sir Desmond O'Callaghan wrote delightful letters. Since he wrote me as follows the loneliness of life has left him, and he now wanders in the Elysian fields:

". . . In the long ago I spent a very pleasant week with you all at Newlands and played in *Sweet Lavender* in which you, your sister Shelagh, Gordie Wood and your brother took part, and you two sisters sang songs afterwards. . . . Your intensely interesting memoirs brought you very vividly before me. What you, a big-hearted woman, must have suffered one can but try and realize, and I read it all with infinite sadness. You still have your boys and I by going

[1] Field-Marshal Prince Edward of Saxe-Weimar (1823–1902), m. 1851 Lady Augusta Gordon Lennox, d. of the 5th Duke of Richmond and Gordon.

into far countries have accustomed myself to being alone. I used to meet your sister very often while I could skate, but I am within a month of eighty-six and that is too old for skating. I would so much like to see you. . . ."

Of the countless letters I received, few, if any, gave me more lasting pleasure than this one from the late Lord Lamington:

"*Lamington, Scotland,*
"25*th Novr.*, 1928.

"Dear Lady of days bygone, so many in number that your memory of me must be certainly dimmed if not quite obscured. But I have always kept a true vision of angelic beauty and think of you singing seated at a piano at Newlands; materially, too, I have been in touch with you as day in day out I have carried a gold pencil case inscribed 'Wallace from Daisy, 1895.'

"However, I only trouble you with these lines to offer my congratulations to you on your book, so vivid in its descriptions, so frank in its opinions. It is a historic work of real interest. I don't know your address so I send this to Lady Adelaide Taylour to ask her to send it on.

"There are references in your volume that you were not strong; may this not be now the case, but that you are able to enjoy life. You have seen so much and have played such important rôles that you are to be envied in the mere contemplation of what you have done.

"I won't weary you more,
"Yrs affec.,
"LAMINGTON or WALLACE of old.

"*P.S.*—The news to-night is that the King has had a disturbed day. We are going through critical days in this country and it is to be prayed that he may recover for the country's sake as well as his own."

I am not a very "bishopy" sort of person, although I know a few. The dear Archbishop of Wales [1] who married me; the funny little Catholic Bishop of Cannes who, for all

[1] Right Rev. Alfred George Edwards, D.D., Bishop of St. Asaph 1889–1920; Archbishop of Wales 1920–1934.

his episcopal ring, pastoral staff and trailing purple robe, is just a Provençal peasant. There was a Cardinal—at least I think he was a Cardinal—in Breslau whom we saw sometimes on official occasions; he was tall, dignified and silent and never, so far as I remember, came to Fürstenstein which, I suppose, was too hopelessly Protestant. When staying with darling Aunt Ethel Peacocke at Efford Park I met a real Irish Bishop and, of all bishops anywhere, the Irish are quite the most human and least "bishopy." Dr. and Mrs. Dowse and I became great friends and corresponded occasionally. Here is a charming letter from him:

"*The Palace, Cork, Dec. 22nd,* '26.

"MY DEAR PRINCESS,

"It was so good of you to think of us and to send us such a beautiful remembrance. We loved hearing from you. It is very nice of you keeping us in your mind. When you are next with Mrs. Peacocke,[1] we shall be delighted to welcome you to our very humble Palace. I am just sending you a specimen of our Irish cards, a great contrast to yours! Mamie sends her love, and as I gathered up all that was over of yours to her for myself, perhaps may venture to send you mine in return.

"Please give our very kind remembrances to Dolly. We are looking forward to seeing her with you when you come. Hoping you will have a very happy Christmas,

"I am,
"My dear Princess,
"Yours most sincerely,
"CHARLES CORK."[2]

[1] Ethel Cornwallis-West, aunt of the Authoress, m. in 1875 Warren William Peacocke, of Efford Park, Hampshire, who died in 1877.

[2] Right Rev. Charles Dowse, D.D.

CHAPTER XI

DER ROSENKAVALIER

I

"I wish your Highness a real blessed New Year and a happy future. Have you been able to find out anything about our friends? Heart's innermost greetings.

"365 *s.s. Noyon*, 31/12.

"ADOLPHUS FRIEDRICH."

That was my 1915 New Year's greeting from the last reigning Grand Duke of Mecklenburg-Strelitz. Before the war broke out I knew him well, but not intimately. He knew Shelagh and Bend Or, and had been their guest at Grosvenor House and Cowes; he was my squire at the Earl's Court Tournament in July, 1912. Little did I anticipate that the fierce fires of war would test and forge our friendship and that in darkness, loneliness and isolation he would indeed prove a chivalrous and loyal squire. He had many friends in England and it is to those amongst them who were already killed or missing that he refers in the telegram—one of them being young Percy Lyulph Wyndham, Bend Or's stepbrother. His dear beloved grandmother, then aged ninety-two,[1] and almost the same age as Granny Olivia, was indefatigable until the day of her death in helping to find out about English soldiers missing, wounded, or prisoners of war, her great prestige in Germany and her position in England as aunt of Queen Mary giving her many advantages in carrying out her self-imposed task. Quite literally, she was related to every Royalty in Europe.

[1] *See* p. 32 (footnote).

Then came the Döberitz incident and, as a consequence, my banishment to Bavaria. I asked the Grand Duke to help me, or get his grandmother's permission to allow me to stay for a time in Strelitz.

Then apparently, I suggested that he should visit me and the children and he replied as follows:

"Surely I will manage later to come and see you at Partenkirchen. I had no idea what had happened when I wired; I could not do so now, as I have rather much to do at this time. Please do not think I am a person who leaves his friends in a situation like yours. I am only too glad to be of some little use to you, dear Princess. In about a week or so I hope to see you; I will come quite incognito to Partenkirchen (as I have not yet paid an official visit to the Bavarian Court), travelling as Count Wenden.

"Will there be room for me at your *Landhaus?* I thought of motoring from Munich if I can get a car there. As soon as I can fix a date I shall let you know.

"To answer your question about Strelitz. My house will always be open to you and I will be so glad to have the honour of receiving you.

"With best compliments,

"Yours very sincerely,

"ADOLPHUS FRIEDRICH.

"My grandmother has again made inquiries about our friends; I hope I can bring you good news."

The Grand Duke duly arrived and we all became the greatest friends. Every morning he brought or sent me flowers from King Ferdinand's little shop at the corner of the Ludwigstrasse. The children, to whom he was an angel, at once adored him. I remember his sadness because, even with the aid of his grandmother, he was not able to bring with him the longed-for news as to the whereabouts of relations and near friends; these, at that moment, included Bend Or's uncles, Gerald and Hugh Grosvenor, and many more. During the autumn of 1914 and spring of 1915, so far as reliable information about one's English friends—soldiers or civilians—was concerned, we in Germany lived in utter darkness. Later, principally through the extraordinary activities, so brilliantly organized in Madrid by King Alfonso the Thirteenth, the obtaining of information about the missing, wounded, and prisoners became much easier.

Then, all too soon, duty claiming him, the Grand Duke returned to Strelitz, and, as one does when one is lonely and unhappy, he kept recalling our earlier meetings before the war. As his letters show he was, for a young man, perhaps too much inclined to look backward, and that is always a mistake. But what is one to do when there is no discernible future?

"*February 23rd,* 1915.

"Oh, D.! the world is too vile. I have no words to express my rage! It's too shameful that they *dare* do things like this to you. Hatzfeldt[1] must help you. Do you think they have opened letters of mine to you? With my initials and sealed with my crest—it would be a bit too strong. Do you remember your telegram they sent to be censored before delivering it to me—even though I had arranged it through Z. whom I then thought your best friend? Alas, now I know what kind of person he is, and think it quite likely that he is at the bottom of it all! I hate him; he has behaved too badly to you! Oh, D.! I think of you so much and so sincerely.

"Do you remember it's to-day, one year ago, that I had the great pleasure to arrive at Pless and we had such a nice cosy little dinner in your dear home. I remember every detail. In the morning I had arrived and was shown into your anteroom and after having waited only one minute you came in. I was very shy, but so happy and you so kind; you looked so handsome and I was madly in love. Then you gave me an excellent English breakfast and we went out in the sleigh and had such a happy time.... Oh, D.! it was the time of my life. It was too good and happy *for me* to have the luck to come again.

[1] Hermann, 3rd Prince of Hatzfeldt and 1st Duke of Trachenberg (1848–1900), then Viceroy of Silesia, m. 1872 Countess Nathalie Benckendorff (1854–1900), sister of the last Imperial Russian Ambassador in London.

"But, darling, you must recover happiness and I will do what I can to help you.

"A visit to Switzerland would do you good, you must have a change and see nice people; here, I am sorry to say, they are too vile.

"I perfectly loved your dear long letter, and also thank you so much for the postcard. I had it framed and it stands on my writing-table. My grandmother and I adore the illustrated papers. I'll collect them here and return them later to you. Muriel Münster[1] sent me some yesterday with a nice letter and hopes to come here and see the Grand Duchess. Please do let me know if you go to Berlin before coming to Strelitz. If so, I'll manage to come if possible; I would love it!

"Oh, I am in all my thoughts with you; and I hope everything will be settled to your satisfaction! It must. Please have confidence and hope. God will help you quite surely. Oh, D.! I pray for you.

"Ever yours,
"A. F."

"*Neustrelitz, March 20th,* 1915.

"DEAR PRINCESS DAISY,

"Only to-night I find time to send you a line to thank you ever so much for your dear letters. Since I returned I have been kept so busy; all the time people come, and I had to settle a great deal, often rather important things, and I had no time for myself. . . .

"You know I should love to start a *Lazarettzug* and it would be my greatest pleasure to fulfil your wish, but it is more expensive than I thought—eighty thousand Marks and eight thousand monthly for upkeep. Please don't be X, or think I have forgotten dear 'Sister Daisy,' but I have so many charity things here, and naturally I prefer to help in my own country first of all. I am quite miserable that I must give you this nasty answer; all things that have to do with money are so unpleasant; please, please forgive me!

"I so much hope I may see you next week in Berlin or

[1] *See* p. 117 (footnote).

Potsdam[1] and we will talk it over. When you get this line please send me a wire saying that you are not too X with me; I hate to disappoint you! What can I do to show my great friendship? The first thing you ask me to do for you I refuse. You must think me a perfect brute, and imagine that as soon as I left Partenkirchen I forgot all about the *dear* new friend I was so lucky as to find. All my thoughts are with her and I *pretend* all the time to be with her; in my mind I am living through all the lovely hours I spent with her. It is like a glorious dream and it seems to me a long, long time ago. Here it is so cold and lonely, and I have nothing to do but business all day. I long to come to Berlin next week and have a nice talk with you; please don't be X with poor me. I may not express what I would like to write to you—but you may guess it.

"My cousin[2] gave me no answer yet about my visit to Schwerin, but I suppose he will have time for me next week, and on Saturday or Sunday I shall have the great pleasure of seeing you. Please thank Metternich[3] for his kind note and give him my love as I did not take leave of him.

"I hope dear Lexel and darling Baby are quite well; I love them both and send them all my best love. Did you write to Patsy? I enclose some cuttings and the letters you sent me from Schönborn.[4]

"God bless you,

"Yours, a friend always,

"ADOLPHUS FRIEDRICH."

"*Neustrelitz*, 24 *March*, 1915.

"DEAR PRINCESS DAISY,

"All my thoughts are with you and I pray to God to console you. I only hope you may have better news of Lady

[1] The Grand Duke's Regiment, the 1st Uhlans of the *Gardes du Corps*, had its depot at Potsdam.

[2] Friedrich Franz IV, Grand Duke of Mecklenburg-Schwerin, b. 1882; m. in 1904 Duchess Alexandra of Brunswick-Lüneburg, Princess of Great Britain and of Ireland. Abdicated Nov. 14, 1918. (*See* p. 122.)

[3] *See* p. 133.

[4] Count Clemens Schönborn-Wiesentheid b. 1855, m. 1892 Baroness Maria Rosario von Welczeck, b. 1875. Their d. Maria Katharine (Cissy) m. 1924 Prince Hans Heinrich (Hansel) of Pless. Count Clemens was at the time a member of the *Reichstag* and one of the heads of the German Red Cross.

Olivia FitzPatrick, and that you will have the happiness of seeing her again after this terrible war. I can't tell you how I feel for you, you who love your grandmother as I do mine. And to have no news—all letters taking such a long time.

"Last night I at once told all to my grandmother; she also takes great interest, and remembers quite well Lady Olivia, whom, she tells me, had been very handsome with curls of lovely fair hair. Surely in her youth she was the image of you!

"I hope all the same that you have a little change at Munich and forget all the unpleasant things of life.

"Surely by now you have got my note about the *Lazarett-zug*; I am quite miserable, but it is rather impossible for me to pay the great expense. Please, please do not be too X; we will talk about it once more. I long to see you again; please let me know what time on Sunday the 28th, I may come to see you at Potsdam? I will order Kimbel to go on Monday to Potsdam.

"Your very dear letter gave me such immense pleasure; every detail of what you do interests me so much. I so often think of you and the lovely time we spent together.

"*Au revoir,*

"Yours, a good friend always,
"ADOLPHUS FRIEDRICH."

"*Neustrelitz, March* 25, 1915.

"DEAR PRINCESS DAISY,

"Just now I received the very dear letter you wrote to me yesterday. It is quite shameful that the people in Berlin dare treat *you* like this. I have no words with which to express my rage. I only want to tell you that you have my deepest sympathy, and I feel the harm they do to you as if it were done to me! Oh, these Prussians!

"I may not write what I should like, but you will surely guess. And now you will be escorted or protected, as your family orders, by your H.H.; it is really, beg your pardon, a farce and I cannot help laughing. But I only laugh a moment, for I am nearly in despair. What will become of my visit to you at Potsdam? Will your family sit upon you all the time, and what will H.H. say if I come? I so long to see you and have so much to say that I cannot write! Please send me a line and advise me how I shall behave. . . . The delightful plan of being with you at Partenkirchen for Easter is, I am so sorry to say, impossible. I long to hear your dear voice and will try to ring you up at Munich.

"All my thoughts are with you—could I but be with you in person. Bless you, darling,"

"Ever yours,
"ADOLPHUS FRIEDRICH."

Then, although not really called upon to do so, but deeming it his duty, he insisted on returning to the Western front, having arranged for the government of his little State during his absence. His letters will continue the story:

"*Neustrelitz, March 30th,* 1915.

"DEAR PRINCESS DAISY,

"Only one line, but I must send you this. All the time my thoughts are with you and I have still a big lump in my throat; I am quite miserable to have left you. You have been such a dear and kind friend to me again. I loved the short hours we had together and thank you for all your graciousness. I only wish I could be of some use to you in this terrible time through which you are passing, but I have not the power. I only can be your true friend and pray to God; the Almighty surely will help you. Be strong and wait till after the war, then all will be settled and you must have the happiest life you can think of. All the nice people are on your side and you are such a dear and all will end to your advantage.

"I thank you so much, you have been so nice to me, disappointing you as I had to about the *Lazarett.* You see I have also sometimes intuitions, and I had to advise you not to go there! It almost broke my heart, as I saw your disappointment, but I did it for your sake. If I did not care so much for you, I would never have done it, but in this war time I have the duty as your friend to protect you from all the nasty people who want to do you harm.

"I hope you arrived safely at Partenkirchen at your nice little villa, and will have some peaceful days there. I am so glad I know it and can be in my thoughts all the time with you there and know where you sit and write, and the chair you rest in! Those days in Berlin and Potsdam I was so glad to see and speak to you and it would be ungrateful to say I was not happy, because being with you is happiness for me; but it was not peaceful, you surely felt the same. Please send me soon a line, I long to have news from my darling!

"Ever your ADOLPHUS FRIEDRICH."

I had been to Potsdam for the confirmation of my eldest son, Hansel. It is a very important ceremony in the Lutheran Church. My husband, who was at the Western front as his A.D.C., got special leave from the Emperor to be present; as many relatives and friends as possible came, including the Grand Duke.

If they did not allow me to nurse in a military hospital, I was determined somehow to do so in a *Lazarettzug* or Red Cross train. The Grand Duke, like many of my friends, did not approve of the plan. Looking back now, I dare say they were right but, had I not succeeded in doing so, I should have gone mad—that is, madder even than some dear friends declared me to be!

"*Neustrelitz, April 2nd,* 1915.

"DEAR PRINCESS DAISY,

"Your dear telegram last night gave me great pleasure. I longed to hear from you. I hope you have a pleasant time at Partenkirchen; surely it is more peaceful than in Prussia! Please sometimes think of someone who cares quite terribly for you, who longs to be with you and help you.

"I must tell you about Kimbel, who was here the day before yesterday. We have looked through all his plans and my *Hofmarschall* was delighted and approved everything. In the dining-room he had the very good idea of having a door opened out to the terrace. (This is where Kimbel had thought of the dummy door.) It will be a great improvement. About the panels: I thought of putting them where Kimbel proposed and I hope that you will like it. All the alterations we spoke of together will be carried out. In the *Schloss* I showed Kimbel some furniture and pictures for my new home and he was delighted, especially with some old English coloured prints (not the rather poor set of the *Cries of London* I showed to you). About the 10th of April he will return and then again go and see you.

"I gave your messages to my grandmother and she will send your letter as soon as she writes to Daisy of Sweden.[1] She is quite miserable about all the losses of ships and lives by the U boats. What news have you of your dear grandmother? I so much hope she is better and that you may see her again. She must be a darling, surely, so much like mine.

"All my thoughts with you, d.....t, Bless you,

"ADOLPHUS FRIEDRICH."

"*Neustrelitz, April 7th,* 1915.

"DEAR PRINCESS DAISY,

"Your so very dear letter has given me great pleasure; I read it over and over again and thank you ever so much. You ask why or for what I thanked you last time we met. You say I am happy and you could give me nothing; I had everything I wanted. I beg your pardon, I want a great deal and you have given it to me.

This war makes me almost as unhappy as it does you and I long for someone who understands me. You do, and therefore I love to talk to you about it. You may think my dear grandmother understands me, but only in a way; she has not been to England for so long and her point of view is, I dare say, for our days, sometimes old-fashioned. You know I love her so much; but I can't follow her in all her political feelings.

"I will never forget what you have been to me in this terrible wartime and what we have gone through together. I will not mention what a great part you play in my life, but you will guess! And I can't thank you enough! I miss you so much and would love to be near you. Please often send me a line; I long to have news of you. I hope you are well. Do you get the English papers from Ascher of Berlin? Give my love to the darling Baby, so nice that he thinks of me:

[1] *See* p. 116 (footnote).

I would love to be with you and play the part of Baby's nurse. On the 15th of April I go to the front again. I am quite miserable without someone I care so terribly for. Bless you.

"For ever yours,
"ADOLPHUS FRIEDRICH."

"*Neustrelitz, April* 10th, 1915.

"DEAREST PRINCESS DAISY,

"Only one line to thank you ever so much for your very dear letter of April the 8th. I perfectly loved it, but it made me very, very sorry to think you imagined I was cross with you. Never such a thought entered my mind, and I have not one reason to be! You are such a darling, I care for you so much, please, please never think such a thing of me again. As I wired to you to-day, I have sent three letters to Helene[1] for you, since Potsdam; I hope you have received them. All about Patsy dear, and your grandmother, has pleased me so. I hope God will protect the dear old lady for your sake! Please thank Patsy with my very best love for her kind message; I am so delighted she approves of my being with you at this terrible time. I would love to be more with you, all the time, but alas, I have duties also. On Thursday the 15th I go to France again and my address is: My name and *Stab des IX. Armee Korps;* this will find me at all places at the front. Here it is too lonely, I must leave, as I cannot come and see you again just now; what would all the jealous cats say?

"Kimbel is coming on Monday and I will tell him to wire to you asking what day he may come to you. It would be a great pleasure to me if you would see him and write to me whether you approve of all we settled here. Your good taste I will always follow! And I will always love my little country home because you helped me to make it cosy.

"Bless you. I am miserable to be so far away and lonely, and long to be with someone I care quite terribly for!

"For ever yours,
"A. F."

[1] Fraulein Helene Wagner, Private Secretary to the Authoress, whom she accompanied everywhere throughout the war.

"*Noyon, April 19th,* 1915.

"Dearest,

"I am longing for news, my Darling. Please send me soon a line, it will give me such pleasure.

"What shall I tell you about here? I am living in the same little villa and sitting at the same table and all at Noyon is the same—but I am not the same. My thoughts are somewhere far away in the mountains in Bavaria with a darling friend whom I would love to be with in her little room with its comfy chairs and be cosy and happy together. Alas, it is war-time and I am sitting here far away, and I must say I prefer it to being at Strelitz quite alone. All the dear little things you gave me are here with me; your photo stands on my table, your cushion next to me on my arm-chair. Did Kimbel at last come and see you?

"The other day at St. Quentin I went to a curiosity shop hoping to find something nice for you, but I had no luck; so I only got some furniture for my house, a quite nice Recamier sofa and a writing-table. I also went to see the Museum and was shown some very fine pastel pictures by De La Tour, who was court-painter *sous* Louis XIV.

"I am so delighted to know you will soon be busy at work in a hospital again. You will understand my ending these lines as I have to visit the *Lazarett* here, because last night some of my men were badly wounded. Please think sometimes of someone who cares quite madly for you! Bless you, darling!

"A. F."

"*Noyon, April 20th,* 1915.

"Only one line to tell you that no letters are allowed to be sent from here for about ten days, so please do not think it is my fault that you get no answer. Your letters will be delivered to me. This letter business is a great secret and so I beg you not to mention that I told you.

"Your very dear letter you wrote to me in the night of the 13th to 14th April only reached me yesterday afternoon. Thanks so much, but all the same I am quite miserable about all you write of yourself. I implore you do not think of such terribly sad things. God made you to live and will give you strength and patience to bear up. Please believe me, I implore you! Have courage and wait; times will change and you will surely be happy one day. Could I but be with you and offer you my help and be a good and true friend. Therefore I came to Partenkirchen to be with you and what did the people make of it? I only wanted the best for you, and now they speak nastily about it. Alas, it is because of my position, and it makes me sad for your sake. Darling, be brave, as you have been all your life; after the war you will see all will be settled as you wish.

"Nothing new here to tell you, only that I would love to be with someone very dear and so nice. Good-night, my dear, it is late and I hope to dream of you.

"Ever yours,
"A. F."

"I am motoring to-morrow to see a relation and to post this at Cambrai. Yesterday I posted a letter to you from Chauvy."

"*April 27th,* 1915.

"D. . . . I hope by now I shall be able to send off letters again, and I want so much to give you news and to thank you ever so much for two so very dear letters of April the 19th and 23rd. It makes me quite miserable to know that you are so unhappy and I cannot help you. I implore you, please never think of that little Island you wrote me about again; it would *not* be God's will! God Almighty sends us bad times as well as good ones and we have to face them. Both are very difficult, but it is always for our good. We have to be strong, and one day it will show and will give us eternal happiness. What I say is only quite generally sad; you will surely have better times in a little while. Please have patience. After the war you will show what you have gone through, and all will be on your side and they will look up to you! Never does one misfortune come alone, and I pity you so much about Ruthin and all the trouble your family gives you. Alas, while the war lasts nothing can be done; I hope I may help you one day!

"I had a line from my grandmother saying she had sent you a letter from Daisy of Sweden to your Munich address;

did you receive it? You write about a man who is married to an American; now I perfectly understand. I always *disliked* him and now *hate* him; formerly I had to see him because of the woman I was with at the time. I will tell you more about him and all the story when we meet again. Surely he has spoken about you and me—this creature.

"The books about India are surely in the bookstand again; you remember we looked at them and left them on the sofa in the dining-room. I only hope they are not lost. Your letter of April the 23rd I received last night and I loved it. So glad you had such a long talk to Kimbel. I will do all you wish about the hall, and mahogany will be very nice, so please order Kimbel to do it so. My *Hofmarschall*, von Yorck,[1] is at Strelitz.

"To-day I have got the little anchor I ordered for you and I hope you will like it and that it will remind you of happy hours! Bless you, and please remember someone who adores you is praying for you.

"A."

"The frames have not yet arrived."

"*May* 13*th*, 1915.

"D. . . . Ever so many thanks for your darling letter with the nice photos; what a charming little remembrance of our last meeting. All the time I am thinking of someone I care for with all my heart and would love to be with! Sometimes I pretend and I shut my eyes and sit by someone's side and feel so happy and go on pretending! What a terrible time you must have gone through again. I pity you so much. Surely they flew flags at Pless; here they were quite mad with joy about the *Lusitania*. All the poor innocent lives that were lost; I only hope you had no one you knew on board?

"If war with Italy breaks out this blood-shedding will go on. I do not see myself at Abbazia swimming—with bombs and torpedoes in the Mediterranean. I fear we shall have to give up this plan, but where could one have a peaceful time? What a pity Prince Ludwig Ferdinand of Bavaria cannot have you at his hospital; but what about the other professor you wrote me about, who longed to have you?

[1] Count Ernst von Yorck von Wartenberg (1873–1931).

"I am so happy the little anchor gave you pleasure, I would like to be at its place. As you did not answer my telegram, I trust Baby is quite recovered again; my very best love to him please.

"Here it is quite lovely; all the blossom is out and it is beautiful to ride in the woods. I had the chance to find a quite nice thoroughbred French horse, which had been taken by our men out of a stud not far from Paris, and was now here with a cavalry regiment. Luckily the hospitals here are rather empty, but all the same I go there every day and help as much as I can to give the poor wounded a little pleasure.

"Last week I asked to see the Emperor at the *Hauptquartier* to bring him our Mecklenburg-Strelitz war medal and got an answer from old Plessen (is he staying at your place?) to tell me that he could not see me now. If he is at Pless I hope he has sent you a nice message! But you must be proud, very proud, and wait till they apologize. Could I but help you, but I have nothing to say. It will please you to hear that Fritzi Schwerin asked me about you the other day and I could give him details about all that happened in Berlin; he had great sympathy with you and was quite astonished. I pray all the time that things may change and peace will come. All my best love and many nice things to someone I adore so very much! Bless you.

"A."

"*Neustrelitz, May 29th,* 1915.

"D. . . . What a pleasure for me to hear your dear voice this morning. Alas, it was only by telephone and in German! It would be quite divine if you could come here. I have spoken to my grandmother and the darling naturally will be delighted to see you. I think the best way will be if you would kindly announce yourself at my grandmother's and arrange to come with Muriel Münster. She has already had the idea of coming here and had to give it up because her son returned from the front. So it would be quite natural if you came with her. You know all the people are so narrow-minded here, and I as bachelor have a rather difficult position. If you would come, you would be my guest and I would have the great pleasure of seeing you in my home. But to the people you would come to see my grandmother only, and I would show you about the place. Nothing is really nice this year; the *Parkhaus* and all the details are not as I should like them to be, but I have not yet had time to have things altered as I want. So please do not be too critical. Also, the gardens are not nicely kept; we have had no rain for months and no men to water everything. But all the same I will show you all I want to do some day. You have seen Mecklenburg, so you know what it is like and what can be done.

"Please do come and please ask me to send my motor to Berlin for you; it will be much nicer.

"I should love to go to the sea with you; what a great idea, but don't you know the name of the place? It's surely nice and cosy. I may not write what I think of it and how mad it makes me. Oh D. . . . I adore you and please do come . . . It is really too bad, I am furious! But please have patience, in time all will be, must be, arranged for your sake. About the war I cannot write, it is too bad! Bless you D. . . .

"Ever yours,
"A."

"*Neustrelitz, June 10th,* 1915.

"D.! Only a line to thank you ever so much for two very dear letters—the second one I only got this morning. As my hay fever is quite dreadful, and I am more than imbecile, I can write but nonsense. The heat and dust are too awful here; it is quite impossible for me to stay longer and I am sending my *Hofmarschall* to Bansin—the place you are going to—to get a villa or something for me. It is the only thing to cure me; and I long to bathe in the sea. Naturally I would return to Strelitz when you come there; but it would be perfectly divine if you could come to Bansin now. I have, of course, chosen the place because you have written to me that you had the idea of going there—and I think but of you, D. . . . Please do come—I am quite mad to see you and have so much to tell you that I cannot possibly write. . . .

"I must see you; I am quite mad. Oh D.! do be so kind and come. Ever yours—Bless you—and come.

"A. F."

2

I had been to Fürstenstein to meet Hans and had asked the Grand Duke to come there also. But, as he explained, owing to his dreadful hay fever, he did not dare to motor. We therefore met later at Bansin. My Diary must here take up the story:

"*Bansin, July,* 1915.

"On the 29th I left Fürstenstein at half-past two for Bansin. When I left I was very hoarse and since I have been here I have become worse, though to-night I am much better. My voice absolutely went.

"To-night, as the boys and I were at supper, we saw two figures across the private road, and out I ran to see who they were, when there stood Rosario and Clemens Schönborn. I was so glad to see them! We are all going to bathe to-morrow in the *Familienbad*, as the Schönborn girls and the boy are here too, and Lexel is delighted to have his friend of the same age, little Clement, with him.

"These are the funniest little villas—one for me and three maids and a man-servant, and one for Lexel and Baby Bolko with Fräulein Fenzl and Käthi. I have had some six-foot trees planted up against the palings to hide our villas from the houses opposite, and make it more private. Just a little bit away are the woods, and just across the road is the sea, and we have two private little huts on the beach in one of which Baby sleeps.

"The little Grand Duke of Mecklenburg-Strelitz has really been a darling, going about with a small bottle of something which he drops into his eyes and his nose to relieve his hay fever. When I could not go out nor speak to anyone, he took Lexel out, or played with the Baby, and yesterday he took me and the three boys and the dog *Wolf* out in his motor-car, with the most excellent picnic lunch. He and the boys bathed, but the place they found was miles away from anywhere and very smelly, so I did not join them but rested under the trees with Baby. Then we all four had lunch and played the gramophone. After lunch, while the Grand Duke was dressing, the boys and I climbed trees which, as I had only a bathing suit on (I had intended to bathe), it was very easy to do with no petticoats to get in the way. Now he has gone—but will come back in a day or two, and will take us and the Schönborns out in the car.

"Yesterday a telegram came for me from a Herr von Bülow from Berlin telling me he had a letter to hand me from the Queen of Rumania and asking when he might do so. I wired saying I should be very pleased to see him but, to save him the journey, he could hand the letter to Count Schönborn in the Reichstag or the Hotel Esplanade. I then realized that this might seem rude as, if a Queen sends a letter by a special messenger, one cannot refuse to receive the gentleman to whom she entrusts it. So I sent a second wire saying I should be pleased to see him here on Friday as he proposed, and asking him to let me know the time. He comes to-morrow at four. The little Grand Duke made me do this, and he sent the wire off for me.

"To-night I asked Count Z. if he would be present when the gentleman came as, somehow, since all that has happened to me in Berlin, I trust no one; but he said it was not necessary. So then I asked Rosario Schönborn if she would come and she agreed. She told me that this Herr von Bülow is supposed to be the best-looking man in Germany, and was sent to Rumania on purpose to make Germany loved by Rumania, and to become, if possible, a friend of the Queen and influence her in favour of Germany, and that he had succeeded. . . . I said to Rosario: 'How on earth do you know, and, anyway, what difference does it make to me?' and we both laughed.

"So I shall see Herr von Bülow to-morrow by myself. I do not believe that the politics of Rumania are governed by the good looks of any single German. Queen Marie of Rumania is far too intelligent not to know how to influence her people as she thinks best, and far too strong-minded and clear-headed a woman to be misled by such childish diplomacy.

"All the same, if this Herr von Bülow is nice I shall most certainly propose to him to come back to Bansin and stay here and be with all of us to bathe with us and have picnics and so on. One thing I must, however, say. Quite naturally —but very wrongly—he sent that telegram from Berlin telling me he had a letter from the Queen of Rumania, when he had better have let me know by post, as Germany feels that Rumania is still not certain what attitude to take in this war, and that a telegram like that should have been sent *to me* from Berlin will again upset the Germans and confirm their uneasy opinion of myself. I am really almost getting quite proud of the danger I seem to be to this war-demented country.

"My Diary will perhaps some day prove amusing to read, and I will put in later what Herr von Bülow tells me.[1]

"*Noyon, October 17th*, 1915.

"D.D.D. I hope you are in better spirits. Please don't think all the time of failure. In time changes *will* and *must* come for you; do be strong and face the world as you have done so bravely up till now.

"Through Major von Gosler I have had the pleasure of hearing about you; he was delighted with his stay at Salzbrunn, and all he was so kindly allowed to see. I have to thank you so very much for all the trouble you gave yourself with Kimbel, and for ordering the furniture for my Chinese room. As, by your wish, it is to be a 'surprise' for me; he was not allowed to tell me much, but by what I do know, it will be a great success. I knew it at once; because I know your extremely good taste.

"Oh D. . . . do come soon to Strelitz; the Hohenlohes[2] will be there too, and you will, I hope, have a few nice days. Think only of agreeable things, and feel English with my grandmother!

"I am going to leave Noyon for good; my Army Corps has already gone south, somewhere near the Champagne. But everything is so secret that I do not know for sure. The end of this month I hope to return. I have to stay some days in Berlin to see my dentist, and if by any chance I could have the pleasure of meeting you I would arrange it. I also could go to Strelitz at once, and from there could come over to Bansin for a few days. Please think it over. My address at present is: *Feldpoststation* 39, 15. *Landwehr Div.*

"My visit to Lille and Ostend was rather interesting. At Ostend I found a great difference! The coast was quite

[1] *See Daisy Princess of Pless*, p. 358, London, John Murray, 1928.

[2] Prince Gottfried and the Archduchess Henriette, *see* p. 62 (footnote).

altered by the fortifications all over the place. I sent a love message over to England from you on seeing the sea that I longed to cross. Please keep this to yourself; if they knew they would kill me at once!

"Eitel Fritz of Prussia has come here with his troops last night. He came and called on me; I was terrified to see how fat he has become; but he was very nice and will dine with me to-morrow night. I have only spoken a few words to him, so I could not begin about you, but hope to do so then.

"Please kindly send me soon one line; I long to have news. I have had none since I wrote last.

"Bless you, and do think of one who is so grateful to have your cross and anchor to protect him from all evil.

"Yours,
"A. F."

"*Neustrelitz, Dec. 15th,* 1915.

"D....A D.....g D...y. Oh! Oh! Oh! I loved your darling letter and thank you a thousand times. Please do take care of yourself and come home quite safe. I am so troubled to know that you are travelling in a *Lazarettzug;* it is really too much for you; do think of your so precious life, and of poor us who love and worship you. I send this short line to Helene and hope to get news as soon as you have got back safely to Partenkirchen. To-morrow morning I leave for the front where I shall be on Friday night. My address is *Armee Oberkommando,* 3. *Armee.*

"Yesterday afternoon *Schwester* Martha came to see me with a message from your brother-in-law, Fritz; she was sent to Germany from Constantinople to beg for Christmas gifts for his *Lazarett*, and hopes to be back there with them in good time. She gave a very interesting description of all she had gone through; it is very hard work there; she is full of admiration for the Count. It has taken her eleven days to travel to Berlin. She also went to Potsdam to see the Duchess of P.[1]

"Through your letter to my grandmother I hear to my surprise that you only left on Monday; in my thoughts I was

[1] Countess Mathilde of Dohna-Schlobitten, b. 1861, m. 1886, as his second wife, Hans Heinrich XI, Duke and Prince of Pless, father-in-law of the Authoress.

already for days travelling with you to Servia! I only hope you will be back in time for Christmas to be with your dear children. I had a letter from each of them thanking me for a trifle I had sent them; they wrote so sweetly and nicely to me, and are longing to have you back.

"It is so late and I have still to see if all is ready for my journey. All the time my thoughts will be with you, and I will pray for you that better times may come soon. You shall and must be happy once again! Oh! D...y. What may I do for you? Please do think of someone who adores you. Bless you.

"Ever yours,
"A. F."

"*Vouziers, A.O.K.3.*
"*Dec. 19th,* 1915.

"At the moment I was leaving Strelitz I had the great pleasure of receiving your very dear letter from Görlitz. It was so good of you to send me the little card with the green fir trees; it will remind me of someone I care so much for and so often think of. At Xmas I will put it on my table and think of that person and the good times I spent with her in the green woods. It seems to me ages ago, but I *do* remember everything. My thoughts will be with you in the little cosy room with the arm-chairs on Xmas Eve. I hope so much that you will be there in time to be with your dear children. They are so fond of you and wrote so nicely to me the other day that they do await you.

"I only hope nothing happened to you in Servia and that you are not too fatigued; it's really too hard work for you. In Berlin the other day I saw my sister Charlotte[1] with her eldest boy; they are not coming to Partenkirchen as the doctor does not want to send him into the mountains; but L. H. is at the Hotel Gibson—it won't please you much! One more to watch you! Oh! D.... what shall I do. I can't come there; they would only talk about it again. It is such a bore! Oh! why are they all so jealous and nasty?

"Before leaving Berlin I dined with the Gottfried

[1] The Grand Duke's second sister, b. 1880, m. in 1899 the Crown Prince Danilo of Montenegro (1871–1900).

Hohenlohes. Like the last time, someone was missing so much D.... Oh, I do long so intensely to hold and kiss someone's hand!

"Here it is not nice; the poor troops have to suffer a great deal of bad weather, wet trenches and much artillery fire. Vouziers is a very dirty little place with no roads on which to ride. There are many hospitals; I'll go to them to-morrow.

"I often read your books and think of someone very, very dear.

"Please send me soon a line; I long for news. My very best wishes for Xmas to you and your children. God bless you.

"Ever and ever yours,
"A. F."

"*Vouziers, midnight, Dec. 30th,* 1915.

"Thank God you have returned safely! Oh! D...y, I was so sad all over Christmas, as I didn't know where my thoughts could find you. Now I can be with you; alas, but in thoughts, in your cosy little room! Why can't you sleep? Please do think of your precious health and don't overwork yourself. Is good Seidel there and does he take care of you? Do tell him from me to give you the food you like and have it cut before it is put on your plate. I would love to be there and be of use! Your dear note made me so happy; but I would wish you could be happy too. Thank goodness you are not going to Konstantinople; I was so troubled lest you should; I send you the cutting I saw in the paper. I hope Servia will be safer and more interesting too.

"It is really too kind and good of you to send me the three-leaved shamrock; it will have great value for me, as it has belonged to you, and come from dear Patsy's garden; a thousand thanks.

"Here, or better to say at Charleville, I went over the French shops and found again some perfume—it's where the *Hauptquartier* is—I hope you will kindly accept it. I must laugh sometimes when I remember the strange things like soap or biscuits which I have had the pleasure to offer you; it is war-time! It's a quite terrible time, but all the same I am so thankful that I found a dear darling friend with a golden heart! D.....t, all my very best wishes for 1916; may it be more happy than the last one. We will hope that it brings peace and that you will see Patsy again! Please give her my very best love in your next letter. Had you good news lately? At midnight our thoughts will unite! God bless you D.....t

"Ever ever,
"A. F."

"Here nothing happens that might interest you; it's rather tiresome as the front line trenches are far away; so I see little of the troops. It's much like the *Hauptquartier!* Sometimes I see the young Crown Prince of Saxony; quite a charming boy."[1]

"*January 7th*, 1916.

"Oh, D... I thought *so much* of someone at New Year and I hope our thoughts met and that my very best wishes for 1916 arrived in time.

"I have had quite enough of my stay at Vouziers and I will return to Strelitz on the 11th. There is nothing much for me to do or see here; it is too far back and too much like a tiresome *Hauptquartier*. This morning I went to see a *Lazarettzug* and the way they bring the wounded in. All the time I thought of '*Schwester* Mary Theresa.' Here they had no nurses; but it was only one-third of the train. Will there be a chance to see you? Please do be so kind and arrange it; I would love it. On Wednesday the 12th I am in Berlin, but only for the day, and leave in the evening for Strelitz; but later I could return any day or time you would order me. I now stay at the Adlon; it is much nicer as all my friends are there! (I said nothing about your coming to that hotel.) Charlotte Reuss[2] and the Grand Duke of Schwerin go there often.

"Once I got some English papers in which I read about Pietri's[3] funeral; what a loss for the Empress. All the other

[1] Georg, b. 1893, served in the Cavalry of the *Gardes du Corps*; now a member of the Society of Jesus.

[2] W. of Heinrich XVIII. Prince Reuss (1847–1911) and her brother the then reigning Grand Duke (*see* p. 122 *ante*).

[3] Franceschino Pietri, a Corsican, the devoted servant of Napoleon III, he continued faithfully to serve the exiled Empress Eugénie until his death at Farnborough Hill, Hampshire, in 1915, at the age of eighty-two.

news was so sad also! This war is too terrible; nothing but killing! All think it can last for ages.

"I hope you have had good news of Count Fritz Hochberg; he is a marvel; *Schwester* Martha told me all about him. What is dear Patsy doing? And what is her darling daughter doing? I do long to be with her and tell her so many nice things I can't write! Oh! D... Bless you, and take care of yourself for all of us who worship you!

"A."

"*Neustrelitz, Dec. 4th,* 1916.
"*Monday night.*

"It seems to me ages since I have written. Please don't be cross! I am so very depressed because of my darling Granny and am not in the mood to do anything. But I must send you one line to thank you for all the kind words you sent me. I know that all your sympathy is with us, and also your thoughts. But by the wire you sent me to-day I see you do not realize the hopeless state the poor darling G.D. is in. Next Thursday she will have been four weeks in bed without any food, but some wine and water. Last Tuesday, the 28th of November, was the last time she spoke to us. Since that time she is sleeping—the doctor having given her injections—so that she has no pains. The heart is working quite strongly. She told us last Tuesday that she was feeling her end, and was only hoping that God would take her without suffering a long time.

"I can't tell you what it is to me, watching the most dear Granny, and not able to help her. In my thoughts I already imagine what my life will be without her; but all the same I pray to God that the Almighty would kindly deliver her from her pain.

"My thoughts are so very often at Berchtesgaden with someone so dear! I have not time to write more; I have to go to see the darling Granny who is now lying quite peacefully. Your brother-in-law Fritz will tell you all about here and the *Parkhaus*. I did enjoy his visit so much. I went to see him at the Sanatorium the other day in Berlin. Did he tell you about his operation? luckily all went off so well.

"The Almighty also has taken notice of my prayers; I am so glad your dear father is better. Have you had news again? All my thoughts are with someone so dear.

"Ever yours,
"A. F."

"*Heringsdorf, June 27th,* 1917.

"DEAR PRINCESS DAISY,

"So many thanks for your very kind letter; all you said gave me great pleasure and you must know that my thoughts are so much with Patsy's dear daughter!

"I haven't written you a line for ages, but had so much to do, and felt so very bad with hay fever for the past three weeks. It began again at Dresden, where I went to settle about my darling Granny's old home, and to say where all the dear things had to go. With my sister's help all was arranged, and we shall sell the place later on. I had hoped to go there earlier, but my cousin from Schwerin kindly offered to come to Strelitz for my birthday, and so I had to stay, and also to ask my sister Marie to come with her husband, Julius Lippe. While she was here I took the opportunity of arranging all kinds of old things of my Granny's. Mostly things belonging to her wardrobe, and other most interesting old clothes of the family. Her former maid took care of them, and was waiting all the time to show us the things and then to leave. So I had to stay and help my sister and mother.[1] The heat was quite terrible and I suffered agony with my hay fever.

"Last Saturday night I was at last free to motor here, and the first letter I write is naturally to Patsy's daughter. I only recover quite slowly and try to take a kind of rest-cure. Early in the morning I go for a ride followed by a very refreshing sea-bath. All the day I stay indoors, taking a short walk after dinner. Up till now I saw no one, and don't want to. The only person I have met is Princess Gottfried Hohenlohe; she had been here for some time and is leaving; the children are staying on. I hope my sister is coming next month with all her family to Heringsdorf, but I must first discover if it is possible to find lodging and food. So you see

[1] Princess Elisabeth of Anhalt b. 1857, m. in 1877 Adolf Friedrich V, Grand Duke of Mecklenburg-Strelitz (1848–1914); the writer of these letters was their only son.

I am not fit to see a dear guest! I only hope you will have a peaceful time and good rest at Nauheim. Will Frau Eiselz be with you? Surely no one thought of insulting you at Fürstenstein or dared to do so. I have no words for your uncle's letter! Count Dankelman's was such a gentleman-like one.

"... I am so glad Hansel is doing so well; I had that impression from the beginning. In quiet minutes I often find my thoughts far away in the beloved country Patsy's daughter was born in; I think of the best time I ever had in my life and the dearest friends I ever made. I shall never forget the delicious time at Ruthin with your most kind parents. I hope you had news of your father's health lately; as I pray daily for Patsy's daughter, I also pray that she may see her parents, both strong and well, after the war. But alas! I have the feeling—as you had since the beginning—that the war will last for ages yet.

"And the day after to-morrow is your birthday. I know you don't like me to take much notice of it; but I may send you all my best wishes? May the Almighty protect you and help you in all you do. Please don't forget a friend; his grateful thoughts are with you all the time. I wonder if you have left for Nauheim or where you will be on that day. I thought your birthday was to-morrow, but you say it isn't.

"I brought all kinds of interesting old letters and books of my darling Granny here, and love to read them; everything reminds me of her and only now I see and read lots of most interesting and historical affairs I never heard of. By this post I send you the last three *Vogues* and would much like to see some of the dear English picture papers. Would it give you much trouble to send me some? My very best wishes once more. My love to Baby and Lexel and Patsy's daughter.

"Ever yours,

"A. F."

In July I lost my beloved father. One of the most terrible things about the war was that it prevented us being with those we loved when they were at the point of death. There were so many thousands of unsaid good-byes. One of the results of the death of Poppets was that Ruthin was sold.

I hated this. It made me feel as if my childhood and girlhood were being destroyed as high explosives uprooted great masses of soil on the Western front. With this feeling, with my grief, and with little Patsy's tragic loss the Grand Duke was at one. His own grief was only six months old:

"*Heringsdorf, Aug. 9th,* 1917.

"What pleasure to get news from someone from whom I longed to hear so very much. I got your most kind letter this moment and do hasten to send you a line at once. I sent my last letter to Fürstenstein, I don't know if you ever got it. So I will send this to Helene, as I have not your address in Nauheim. My thoughts have been with you all the time and I do hope you have had a most pleasing stay with your dear friends in Austria. Thank you once more for your so very kind long letter; it made me quite home-sick to get an English one, and all you said reminded me so much of times long ago; times of peace at Ruthin and times so peaceful at Partenkirchen. What nice little jokes we had and what fun on the bob sleigh with Lexel—quite like children. It makes me quite miserable to think that the lovely place of your childhood has to be sold; can nothing be done? I do hope dear Patsy is quite well, do kindly remember me to her; I do pity her so much. All that is going on in your country makes me feel very sad. In my dreams I am so often there with all my relations and friends, quite as in bygone happy times; also I dream so much of Patsy's daughter, and we discuss together all things of interest; then I find me at Ruthin in the lovely garden, pushing her about in an arm-chair. Do you remember that night—what fun we had?

"It is quite terrible to have no darling Granny; I long to talk to her and to discuss politics, and all those I love. Here I have lots of her interesting old letters and political things and for hours and hours I sit and study them. I then forget everything about myself and live in olden times. All I find is interesting—things she once told me about her youth, and later. But then my thoughts return, and I find I am sitting here at Heringsdorf quite alone in this terrible war. And then I think so much of last year with dear little Baby here, his accident to his poor little arm, and your dear visit with Lexel.

It was about just now that you were here. Schönborn came, and you sang to us!

"So you have been at Nymphenburg again and our dear arm-chairs are there; I so often think of them, so cosy and so nice it was. I had to go to Buchenhof the other day; a Countess Roedern who was staying there this year asked me. It all reminded me so much of times long ago, so cosy and so nice!

"Please forgive. I have quite forgotten to thank you for having ordered them to send me the quite lovely lace *Bettlaken* for my lady guests. I love them—so very *distingués* and quite what I like. They didn't send me the bill. I also loved the English papers; I will return them later, not to Nauheim. They sent me no more *Vogues;* would you like them? If so I will again have them sent direct from the shop.

"I so much hope the cure at Nauheim will do you good and that I shall have the pleasure of seeing you once when you return to Berlin. . . . Here I sit quite lonely. Please remember that someone is praying for you!

"Ever yours,
"A. F."

"*Neustrelitz, January 10th,* 1918.

"Dear Princess Daisy,

"Your very kind letter gave me the greatest pleasure and I have to thank you *ever so much* for your Christmas gift. It is exactly what I like and it will surely bring me luck; it arrived here (sent by Helene) on Christmas Day and I so often open it and think of 'someone.' . . .

"Your singing to the wounded on Christmas must have been touching! My mother and I went to all the hospitals here; the wounded are always so grateful, and so pleased with the little presents. It is so very difficult to find suitable gifts now. As it was my first Christmas here without my darling Granny it was very painful. I am so grateful that you mention her in every letter; she was a darling! All the time I am arranging my *Parkhaus*. I have had old coloured prints framed, some of them English, and hung them in the passages. All the furniture Kimbel arranged under your direction in the hall has naturally *not* been changed. In all I do to the house I think of her—what would She say—would She like it?

And one day I *do hope* she'll come and stay there. Oh! all my thoughts are with her and I pray for her daily. Better times will come and she'll see Patsy, Ruthin and all the dear places and friends.

"Just the same,
"A. F."

An extract from my Diary must tell of the tragic ending. Even now, after the lapse of years, I ask why, oh why? On reflection, I find it curious that during the war, out of the depth of my depression, I more than once spoke or wrote to the Grand Duke about suicide, while he never once mentioned the subject. Of course he *may* not have taken his own life; all one can say is that the circumstances pointed that way.

All sorts of quite trivial incidents united us, as the smaller things of life do unite those who are true friends. And how, even during the war, we could laugh together when we recalled some of them. We loved to laugh over such occasions as that on which he, Lexel, Lexel's tutor and I motored from Partenkirchen to Innsbruck to try to buy some nice pieces of old furniture for his new *Parkhaus*. We wanted to go to church on Sunday morning as there was some special music. They got to know of this and spread red velvet over a reserved pew for us. As we came out a woman in the crowd that had gathered exclaimed: "And that is the Grand Duchess." I stopped and, turning to her, said: "No; it is not. I am the Princess of Pless, this is my son, and this gentleman is his tutor."

And my friend was everlastingly doing such kind and charming things. He helped my Lace School in Silesia by purchasing lace-trimmed sheets for his women guests at Strelitz such as he had seen at Pless. We used to talk about London, and Queen Mary and King George the Fifth, and Cowes. He particularly liked recalling his visit to Ruthin; I had got Patsy to invite the Grand Duke Michael and Sophy and their two attractive girls Nada[1] and Zia, to meet him,

[1] Countess Nadejda Torby m. in 1916 Prince George, e.s. of Admiral of the Fleet Prince Louis of Battenberg (later 1st Marquess of Milford Haven) and H.G.D.H. Princess Victoria of Hesse and the Rhine, sister of the late Princess Henry of Prussia.

hoping that one of them would fall in love with and marry him. When I confessed this plot to him one day at Partenkirchen he said it would have been impossible as the marriages of their father and grandfather[1] were both morganatic. Another delightful recollection was his first visit to Fürstenstein three years before the war. Shelagh, Muriel Wilson, Bee Pembroke, Muriel Beckett and several other delightful women were there, and we had a marvellous time. . . . But to come to my Diary:

"*Reserve Hospital Brcko,*
"*Deutche Feldpost* 25, *Belgrad,*
"*March,* 1918.

"The little Grand Duke has passed to God by his own hand. He who gave me everything he could that I wanted—little things which were useful in the *Lazarett* train, a paper-knife for my table here, a blotting-book which I use now—are all, all from him, and now even *he* has gone. I have no one left. They wanted me to find him a wife. I try to do so, and she was nice, and had even been to Newlands to little Mother. I thought *this* would please him—to think of this—but—somehow—what can I say, what can I think, except of the great masses of flowers he used to send me to Partenkirchen three winters ago. Afterwards he came there himself, and then later to Berchtesgaden. Well—what I think I will not say. What is the use?

"I can see myself now in Partenkirchen in bed and the nice housemaid Anna coming in with a great bunch of red roses, saying: '*Seine Königliche Hoheit schicken Durchlaucht diese Blumen.*'[2] *Rosenkavalier* we used to call him, and his Granny loved me. Somehow it seems incredible that, in spite of everything, in spite of all my sorrow and all the woes I think of, my wretched face remains more or less the same. I don't look old, and no one guesses how old I am—in fact, upon my

[1] Their grandfather the Grand Duke Michael, son of Tsar Nicholas I m. in 1857 Cecile, d. of Leopold Grand Duke of Baden; this marriage was therefore not morganatic. Their father the Grand Duke Michael Michailovitch m. morganatically, in 1891, Countess Sophie Meremberg.

[2] His Royal Highness sends your Highness these flowers.

word at the present moment I don't know it myself. I see in the papers how old he was—just over forty—I thought he was at the most thirty."

Perhaps I saw, still see, the *Rosenkavalier* through rose-coloured spectacles. Then let Fräulein Staehle, Bolko's excellent and very intelligent governess, speak of him. She knew him well, yet saw him objectively, as the difference in their respective positions necessitated:

"*Partenkirchen, Feb. 26th,* '18.

"MADAME,

"Your Highness cannot imagine how grieved I was when I read in yesterday's paper about the death of His Royal Highness the Grand Duke of Mecklenburg-Strelitz.

"My very first thoughts went to Your Highness. Why is Fate so unkind to take away from you within but a few months the beloved father and a dear friend?

"Life is so cold, so empty without a friendly hand stretched out to help one along—how very sad to see one after another vanish. The only consoling thought in this sadness is the belief that we shall meet again with those we cared for. The souls will meet in higher spheres and nobler surroundings and will partake of joys and delights far greater than ever in this life. I feel sure of it, don't you?

"Your Highness will feel so weary, life will seem such a burden; I pray to God that He may send you strength and courage—always strength and courage, although it often seems hard to know where to take it from.

"Bolko is very well and quite pleased to be here; we like our tiny, weeny little house and feel cosy in it. To-day the weather has been very fine, but there is a thick mud on the roads as it keeps on snowing and thawing.

"Baby wishes me to send Your Highness his most affectionate kisses and a lot of love.

"With all my heartiest thoughts I beg to remain,

"Your Highness's most respectfully

"OCTAVIE STAEHLE."

"My wretched face remains the same. . . . I don't look old. . . ."

That was seventeen years ago. Now, as I recall it all, I think of Richard Strauss's *Rosenkavalier*. The Princess sings of her vanished youth and beauty, and wonders how she can have grown old, wonders how the young *Rosenkavalier* can love her. In the German, Hofmannsthal's libretto is beautiful; the English translation is awful and I doubt if I can amend it—but will try:

"Can it be . . . that I am that young girl of long ago . . . and that I shall be called 'ere long the old Princess . . . there goes the old Princess Theresa . . . how did it come to pass . . . for I am I and never change. . . ."

Nevertheless the music paints with ravishing melancholy all that a woman feels when youth has fled and beauty swiftly follows. . . .

If our dear *Rosenkavalier* remembers he thinks of me as, like himself: still young. Still beautiful.

My boys loved him and called him "Uncle Strelitz." And he loved them. We shall all meet again. *Auf Wiedersehen . . . Rosenkavalier*. . . .

CHAPTER XII

INTERROGATIONS?

I

EVEN this chapter heading is followed by a note of interrogation. Well, why not; after all, what is life but one long—or short—note of interrogation? An interrogation to which so many offer their own answer, answers which are for the most part merely evasions of one sort or another.

Poring over my old Diary and looking through the hundreds of letters that I have preserved I am struck by the mass of glittering names and their relative insignificance. This sets me wondering, and makes me ask myself if I have ever known any truly great men, or have I met only eminent personages? Because one can *know* a great man or a great woman; it is difficult, almost impossible, to know those who are merely eminent. That is because mountain streams are crystal clear, whereas valley rivulets are invariably muddy. They are too far from their source, or they rise at too low a level.

Have I had any great contemporaries? That is using the word exactly as meaning people of approximately my own age. Without knowing it I may have had; because sometimes greatness is only discernible after it has vanished. I can only say that I never met any men or women to whom I would unhesitatingly, and without any qualification, concede the adjective great.

In England, Shaftesbury, Gladstone, Salisbury, Dufferin, Florence Nightingale, Elizabeth Barrett Browning, George Eliot, the Brontës, the Baroness Burdett-Coutts, General and Mrs. Booth, the Great Queen herself, were all really long before my time. Balfour, it is true, was alive throughout my active life, but then he was posing as a politician and was, or so I considered, an inept one, whereas his true elements of greatness were as a philosopher and writer, and these were hidden from me. Both Lord Rosebery and George Wyndham undoubtedly possessed an element of greatness, perhaps even of genius, but in each of them it was stultified by some unseen inner weakness that never showed on the surface. Campbell-Bannerman and William Harcourt were merely successful (and lucky) politicians. Little Bonar Law had, I think, a strain of greatness, as had both Milner and Curzon. There was Alfred Gilbert the sculptor; and they tell me that greatness may be ascribed to composers such as Elgar, Delius, Vaughan Williams and Bax; I don't know enough about music to say.

When I first arrived in Germany, Wagner was but lately dead; Bismarck had left the stage; the Emperor Franz Joseph, who undoubtedly had an element of greatness, reigned in Vienna, but he was the embodiment of the eighteenth century, and had nothing to do with the nineteenth. Tolstoy was still alive, but by the time I had become conscious of him he had largely forsaken creative work for propaganda and pamphleteering. Of the Emperor Friedrich I do not know enough to speak, nor was he really tested, but I am convinced that the Empress Friedrich had in her certain elements of true greatness, although fate denied her opportunity. The very fierceness of the venom with which Bismarck pursued her is to me proof that he recognized her essential qualities and feared them. It was not given to any other woman in history to make the Iron Chancellor put on all his armour and unsheathe his sword. And in those days it was all the more wonderful because in Germany women were absolute nonentities, to be seen, but never heard. (As a matter of fact one could hardly help looking at them, they were, for the most part, so massive, so annoyingly meek, and so dowdily dressed.)

Great soldiers? I don't think there were any, although there were some successful Victorian ones such as Wolseley and Roberts. But, after all, their battles were won on a small stage and, comparatively speaking, were but modest. Of the soldiers of the Great War it is too early to speak, although the position accorded to Foch would seem to be unassailable. Kitchener, like Jack Cowans, was a great administrator, not a soldier. As someone wittily said of dear Jack, he never in his life saw a shot fired in anger—except perhaps by an angry husband!

During my time there were, of course, a great many successful business men flourishing in both Germany and England, but the circumstances of my life and surroundings gave me but few opportunities of meeting them. The only two prominent ones I really knew were Albert Ballin and Ernest Cassel; both Jews and both Germans; neither aroused my admiration. I met many members of the Rothschild family, but only socially and at infrequent intervals.

I do not of course forget the magnificent work of great scientists such as Simpson or Pasteur. Of inventors I do not speak for two reasons: First of all I am not competent to judge them; secondly, it is far too early to say how far-reaching their discoveries are. It is certainly much too soon to decide how many modern inventions are a blessing, how many a curse. I am not, for instance, one of those who think that everything can be measured in terms of speed and movement.

So far, aeroplanes have been employed mostly as artificial vultures . . . birds of prey. Vultures are, I am told, amongst the swiftest of birds and have been scouring the Eastern heavens for untold generations; yet they remain what they were at the beginning—mere birds of prey. It is not speed itself that is significant, but the purposes for which it is employed. Therefore such men as Edison and Marconi leave me cold. The most I can concede to them is to suspend judgment. A great deal of interested nonsense is talked about the value of rapid means of communication between the various parts of the Empire and the different nations of the world. We are so intent on the means, so childishly obsessed by novelty, that we do not pause to envisage the end. Rapidity of intercourse is clearly just as liable to destroy, as it is to promote, concord. If it were not so the world would by now be one great brotherhood instead of being, as it is, more filled with hatred, jealousy and all uncharitableness—spiritual, political and economic—than ever it was. One has only to think for five minutes of the inside history of one's own family, or any other family we know, to realize that personal proximity and rapidity and frequency of intercourse can be very potent and lasting sources of friction, anger, and even hatred. Nowadays politicians rush to the telegraph, the microphone and the newspaper and, throughout my whole life, it has been my experience that when they do so they are unlikely to be fulfilling the Anglican Prayer Book injunction to seek peace and ensue it.

That silly democratic dogma labelled "open diplomacy" has done much mischief and, if persisted in, will do much more. Invented by newspapers for their own ends it did a great deal to ruin the relationships between Great Britain and Ireland, and by its continued practice politicians everywhere keep re-opening closed sores. I suppose the telegram of the Emperor Wilhelm the Second to Kruger, his famous *Daily Telegraph* interview, and his many flamboyant and provocative speeches might all be described as "open diplomacy." If so, give me the old-fashioned, slow and premeditated variety.

But (as usual) I have wandered away from my subject.

It seems to me that the chief difference between earlier generations and my own is that the Victorian age had many great men; mine many eminent ones. There is, it would almost seem, a bigger and more unbridgable gap between true greatness and eminence than there is between man and the higher apes. The whole tendency of modern life and modern education appears to be to raise the general level somewhat, and to reduce, if not indeed eliminate, the possibilities of producing undeniable greatness. As an unrepentant individualist, one who sees all progress as the result of the lives of a few outstandingly illustrious men and women, such a conclusion is melancholy. Modern nonsense about giving every budding genius its chance is absurd. Genius does not need chances; it makes them. Speaking to a lady who had mentioned the word opportunity, Napoleon said: "Madame, I am opportunity." And he was. A good deal of political chit-chat about educational facilities for the many is also nonsense. If it were true, look at the hordes of geniuses Oxford and Cambridge alone would have turned out during the past five hundred years. Christ was not a university man. Let us recall at random some others who were not at universities. Mohammed, Buddha, Saint Paul, Saint Augustine, Santa Teresa, Saint Francis, John Bunyan, Abraham Lincoln, Emerson, Carlyle, Cobbett, Joseph Arch, George Borrow, H. M. Stanley, Dr. Barnardo, William and Catherine Booth, Florence Nightingale, George Eliot, the Brontës, Queen Victoria—thousands of others—some humbly born, some highly, some educated, some not at all, but none of them, so far as I can remember, graduates of a university. Self-made men and women in the only true and valid sense. Moreover, to come to our own day: Clemenceau, Lenin, Pilsudski, Mustapha Kemel, Masaryk, Benes, Roosevelt, Lloyd George, Mussolini and Hitler—although one or two of them were at a university—none of them could be described as typical products of Eton and Oxford.

One must ask oneself why our period is sterile compared with the immediate historic past? Perhaps it is impertinent for me to seek to try and answer it. I do not know enough. But is not the child with the string in its hand justified in trying to untie the knot? Of course the child (that's me) is not a great historian or philosopher, made with large discourse—looking before and after. But, it really had the string in its hand and has even seen some of the knots being made!

My own opinion then, for what it is worth, is that my contemporaries were without vision, as are their children after them. The dust of material success blinded them; the unabated noise of pleasure and enjoyment (as it always does) dulled their hearing; so many roads were open to them that they continuously lost their way. They had no sense of direction, no beliefs, no ideals, no shining hope of a promised land. They achieved and were satisfied; and achievement that satisfies is death.

2

The Victorians—the generations immediately preceding my own—may have been absurd and misguided in many ways; at least they had beliefs, and held fast to what they did believe. Surely any anchor is better than eternal drift.

And were their beliefs so very absurd?

Let us look cursorily at what some of them were. They believed in the Church of England, in public morality, in reticence, in abstract virtue, in respectability, in snobbishness, in the British Constitution (whatever that may be), in getting on, in wearing a great deal of clothing, in vintage port, in comfort, in masses and masses of good substantial food, in Mrs. Grundy, in large Academy pictures in rich gold frames, in massive ornate expensive mahogany furniture, in Tate and Brady, Barnum and Bailey, and Moody and Sankey. They believed in Great Exhibitions, the divine mission of the English to turn black people into a nice light amber and brown, and yellow people into a genteel saffron. They foresaw the whole world as moderate Christians, correctly mannered, prolific, law-abiding and—of course at a respectful distance—British.

They knew Germany existed because the Emperor Wilhelm the Second was always tactlessly, indeed almost truculently, reminding them of the fact; he was even beginning to build ships, which occupation, by divine ordinance, had been the sole prerogative of the English people almost since the days of Noah. There was most certainly, somewhere about, a place called Russia. Had not one of Queen Victoria's granddaughters married its Emperor? Therefore it must exist. It was "great," and "white," and (happily) very far away.

Without question, there was always France, the ancient enemy, but the Almighty (who had a strange but undoubted penchant for the English people) had, geographically speaking, been somewhat tactless in placing it so near to the shores of England. On the other hand He had perhaps to some extent redeemed Himself by placing the United States, that errant daughter, quite comfortably far away. The Victorians never cared to be reminded of the existence of offspring that had "gone astray"! Not only had He done this for England but He had thoughtfully provided large tracts of country, long called the Plantations, to which unsatisfactory sons (and daughters-in-law) could be shipped and safely tethered there with a rope known as a Remittance.

There were other places.

There was Africa where ivory, elephants, Lobengulas, and, towards the end, President Kruger, Cecil Rhodes, and Jameson went on raids, and other awkward and rather tiresome animals disported themselves. It was quite well known, but rather unfavourably in a social sense, because there Mr. Stanley accidentally met Mr. Livingstone the well-known missionary and they spoke without even being properly introduced! Which went in search of which I can't remember. This, however, although bad enough, was not quite so shocking as the affair of the eccentric Miss Nightingale (it was before people began dropping her prefix) who went off uninvited to the Crimea, wrote angry letters to no less a person than the Honble. Sidney Herbert at the War Office, while all the time mixing in an unseemly, indeed dangerous, manner with unmarried soldiers. It was even said that without, so to speak, averting her eyes, she held aloft a lighted lamp while doctors dressed wounds on parts of the male body (such as stomachs) that no unmarried female was supposed to know anything at all about—much less look at! This also had some uncomfortable connexion with Russia.

Japan was merely a vague and unimportant geographical expression.

Then there was China. There must have been because it had a Customs Service to which younger sons who were not always too bright mentally, were sometimes banished. Some people in England had large pieces of Chinese porcelain, not uninteresting and which "went" well enough with "old" oak—just then coming in—but not at all well with mahogany —just then going out—much less with modern furniture of satinwood, birds'-eye maple or, more popular still, walnut. China had bandits and no real Constitution, therefore, in spite of its temples, cities and people—all largely redundant and overdone—it could not possibly be a civilized place. And anyhow short feet and long pigtails were quite odious.

India was assumed to be a place of some importance because, in a way, it belonged to the Empire. Queen Victoria herself had been proclaimed Empress of that place, which of itself gave it a sort of sacredness. That very odd Mr. Disraeli had, somehow, something to do with this. It was even said that Her Majesty had been so gracious as to make friends with one or two of the native Princes, many of whom were very rich and several of whom were quite good sportsmen; and had she not on one famous occasion—although this had really nothing to do with India—personally presented a coal-black Native Chief with a white English Bible. Once, but this was later, the Queen's youngest son, the Duke of Connaught, had held a military command in India; the Prince of Wales himself had visited the country and declared that he found it enchanting; several retired Viceroys such as Lord Lytton, Lord Dalhousie and Lord Dufferin spoke with warm admiration of the place. Therefore there must be a good deal to be said in its favour. But it also was very big and very far away, although a wonderful field of opportunity for devoted missionaries. It also provided a somewhat unusual background for a new writer, a Mr. Kipling.

Of Australia and New Zealand one did not hear much. They were even farther away than India. Canada, on the other hand, was much nearer and really seemed quite worth while. So much so that the Queen had sent her daughter, the delightful Princess Louise, out there as Vicereine, her husband, Lord Lorne, of course accompanying her to protect her from bears and bandits and to act as Viceroy.

There was a subconscious feeling that such huge geographical units as Russia, China, India, Australia and even New Zealand were somehow unwholesome. Had not history proved that the small nations like Greece, Rome and Great Britain were by far the most civilized; indeed, had not Providence itself sanctified this feeling by so arranging things that the English Bible was written in Palestine—a place so small that you could hardly find it on the largest pair of schoolroom globes!

Then the whole thing fell to pieces.

The Great Queen died: It did not seem as if she could.

Her two Jubilees, more particularly the second one, had somehow made the hitherto far-away Empire seem much more real. Several contingents, for example, of picturesque-looking cavalry, many of whom rode undeniably well, a number of Indian Princes, Imperial statesmen and official representatives of the various Colonies joined in, and the whole made a varied and imposing impression—particularly it was to be hoped on the rather upstart foreigners—and was therefore quite worth while. Besides, with a growing population ever-increasing markets were essential. All these people, however dark their complexions, however exotic their morals (if indeed they had any at all), and however odd their manners, represented markets.

We were by now without doubt a great Imperial people, in fact, quite like the old Romans. Yes; the Empire was, after all, certainly well worth while. Anathema to all Little Englanders.

But what was to be done now that the Queen, who (under Divine Guidance) made all this, was gone?

We may poke fun at and be ironic about the Victorians. Why not? But let us play fair, poke fun at and be ironic about ourselves. It is a wholesome occupation. The Victorians had faith. We have not. They believed very often in all sorts of quite fantastic things. But surely any totem is better than none. If they were too ready to believe in almost anything we are far too much inclined to believe in nothing.

But I had forgotten. We do believe in something. One unassailed and unassailable dogma has survived from the Victorian credo. We still believe in "progress."

It was not the beliefs of the Victorians that were absurd. Far from it. Often they were fine: It was their make-believe that was ridiculous and, to the younger generations, even revolting.

What will our descendants two or three generations hence think of our beliefs and make-believe?

3

At this point we cannot avoid asking ourselves why greatness, and admiration for greatness, died out with the Victorian era, leaving behind, as it were, a few trailing clouds of shabby glory? Because a reason there must be. As, at our present stage of development, we are quite unable to discern what that reason is, we must each of us hazard a guess which, inevitably, will be largely an expression of our personal hopes and temperament. My own feeling is that, first of all, we have lost greatness because we have lost reverence. We know well that to obtain certain desired results in the scientific world we must provide the right conditions. The spiritual world, surely, must also have its laws and there, as elsewhere, if we will the end, we must carefully devise the means. Everything that is said anywhere is, as we now know, automatically recorded in the ether and always has been, but it was only the other day that we became conscious of the fact. Being ignorant of the possibilities we had not sought for a suitable technique; the potential powers of human intercourse were always there, but our ignorance and, shall I say, deafness? kept us in darkness. We could hear but not, as yet, overhear. To alter the poet we might say: Heard melodies are great, but those unheard are greater. We had no powers of receptivity because we had no belief and, therefore, no hope.

Generations that enjoy great material success and, at the same time, lose their ideals and spirituality, are bound in the end to prove sterile. Where there is no vision the people perish.

Having missed the highway, the men and women of my generation, as I have already suggested, wandered down all sorts of crooked paths. Panaceas were everywhere in demand: short cuts to a millennium, largely materialistic, were everywhere proclaimed; the serious-minded were infatuated by "isms" of all sorts: Communism, Socialism, spiritism, pessimism, defeatism, feminism, occultism, paganism, nudism —and a hundred other cure-alls were loudly shouted from every housetop. Old-fashioned unsensational virtues such as patience, courage, hard work, charity and patriotism were jeered at; for the frivolously-minded, motley was the only wear.

When either nations or individuals leave the broad highway for the crooked by-paths they must not be astonished if one day they suddenly find that, after many gyrations, they are back exactly where they started.

An age that knows not heroisms knows nothing. The loss of faith and reverence led to the practice of what was in America called, I understand, "debunking"—an ugly name for an ugly thing. In that country nothing, not even Washington, Lincoln or John Brown's body, were safe from these ravishers, and, in England, not very much. Not even Queen Victoria. That the leader of the gang was gifted with uncanny literary skill made him all the more guilty. Looking at him and, more particularly, at his meagrely endowed imitators, one is inevitably reminded of dirty street urchins pulling faces at the West front of Chartres Cathedral and at the same time bespattering it with rotten eggs. Greatness always angers the mean and impotent.

The post-Victorians are allowed neither delusions nor illusions. This, perhaps, is inevitable inasmuch as a common age makes all things common. Its children, unable or unwilling to climb up towards heroes either dead or living, vented its petty spitefulness by engaging assiduously in striving to pull all things down to their own debased level. Men and women, some few of whom were entitled to the noble name of artist, entered into a competition of biographical unsavouriness.

For a moment, during the Great War, the peoples were blessed with a glimpse of their lost inheritance. Then, reaction setting rapidly in, they became a hundred times worse than before . . . and the end is not yet.

An age of disillusion cannot avoid being an age of decay, and irreverence is death.

4

What nowadays do men and women seek from life? Do they know? Do they ever stop to think, or is that just what none of us dare do? Stop. Think. Have we ever time to contemplate? Are all our spiritual, and most of our intellectual faculties atrophied? Are we just corks on a relentless, chaotic stream; or do we come from somewhere? Get somewhere? Go somewhere? Why do we attempt anything? What virtue is there in mere activity? As we cannot foresee, much less will, the end, what value or satisfaction lies in pretending that the means are important? Why do you read this book? Why do I write it? Why? Always why?

To struggle towards an undefined and indefinable goal is surely an illogical proceeding. Hating it, or fearing it, we all hurry towards death. Why? Is struggle a biological and psychological necessity and, if so, what is its basis?

Putting aside with respectful admiration the many, all too many, millions whom poverty constrains, and putting aside also, but without either respect or admiration, money-grubbers and ambitious worldlings, why do the remainder fight, struggle, battle on, seek achievement? In an age of faith or in an age of reason such conduct would be explicable; but, in an age of pessimism like our own, it is simply incomprehensible.

Personally (and I must once again be forgiven because one can only speak personally) I have never, thank God, had to struggle for any of the more vulgar things of life. Birth and breeding for what they are worth and, up to middle life, health were mine; big houses to live in, money, social position, friendship and intercourse with the prominent, lovely surroundings, music, books, pictures, travel, variety, responsibility, motherhood, matchless friends, flattery, sincere admirations, some measure of success in playing the rôle for which I was cast by fate—all these and much else were given to me—yet I continued to struggle like a small bird in a big gilded cage!

Why?

Probably because I know no better. It takes many of us years to learn that what are called the big prizes of life seldom really matter. Death, the biggest thing of all—and the only human experience that can be said to be in any sense final—we conspire to ignore. All the other things (save love and human-kindness) are so worthless. We cannot prevent earthquakes, rescue masses of people from misery, help individuals to success or happiness—cannot, in fact, deputize for God. But we can, by acquiring patience, serenity and quietude, enjoy the lovely little things, savour them, share them. My far-away cousin, Margaret Sackville, puts it exquisitely in her latest volume of poetry:

> The seed of happiness is little things—
> A feather fallen from an angel's wings
> Drifted towards earth—a song, a rose, a leaf;
> Joy, overweighted, turns at once to grief.
> Small flecks of sunlight to our weakness, are
> More than the conflagration of a star.
> Not limitless our hearts which cannot hold
> Ingots, but rather powder of pure gold.
> Lest man be blind with light, to him is given
> Only the shadow of diminished heaven.
> Wherefore let me on earth's adventure go
> Accompanied by pleasures light as snow.
> These ecstasies confound me—I would rise
> By nicely graded steps to Paradise.[1]

[1] From *The Double House,* London, 1935, Williams and Norgate, by Lady Margaret Sackville, d. of 7th Earl de la Warr, Authoress of *A Hymn to Dionysus, Hildris the Queen* and many other volumes of poetry and prose.

5

The basic tragedy of all human relationships is that we are always similar . . . but never identical. We build too much upon and hope too much from—the similarities. This is a mistake because they are only accidental and unimportant. This may be the fundamental reason why all the achievements of our civilization begin to look suspiciously like failure.

In international affairs, Leagues, Alliances and Empires are based upon the theory of similarities; in religious affairs, creeds and churches; in national affairs, class distinctions, education, political parties, organizations and propaganda; in personal affairs, love, marriage, children, homes, communities.

Supposing we dismissed all this. Recognize frankly and unashamedly that it is only our purely animal and emotional necessities (that is our loves) that bind us and, paradoxically, it is they also, and all they entail, that divide us and make us sometimes hate one another.

The moment that a man or a woman becomes self-consciously capable of any sort of achievement whatever, he or she forthwith mentally cut themselves off from the crowd. This is universally true. I remember two Hampshire butchers in what is called "a small way of business," and one scorned the very idea of any social intercourse with the other because, as he put it, "he killed his own meat" and his rival didn't.

What poet, writer, painter, composer, sculptor, scientist, actor or singer, or even politician, would be pleased if you said they were in any way like one of their rivals. Indeed, so assertive is this spirit of individualism at the present day, that a modern Communist poet would be outraged beyond all pacification if you said that he derived from Byron, Shelley or Keats; he might feel faintly pleased if you said he had affinities with Shakespeare, Milton, an unknown Negro versifier, or some obscure and unheard-of rhymester of the sixteenth or seventeenth century; but, if (of course in a spirit of pure brotherhood) you wanted instantly to be bludgeoned to death, it would only be necessary to hint that he had once heard of Swinburne or Tennyson.

The very first thing a child does is to exhibit and insist on its own "me-ness"; the next is to say mine; and, at the end, do not we all like to think, quite wrongly, that we are the owners of the graves in which we sleep? Probably no legal authority in the whole British Empire is competent to decide who really does own a grave; but it is quite clear, legally, and in every other sense, that we are only what I might call death-tenants.

Now I for one should like (purely as an experiment) to insist upon, exalt, magnify, glorify—if necessary, exaggerate—our differences; base a new code, a new civilization on that and see what would happen. It seems to me that it is the denial of those congenital differences that leads everywhere to pain, friction, chaos. No two of us are alike nor, so far as can be seen or foreseen, ever will be. Yet we speak of my husband, my children, my family, my friends, my relations, my people, my race, my country, my creed, my philosophy, my church. We even say *my* God. We apply to the great imponderables terms only suitable when we speak of trivialities such as shoes and stockings. What else is ours? We say my cat. But who ever really owned or understood a cat? The most anyone could claim is that the cat owns them. And even that relationship only lasts for so long as the cat chooses. We speak of our house; but we are the merest tenants. More foolish still. We say "my garden." (I do so myself.) We speak of making a garden. Without the active and continuous collaboration of Nature, or God, or whatever it is, who could make a garden? Married people even speak of making a baby.

Men, being egotistical and unnecessarily stupid, go so far as to speak of begetting children; women, ever the modest sex, are content to speak of bearing them—that is conveying them from There to Here. To speak of begetting, if the term is used in any way to imply creation, is egotistical nonsense. We beget nothing in that sense; we own nothing;

nobody, however close, belongs to us; every child born into this world comes from we know not where and goes we know not whither. It is itself. Alone. Lonely. Unique. It is in itself a beginning and an end. It can transmit life and death as a conduit transmits water, but it can no more create life or evade death than the conduit can create the water or determine its function and destiny. But it is noteworthy that the thing transmitted by human agency, which we call being, resembles water inasmuch as it also contains the elements of life and of death. If, as the scientists tell us, there are not two identical thumb-prints in the whole world, perhaps not two identical blades of grass, how then can there be two identical human beings?

Is it ever overcome? This isolation. Momentarily only. In passionate devotion to a religion, a crusade, a cause, a beloved person. During a religious revival in Wales; or the feminist battle for the vote; throughout the war?

The war! Is that, then, the true reason why so many men of all nations in their heart of hearts refuse to outlaw war? Is it only in time of war that we find unity with each other? In a mob? When one is swept out of oneself by mob-emotion, mob action, mob law, engulfed in mob psychology? Does this explain lynching in the Southern American States? Does it explain boxing matches; motorists risking horrible deaths at Daytona or Brooklands; bull-fighting; steeplechasing; motoring at speed?

Does it, by any chance, explain Calvary?

Can man only feel united with man in the presence of blood, of agony? Are we, basically, brutes? Blood-lovers? Sadists? Is all our boasted civilization and education but an egg-shell?

Give.

We must give because nothing we hold is our own. We know not whence it came. Did Shakespeare know where *Hamlet*, or *Othello*, or *Lear*, came from? Of course not. Nor were they his until he gave them away to the world; then, in a sense, they became his. But had he kept them to himself, had them buried with him in his coffin as Rossetti buried his manuscript in the coffin of his wife, would they, then, have been his own? Assuredly not.

All this craving for identity has, it would seem, led to the development of what is most inferior in life, such as exaggerated feelings of nationality, racial conceit, superiority complexes, cities and all the vulgar appurtenances and manifestations of the herd instinct, promiscuousness, "isms" of all sorts, dirt, noise, disease, jealousy, ostentation, acquisitiveness, advertising, newspapers, jazz, cinemas, seaside resorts, gambling, drunkenness, gluttony, even prostitution. The mob must always yell with joy or howl with pain—in company. Greatness always faces great moments alone.

Admit, long before it is born, that the child that is coming from the unknown, that is going to pass a few brief hours at the overcrowded wayside station called life, before passing on to the unknown, is unique, free, entitled to itself and its own destiny, neither good nor evil, perhaps neither significant nor insignificant. Just itself—whatever that may be. Base all laws, customs and conventions on that fact, that one indisputable, impregnable fact, and something valuable, perhaps something definitely significant might be achieved. One can only say *might*. The possibility exists only because it would be a philosophy of life and civilization based on a reality and not, as at present, one based on assumption, illusion and make-believe.

When I listen to a clergyman or teacher of any creed I am at once puzzled and annoyed. If I told him that I never could be made to understand where electricity comes from, where it goes to or why it is so bright, he might say that he couldn't either. If I asked him what life is, or death, or where what he insisted on referring to as my soul came from, or even what it is, he would in all probability meekly confess ignorance, relative if not absolute. But in the same breath he would be quite prepared to assure me that by virtue of having read a certain number of old-fashioned theological books, the acceptance of some very old creeds (with doubtful pedigrees), the passing of some rather mediævally-inspired examinations, the "laying on of hands" and the assumption of a dreary, unbecoming and vastly uncomfortable style of dress, he was fully qualified to tell me all about God, the Creation, the past, the present and the hereafter. I know quite well, and he knows that I know, that his limitations, frailties and failures are similar to my own; nevertheless, in this one respect, the most urgent, important and difficult of all, he claims to be a sure, even an infallible guide! And the great trouble about all this is that one couldn't believe his assertions even if one wanted to. . . . Nevertheless, the world is beginning to learn. We are at last turning from dogma to doubt. Doubt is the beginning of all things. Doubts; Quests; Questionings? The child's first articulate word is a question. The old man's last word is a question disguised as a prayer. The world is either facing stagnation and death or . . . a new Renaissance. Mediocrity is, we venture to hope, being gradually dethroned by science. Science postulates and insists on efficiency leading to perfection. Only aristocracy, that is, uniqueness, matters. Is discontent a limitation or an enlargement? Certainties? We have none, or, at least, only relative ones. Life as we know it seems to us urgent and important merely because it is the one thing we have experienced. And about it we don't, as yet, know much. Death, whether it be an end or a beginning, is only significant because it will settle at least that much. While there is death there is hope.

6

Like everyone else who has reached the age of "thirty-nine and a bittock" I am sometimes asked what I personally have made out about this queer business called life. Not a great deal, I fear, beyond the certainty that, at its best, it is enthralling and, even at its very worst, it is all, somehow, great fun.

I don't in the least want to die; all the same I am not, and never have been, in the least afraid of death. All danger gives me a queer sense of exaltation, of vivid alertness, realization of unity—not with death but with life. In moments of great peril every nerve tingles, everything in and around one is intensified; even our companions stand out for the moment with an extraordinary clarity that can be either disconcerting or reassuring. In recollection one of the most precious gains from such experience is the new and authentic sense of values won from the fact that, for the time being at all events, life itself was stripped of all make-believe and we stood face to face with reality.

I believe this explains why so many heroic figures in history were at their best when things were at their worst. Danger awakens; safety sends us to sleep. It is the frequent recurrence in war of such priceless moments as these that makes men love war in spite of all its horrors; moreover, the quest for such everlasting moments sends them out to conquer the poles, climb great mountains, chart uncharted seas. It is the spirit that has won for the world all therein worth winning. It is the essential salt of the earth.

The explanation is in all probability quite simple: Great peril, whether physical or spiritual, by liberating us and bringing us face to face with reality, brings us face to face with God.

The unforgettable moments are the moments when we have seen Him.

I have sometimes thought that passionate advocates of peace are more active than sensible. They will never win to their cause the young, nor any other persons of high and ardent spirit, by insisting on the horrors of war. Since 1920 there has arisen in all countries, and in Germany in particular, a school of thought that dwelt with an inflamed insistence on what one might call the cesspool side of war. Of course war has its cesspools—physical, moral and spiritual—but so has every home and farm and factory in the world. And are our inmost hearts so pure? The only difference is that in war the plague spots lie open for all to see, and smell, and shudder at; whereas, under what we call civilization, they are politely tucked underground in ugly pipes and drains by those whom we pay to be our moral and physical plumbers and scavengers. If the cesspools of civilized convention were everywhere laid open could the most insensitive for one hour survive!

I have sometimes thought that the League of Nations might even yet do great things were it not for its friends. Peace gains nothing and no adherents of value by an intemperate decrying of war. What must be done with war is not to destroy, but to transmute it: to make it constructive not destructive. Youth, high-spirited and idealistic, will always be at war. Give it, then, something worth while to fight.

One perhaps not entirely regrettable result of the orgy of defamation of war indulged in by unbalanced pacifists is the triumph all over Europe of the spirit of Fascism.

If you scrutinize in any country prominent pacifists and their followers you will find that they are all rather drab. They have, as a class, much feverishness but little intensity. Defending a negative virtue such as peace, they are always at a disadvantage compared with the advocates of a positive heroism like war. My chief quarrel with pacifists and pacifism is that they are largely responsible for making peace impossible. A League of Nations organized and run by soldiers and sailors and airmen who had had personal experience of war might succeed in attracting the young because, obviously, its leaders would at least know what they were talking about. A League organized and run by doctrinaires, as we unfortunately already know, is almost bound to fail. And it is a funny thing that Locarno, and all the pacts within the League, were made by soldiers, sailors and leaders and not by clergymen and theorists. The League was suspect from the beginning by realists inasmuch as its "Covenant" was concocted in a study by a visionary for visionaries—a visionary, moreover, who knew nothing of Europe or of war beyond what he had learned in books—and, apparently, not very much of human nature. The world, one fears, has never benefited overmuch from those who have proclaimed themselves, or allowed others to proclaim them, the direct successors of Moses and Jesus of Nazareth. Outside the Bible the use of the term "Covenant" is an ineptitude, if not, indeed, an impertinence. The debasing of majestic words for little things is characteristic of our trivial age, and is always a mistake. In the old days the word Treaty was a serious, almost a sacred one; now treaties are denounced or disregarded as if the act were a mere whim. It does not seem —if one is to judge by the actions of some of the so-called great nations—that the mighty and splendid English word "Covenant" is now more sacred or binding. To cheapen language is to cheapen truth.

Youth will not listen to us anywhere because we have banished from our civilization everything that there was to fight. Satan, portrayed as a potent figure of fallen grandeur by the Bible, Dante and Milton, has been abolished by the churches. No one now believes hell worth fighting—except the Salvation Army. Evil, morality, veniality, have now become purely personal, even academic questions, and I defy anyone to get up a real fight against an abstract principle —except, perhaps, in Ireland.

7

And this brings me back to the question of what is the most important thing to learn about life. It is—not to be afraid of it. Let me repeat it. You will never capture the imagination of youth or win it to your cause except by the way of courage. And, as the courageous never really grow old, courage wins everyone worth while whatever their nominal age. A modern poetess sings "Give no houseroom in your heart to fear."[1] Let us abolish fear. Let us stand upright and unafraid. Barrie says, "When courage goes all goes." It is true. In modern war the main thing is to break the morale of the enemy. It was the morale of the German

[1] *The Lady of the Scarlet Shoes* and other verses by Lady Alix Egerton. London, 1902, Elkin Matthews.

people that was conquered in 1918, not their armies. Hitler, knowing this, sought to re-establish it and, miraculously, he has succeeded. His methods are not the business of anyone but himself and the German people. He was successful.

Is that by any chance in the eyes of some the unforgivable sin?

To rebuild, reunite and re-inspire the proud and ancient spirit of the German people Hitler had to give them something definite and concrete to fight for, and to fight against, something which, while essentially spiritual, could yet be expressed in material terms. He did. He gave them again, as Charlemagne and Bismarck had done, the ideal of German unity, and he expressed it in concrete terms as the recovery of the Saar; he gave them renewed hope in a combined national effort to conquer unemployment; a new ideal expressed in the common will to obliterate odious class distinctions; he gave them again self-respect through physical discipline; he gave them a deeper loyalty in a new, warming, inspiring love, for the land that bore, and the home that sheltered them. He spoke also of art and beauty, love and death, music and dance and song. He spoke of energy and effort and, by decree, abolished laziness and its child, despair. Above all he demanded of everyone . . . courage.

8

Let me recall here a few examples of courage such as I shall never forget. Examples which, like great music, majestically drown for me the muted reverberations of the muffled drums of death.

Little Patsy sits in her tiny sea-surrounded garden on the Mediterranean—Europe's sea of destiny. Idly ruminating on famous harbours, she thinks she can see the ships of Tyre and Sidon; she sees Helen's fatal face charged with unnumbered woes; the bellying of the sails of Cleopatra's barge; she overhears Cæsar's oarsmen; catches sight of Dante's midnight ferry; realizes quite clearly that just luffing in the haze on the blue waters is the black ship of death: It can now only be a little time till it drops anchor for a moment beside her, picks her up and bears her off into the unknown elsewhere.

Little Dollie is with her. That morning she has been specially in to Cannes to buy a few yards of thick *crêpe-de-chine* of the best quality, ivory-white in colour such as would be worn by a bride. A pair of new silk stockings the same shade have also been bought. Glove-like shoes cunningly shaped to fit Patsy's lovely feet have been found in her wardrobe.

A dress, a long, plain, rather full robe, has been cut out and basted up by the lady's maid, but Dollie must herself slowly finish it. It is to be exquisitely sewn, smocked at the slim waist and at the cuffs of the long sleeves; it must fit, not tightly yet not loosely, round the still girl-like bust.

Every afternoon when the open-air luncheon is over, Dollie sits finishing Patsy's last gown, whilst she watches with more care than she would have exercised over her wedding dress: a small tuck here, a little more fulness there; long, but not too long, for that would be clumsy. Then the conversation goes like this:

"Dollie, are we very white when we are dead?"

"No, madame; I don't think so—not so very white."

"That's good. Anyhow that old ivory shade will cast a becoming shadow?"

"Yes, madame——"

"And Dollie—the box thing. They are hideous. Could we have it lined with something cheerful? Rose-pink taffeta perhaps? You know I hate any shiny material. The pink would indeed make a lovely warm reflection."

"Yes, madame——"

"I don't want to look chill and wan . . . and yellow. I don't want to look dead . . . for I won't be dead."

"You—won't look dead, madame."

"I don't know, Dollie. A shot bird can look so dead. And, Dollie, there must be no faintest sign of fear. No moaning black, or abject white. Flowers and colour and songs. And not sunset songs either. Morning songs. And if they must read something let it be that bit where it says, 'And all the morning stars together sang.'"

"But I don't think that's in the Bible, madame."

"It doesn't matter where it is, Dollie. Let them read it. It will be true. Are you afraid of death, Dollie?"

"Oh no, madame; if I may say so, madame, no one who serves the Cornwallis-West family could be afraid of anything."

"Just so, Dollie. We all like you because, like all of us, nothing will ever stop you laughing or making a joke. But, truly, none of us was ever afraid of anything. . . ."

That indomitable spirit. That serene soul. Patsy had loved life with an exhaustless, abounding love. She did not want to die. But death was inevitable.

The terrible pain which she had suffered in the earlier stages of her illness was, thank God, gone. She knew and adored the birds and the sunshine, the flowers and the sea. The beyond she did not know, could not envisage, but not once in life had she known or even acknowledged the existence of fear and she would not do so at the end.

9

And now let us close with a lovely adventure and a good laugh.

One day we all went out on Starnbergersee. Princess Pilar, Dollie, myself, the owner of the motor-launch and two manservants. The lake is not wide, perhaps three or four miles, but it is very long and enormously deep, they say quite four hundred feet in places. Pilar, who knows her native land, said that it is deep because its site was once occupied by a mighty glacier. The great charms of a lazy day moving about its surface are the ever-changing views of almost the whole range of the Bavarian Alps from the East to the West, and the attractive little villages and many lovely country houses and parks lining its banks. For me another charm, not so much appreciated by everyone, is that, like a lovely woman, it is a lake of sudden moods. Owing perhaps to its great depth, or the way the winds reach it from the Alps, storms can blow up on it almost before one can change helm. We were all rather sleepy in the warm sunshine after much too good a picnic luncheon when, in a twinkling, the sky became a low, heavy, leaden blue and, almost without a warning sign, the waves seemed to beat upon us from every direction. The owner of the motor-boat, to whom the lake was known from babyhood, and whom we knew as a steady, reliable pilot, was plainly anxious. Pilar, sitting quietly in her place, said nothing, and little Dollie kept putting rugs and things around me to try to keep me dry. Presently, thinking that my rather high carrying chair might be swept overboard, they lifted me into the bottom of the launch where I lay comfortably enough in an ever-deepening pool of water.

The motor-boat, lashed about by the contrary winds, began slowly to fill; the owner did his best to keep her nose in the wind in order to avoid being swamped. Progress towards Starnberg was quite impossible. So far as one could observe, the lake was now empty except for ourselves. They had seen our plight from the shore and made futile efforts to come to our help. Even one of the big paddle-steamers that ply regularly up and down the lake refused to put out. To have done so would have been quite useless, because they would never have got alongside us.

Deck-chairs, luncheon baskets, hats—everything movable had immediately disappeared. I lay on the wet cushions quite oblivious of material surroundings, thoroughly alive and enjoying it all. I laughed happily as I listened to scraps of shouted conversation between Pilar and little Dollie. With their hair streaming wildly they looked exactly like the dishevelled Rhine maidens, while the winds made music like the *Götterdämmerung*.

"Whatever we do, your Royal Highness, we must not let Her Highness drown. We must hold her up somehow in the water."

"Yes, of course, Dollie. Take those heavy rugs off her

so as to be ready. Daisy, dear, are you prepared to be held up in the water?"

At this silly question Pilar and I laughed more immoderately than ever.

The two manservants were, I regret to say, by this time green with fright or sea-sickness—or both—and looked too absurd. In my own mind I tried to be charitable and pretend that I thought it was sea-sickness—but I really didn't. Dollie yelled at them:

"You must be prepared to hold Her Highness up in the water. She is an invalid and can't help herself——"

"Oh o-o-o-o-h . . . yes . . . Miss. . . ."

The little pilot never took his eyes off his bow except to glance uneasily at the tiny engine-house now, like the rest of the boat, rapidly filling with water. Pilar and Dollie kept bailing it out with an old tin and a glass tumbler for all they were worth.

What inspires the odd things one says at such moments? The wind kept driving us in on the eastern bank where assuredly we should have been dashed to pieces on the shores of the park surrounding Schloss Berg. Once, when quite close to the tall cross marking the spot where King Ludwig the Second was drowned nearly fifty years before, Dollie said cheerfully:

"What a dreadful thing it would be, your Royal Highness, if another member of the Bavarian Royal family were to be drowned in Starnbergersee!"

"Well, Dollie, if it is to be so, it can't be helped."

"Bravo, Pilar," said I, to cheer things up a bit.

"Bravo, Daisy dear; are you too uncomfortable?"

"No, not a bit. I love it."

"Yes, dear, it's all right; but I don't like entering Paradise in dripping clothes and my hair looking awful."

"Never mind, Pilar—your hair is always lovely, and anyhow, God likes people who are natural."

And what extraordinary things one thinks of at such moments! Where do they come from? First of all I thought, if we are drowned just here will they erect two more crosses, one for Pilar and one for me. No, I mused, that would never do. There can only be *one* not three crosses.[1] There can never again be *three* crosses. Besides, not to have crosses for Dollie and the servants would look like class distinction. Quite obviously there could not possibly be six crosses. Yet, after all, they would be as much drowned as we were. Then I thought, well, if I am drowned, I shall at any rate see Queen Victoria again. I wonder what I will do wrong this time. And I had a sudden vision of myself being presented to the venerable Sovereign when I was only seventeen and wearing my first long frock. I wasn't a bit frightened, and had been told the Queen would give me her hand to kiss. I approached the little upright figure in the low chair, but there were masses and masses of flowing skirts and I couldn't find her hand anywhere. It just didn't seem to be there! Bending forward, to my astonishment, she kissed me on each cheek . . . and I started giggling. And the only other time we met I had inadvertently stuck my blue aigrette into her face when I bent to kiss her hand? Would the Queen remember when we met in Heaven? Would she now take the opportunity of rebuking me? Well, if she did, it would after all be a *heavenly* rebuke!

The older manservant, his teeth chattering with cold and fright and a rosary between his hands, was by now on his knees praying hysterically. Dollie, who I fear is a little pagan, said derisively and angrily:

"Look at that old fool!"

Pilar, who, as a good Catholic, perhaps thought the remark somewhat untimely, said gently but without a trace of nervousness:

"Are you not a Christian, Dollie?"

"No, your Royal Highness, I'm a Protestant."

"Well, Dollie, Protestant or not, I think it would be as well for both you and Princess Daisy to say your prayers."

[1] A high cross in the water marks the spot where King Ludwig II, whom Bavarians call *der Märchenkönig* (the Fairy King), was drowned on Whitsunday, June 13th, 1886.

Pilar's words sounded serious, but I saw a gleam of fun in her blue eyes, whereupon I had such an immoderate fit of giggling that I thought I would die of laughter even before I had time to be drowned. There was the older manservant —perhaps excusably—cringing to Providence with fright, the young one close to him too frightened even to cringe. The brown-faced Bavarian boatman intense, concentrated, fighting. Dollie ineptly confirming Pilar's secret unavowed belief that Protestants could hardly be taken seriously as Christians. Pilar laughingly protesting that she did not like the idea of staining the heavenly floors with Starnbergersee water. Daisy, living intensely, nor caring how it all ended, but hoping it would go on for a long time.

It ended, I don't quite know how or why, about as suddenly as it began. Motor-boats came out to help us; sogging wet, we were somehow transhipped into one and taken ashore and wrung out a little. A wet, pulpy mass, we were packed into the car and driven swiftly back to Munich.

After a warm bath I was sitting snugly in bed drinking tea when they brought me the evening papers. Right across the front page were enormous headlines! "Terrible storm on Starnbergersee. Many boats destroyed and lives lost? Two Princesses almost drowned. . . ." Almost. That was what made it such enormous fun.

10

Then, flinging away the stupid paper, I picked up an anthology and read this poem:

Death comes to set us free,
Oh! meet him cheerily
As thy true friend;
And all thy fears shall cease,
And in eternal peace
Thy penance end.

The only fault I can find with this lovely verse is the poet's use of the word "penance" in the last line. Whatever life may be it is not merely that. A discipline, a preparation, an opportunity, perhaps, but, to me at least, not a penance. I would gladly live it all over again, experience once more every ache and pain and agony. Although my first baby, a little girl, died and each succeeding birth was increasingly difficult, the last one making me in the end a permanent invalid, I would bear all my children over again.

Danger?

There is no intensity, no vividness, no exaltation where there is no danger. Surely the great truth that must be grasped is that we are not meant to be safe. All we succeed in doing from generation to generation is to exchange one danger for another. There are now, it is said, no highwaymen on Hounslow Heath, but the Great West Road is, I am told, strewn with corpses done to death by motor bandits. I suppose that in England few people nowadays actually die for lack of food yet under a civilization that puts "safety first," two million English people are compelled in the midst of plenty to live and die on the edge of starvation. People should not be required to starve; but safety, as such, is a myth and, if it **could** be achieved, would result in atrophy and death.

CHAPTER XIII

FAREWELL APPEARANCE

I

HOW do I pass my time nowadays? Well, I don't quite know; I only know that it flies . . . flies . . . flies. What is the good of crying "Time, you old gipsy man, will you not stay?" Because old men are stubborn and he just won't. There he is, always dodging in and out with his beastly scythe, just when one least expects or wants to see him . . . never still . . . never at rest . . . always calling other people to *their* rest and, nearly always, doing so against their will. In fact, a horrid, cross-grained old man.

For those unknown friends who care for me and my doings, I will say just a few words about my present way of life. First of all, I behave quite disgracefully about my Diary, often not writing a line of it for months. But there is nothing much to write. A few extracts written seven years ago will serve my present purpose because my life has not in any way changed since then:

"*June* 28, 1928. *La Napoule. My birthday.*

"I woke up to find my room full of sunlight, flowers and little presents (the latter given to me by my servants), dogs and canaries. I had visitors coming and going all morning and had very little time to dress; my little maid, Dollie, had made for me a special frock of white georgette with dozens of little frills on the skirt and at the bottom of the wide sleeves. It was really very becoming—at least so they all said when I went to a neighbouring château for lunch.

"It really was quite touching. My host had all his Russian servants dressed up in most picturesque costumes, and they all played instruments and, as I entered, struck up a lively melody; each guest was presented with a 'daisy,' and a big bunch of them was given to me; also several little presents and then some speeches, all of which I thought very nice.

"Although it was a brilliantly hot afternoon, I gave a small tea-party, including Lady Congreve and her niece Miss Drana King, who is supposed to be very psychic, Lady Johnson, Amy Paget, and one or two more. In the evening we had a quiet little dinner under the palm trees. Miss Coles and General Gourdine's sister came in afterwards to drink my health.

"I went to bed very tired about midnight."

"*June* 29, 1928. *La Napoule.*

"I woke this morning with a feeling that something was going to happen, which I afterwards discovered was that we were leaving in the evening to get away from the terrific heat of France. I felt thankful that we should soon be in the cool of Bavaria and in my new home in Munich; when I get used to it I shall really like it.

"6.30 p.m. Just starting, thank God, to get away from this heat. I found at the station several friends who came to see me off—and my banker, who was there to advance me a little money to pay off my second son, who lent me the money a few months before to pay off the banker! I and Dollie had a nice reserved compartment in the train and I awoke to find myself passing through Aix-les-Bains. Although it was hot and stuffy in the train we did enjoy the delicious fruit, peaches and melons."

"*June* 30, 1928. *In the train.*

"At eleven o'clock we arrived at Geneva with its cool, glorious lake; there we changed engines, but not trains. From there we went to Zurich by electricity—which seems to be able to go anywhere—and arrived the same evening at six o'clock. At Zurich we went to a small hotel and took a bedroom so as to have a good wash and rest and dinner before leaving by the eleven o'clock train for Munich."

"*July* 1, 1928. *Munich.* 7 *a.m.*

"We have just arrived at my future home; everything looks like spring, so cool, fresh and green. What a relief after the dried, pale yellow look of France. I immediately had a delightful bath and went to bed whilst the usual unpacking went on. I felt very refreshed and dressed and had lunch in my garden; one part I specially love—I call it my meadow. It is rough and wild with all sorts of long grasses and daisies growing, and beautifully shady, as there are so many apple and lime trees. But my English gardener will, I hope, be here from Cannes next spring, and my specially loved meadow will be a mixture of yellow daffodils and blue-bells. I had tea in my hammock in my rose-garden with the fountain playing, and went to bed after an evening of writing letters, and a small dinner."

"*July* 3, 1928. *Munich. Tuesday.*

"It is a lovely hot day, so we are going to take our lunch and motor to Starnbergersee.

"*Later:* We went out in an electric launch, which was delightful. I, Dollie, the butler and the footman anchored the boat under a tree overhanging the lake and had lunch. We spent all day on the boat, which cost very little money. We gave the boatman his lunch and he was delighted. Bavarians are such simple kind people. I hope to do this often this summer, especially when my boys come.

"Now I can't write any more, dear Diary, as I have other more important things to do, so good-night."

2

I don't in the least know what the "more important things" were! Perhaps my maid had to comb and brush my long hair (I have never had it bobbed), or rub face cream into my face because the Munich water, although deliciously cold and pure, is very hard. Or it might be that *Chang* and *Tusan* wanted to go early to bed and, if so, there was nothing but obedience for Dollie and me—I never really know whether to write Dollie and me or Dollie and I—but I think it must be Dollie and me, as the other feels like putting on a tiara for breakfast. Besides, it's too preposterously biblical. Perhaps I was lazy and wanted to get into my large "comfy" bed so that Dollie might read aloud to me for an hour or so.

She is a good reader and likes it, but I don't believe she is really sorry when I have people staying in the house who are also good readers and enjoy reading aloud. My patient editor, Major Chapman-Huston, for instance, or dear Ella Saltoun Willett, one of my best and most faithful friends. She knew and loved Patsy and Poppets and never fails to visit me once or twice a year either at La Napoule or in Munich; better still, she sometimes does both. She is a great reader and a good judge of books. Sitting by the fire or picnicking in the *Daisy Wiese* above Starnbergersee, with the magnificent stretch of the whole Bavarian Alps from the Watzmann above Berchtesgaden to the Zugspitze above Garmisch, backing in the far distance the blue-green lake, Ella has had to listen—more than once—to every line of this book being read aloud, and her advice and criticisms have been most helpful.

Other visitors come and go. Amongst the most faithful is Priscilla Annesley. Her girlish loveliness, which was exquisite, still amply vouched for by a most handsome and imposing presence. She is a delightful guest because she knows everyone, has travelled far and wide and is also an insatiable reader. Always gay, amusing and witty, she never says a spiteful thing. Her sunny disposition keeps her heart young and is a godsend to her friends.

Princess Pilar comes like a breath of her own Bavarian mountain air. Her mother, Princess Ludwig Ferdinand, sheds in a northern land the warmth of sunny Spain and in spite of her old-fashioned, even dowdy dress, not a little of Spain's incomparable charm and olden dignity. In her presence (on this ordinary, common earth) one sits beside a great—though humble—Christian and a very great lady. Prince Ludwig Ferdinand, gallant, genial, full of compliments, at once a typical Wittelsbacher and a typical Bavarian in his unique mixture of doctor, prince and musician. Fritz and May Larisch drift in from Geiselgasteig for luncheon, bringing with them dear, blessed Olivia—handsome as ever—and her girl who is about to be married. And it seems only the other day at Fürstenstein that I was arranging Olivia's marriage to Hansie!

Newer friends also come, and I am always glad to see them because, as I remarked in my first chapter, one must always keep one's friendship in repair. I am particularly glad to welcome the younger generations. During these last times young Hinchingbrooke, eldest son of Lord and Lady Sandwich, came, as he loves the music in Munich and Bayreuth. Rosamund Norman, whose grandfather, Lord Aberconway, has often entertained me at the Château de la Garoupe at Antibes, comes to see me both at Napoule and Munich. Shelagh comes at least once a year. . . . But the gaps in the garden of love and friendship keep widening. Beloved Aunt Adelaide Taylour and Fanny Sternberg, best of women, will visit me no more.

And so I come towards the end of the programme that I have got together for Daisy's farewell appearance. But I learned from Patti, Albania, and my friend, Nellie Melba, that a "farewell appearance" is by no means the same as a last appearance. The other day I received this letter from an unknown woman friend in the United States:

"*November* 25, 1934.

"DEAR PRINCESS OF PLESS:

"Having read your books for the third time, I have a very earnest desire to tell you how thoroughly I have enjoyed them, and how much they have meant to me—having touched within me something indescribable, something which has enabled me to go on with greater courage.

"And so I thank you—thank you more than I can say—and pray God have you in His keeping."

That sort of letter makes it difficult to harden one's heart and decide that, whatever happens, the farewell appearance and the last shall be one and the same. But, after all, it really depends on what my readers think more than it does on me.

I own that I am sad at the thought that I may never again send out another little paper boat to greet from me old friends and make for me new ones as it struggles to survive for a brief hour on the limitless stream of time. Making this book has given a lot of bother, but I am truly sorry that it is finished.

My first book was begun, and this one is being finished, in my Munich home. For me, as I have said, life goes quietly by. I have little hope of any sudden happenings, any dramatic changes. I am unlikely to make any long journeys and may not even see beloved England once again. Munich to Cannes and the splendid Estérel mountains—Cannes to Munich. My picnics in the Bavarian Alps, the sunset as it sinks behind the snow-clad mountains leaving their faces ragged splashes of deep purples, ochres and blacks, and their jagged profile like the tips and pinnacles of a great, flat, heavenly panorama cut by God and fringed with fire from the touch of His hand. . . . So there comes to us one and all, slowly, soundlessly, unavoidably, the last chat by the warm fireside, the last climbing of the stairs, "the last snow," the last sunset as it streams in splendour beyond the Estérels . . . beyond the Bavarian Alps . . . beyond the edge of the world.

3

One more extract from my Diary and then—no—not good-bye: whatever happens, it need not mean that. Let it be *Auf Wiedersehen:*

"*April* 3, 1935. *Munich.*

"When I finished these pages a few days ago I said nothing sudden, unexpected or wonderful could ever happen to Daisy again. Well, something has. . . . I am going back to Fürstenstein—to the home I unwisely and unnecessarily left over twelve years ago. The place where my children belong.

"However long estranged, surely it is well that we should all come together in quietness and understanding at last."

INDEX

C

F

I

J

R

S

T

Y

Z